IT'S NOT ABOUT
THE HIKE

IT'S NOT ABOUT
THE HIKE

Two Ordinary Women on an Extraordinary Journey

NANCY SPORBORG

BAUHAN PUBLISHING
PETERBOROUGH, NEW HAMPSHIRE
2011

ISBN: 978-0-87233-142-6

Library of Congress Cataloging-Publication Data

Sporborg, Nancy.
 It's not about the hike : two ordinary women on an
extraordinary journey / by Nancy Sporborg.
     p. cm.
 Includes bibliographical references and index.
 ISBN 978-0-87233-142-6 (pbk. : alk. paper)
 1. Sporborg, Nancy. 2. Piper, Pat. 3. Mountaineers--United States--Biography.
 4. Women mountaineers--United States--Biography. I. Title.
 GV199.9.S68 2011
 796.5220922--dc22
 [B]
                        2011006634

All photographs by Nancy Sporborg and Pat Piper, except
photographs on pages 196 and 197 by Stephen Romano,
and photograph on page 343 by Jessica Grant, ©2010, JessFoto.com.

Cover design by Henry James
Book Design by Sarah Bauhan

BAUHAN PUBLISHING LLC
7 MAIN STREET PETERBOROUGH NEW HAMPSHIRE 03458
WWW.BAUHANPUBLISHING.COM

IT'S NOT ABOUT THE HIKE

For more information about
Pat and Nancy's presentation,
visit their website:
www.its-not-about-the-hike.com

Printed in Canada

For Pat

THANK YOU

To everyone who read my hike reports or attended an *It's Not About the Hike* presentation and especially to those who took the time to tell me you were touched by my sharing. You bolstered my belief in myself and that helped me take the next step.

To Sarah Bauhan, Bauhan Publishing, who believed in this project from the beginning, Jane Eklund for meticulous heartfelt editing, Henry James for magical photo expertise, and Ian Aldrich for encouraging me and putting me in touch with Bauhan Publishing. To Steve Smith and Mike Dickerman for the peak-bagging bible, *The 4,000-Footers of the White Mountains,* and for your support of this book.

To all the hikers we've met along the trail—you are the kindest, most incredible people and it is an honor to hike alongside you. To the Challenge Team for sharing your four thousand footer journey with me. It was a privilege to stand on top of Eisenhower with you. To Eileen for telling me over and over that I made a difference in your life until I finally believed you. And to the members of the Views From The Top hiking forum for great articles, advice, support, and reputation points.

To my friends for bearing witness and cheering me on. I am blessed to have you in my life. To the strong fit people in my exercise class for your grunts and groans of support. To Rob for teaching me what true courage and grace look like. To Marty and Kate for being the best posse a girl could ever have. To Ruth Sterling, for your marketing expertise and logo design—you are the best of the best—and most of all for your friendship. To Tracey for being a wise and caring cairn in my life, pointing me in the right direction and showing me how far I have come and to Marcus for helping me find my heart.

To my adoptive parents and family for making me who I am today. To Marge, Martha, Anne, Sam, and Ben for welcoming me into the family. And to Kelly and Jess for being the best daughters a mom could ask for.

To Pat for your courage, compassion, and love, for your consistent belief in me, your never-give-up attitude, and being the best hiking partner anyone could ever hope for.

And most of all to Don for loving me and supporting me every step of the way.

CONTENTS

2008—FINDING JOY

2009—BRANCHING OUT

2010—LETTING GO

INTRODUCTION

For in my tradition, as a Jew, I believe that whatever we receive we must share. When we endure an experience, the experience cannot stay with me alone. It must be opened. It must become an offering. It must be deepened and given and shared.

Elie Wiesel, **This I Believe II**

RIDING THE GRACE WAVE...

Life is up to us. Our choices frame our lives. But is each of us on her own on this journey? I don't think so. I believe there is something greater than all of us out there, shining a light on our next moves, opening up the appropriate doors and nudging us to walk through at just the right moment. I call it the grace wave. The grace wave is life pro-actively steering us toward our next adventure. It pursues me, points me in the right direction and then compels me to take the next big step. If I ignore it, it doesn't go away. It tries again by engaging extra help, a friend or co-worker, or by creating a new set of circumstances to help get me through that next doorway.

I'm clear that the grace wave originates outside of me, but it is also within me. I can feel it. It is persistent, ferocious, present, and focused, quietly poking, waiting for me to notice, to trust, to stop thinking, to follow. There is nothing better than the experience of letting go and riding the grace wave.

I believe we are put on this earth for a reason. Each one of us has a purpose unique to us. I believe if we follow the grace wave, we will find that purpose and along with it the true meaning we long for in our lives.

A BREEZE KICKS UP OVER THE WATER, THE VERY BEGINNINGS OF THE GRACE WAVE . . .

I'm filled with anticipation and a heightened anxiety level. You know how you feel when you are about to put yourself out into the world in a bigger way? That is how I feel. I don't usually invite strangers to do something with me. I wait until it is safer, until I know them better, until I feel they like me. I wait until we have something in common and enough to say to fill the silences comfortably.

I meet Pat at the very first session of a therapy group. I am looking for a walking partner and she seems the walking type. Even though I have only sat in a room with her for a couple of hours, I feel compelled to contact her. It's a strong feeling from within that makes no sense when I think about it.

I know she works at Keene State College. I tell myself it can't hurt to see if I can find her e-mail address. I mean, if I can't find it, then that takes care of that! So I navigate on the Internet to the college website and type in her name: *Pat Piper.* The computer responds immediately, as if, of course, everyone knows her. Her e-mail address, job title, phone number . . . all there.

So, I tell myself, it can't hurt to write the e-mail. Just write it. Figure out what you will say. See how it sounds. You don't have to send it. So I start typing:

Subject: Get together for coffee or a walk sometime?

Hi Pat—I got your e-mail address from the college website.

I was just wondering if you would ever want to meet for coffee, lunch, a walk, or whatever. I don't know your schedule, but I often walk at lunchtime around downtown, and my schedule is somewhat flexible. Or I could meet you for coffee or a walk later in the afternoon.

Please don't feel any pressure.

I sit there and read it over a few times. I like the "Please don't feel any pressure," sentence, which really means if you don't want to do this, don't feel you have to. I give her an out. I sit there with my hand on the mouse. Send it . . . don't send it . . . send it . . . don't.

I hit the send button. It's gone.

I don't have to wait long for a response. It comes the same day:

Nancy—I would love to meet, walk, talk, lunch, whatever. My schedule is pretty flexible. What and when would work for you?

Pat

This may sound like your typical story of friendship blooming. It is that. And it is so much more. It is the beginning of the grace wave. It is the first hint of a purposeful wind blowing over the surface of me, bringing with it the beginning urgings of a journey that will change my life.

THE BREEZE CREATES FRICTION ON THE WATER'S SURFACE AND STARTS A RIPPLE . . .

Pat and I set up a walking date. We walk from where she works to where I work and back again, a total of four miles, giving us plenty of time to talk. We like each other. Our walks become a twice-a-week ritual. There is a connection between us. We are both incredibly thirsty to be seen. That is the gift we give each other. But there is more. There is an unspoken deep inner drive in me that I also recognize in Pat. And there is something else, an unconscious inner knowing of what is to come.

Our walks become the highlight of my week because our sharing feels so meaningful. I feel heard. Nothing stops me from walking with Pat. Once, we even venture out in a hurricane. We walk at least five miles that day. I am soaked when I get back to work. I change into dry clothes, but without a hairdryer and round brush, nothing

can help my hair. A vice president of the organization walks by me, and does a double take. He says, "What happened?" I am embarrassed, but I would go out there with Pat and get soaked all over again.

Pat and I add hills to our walks. We walk a six-mile loop as fast as we can. It gets easier and easier. On one of those hill-climbing sessions, we talk about Katahdin, a five thousand–foot mountain way out in the hinterlands of Maine. We had both heard it is beautiful. I say, "Let's go!" Pat, ever the practical one, says, "Well, we should probably climb a few of the White Mountains to make sure we can do it first." Then she tells me about the sixty-seven mountains in New England over four thousand feet. If you climb them all, you get a patch from the Four Thousand Footer Club, sponsored by the Appalachian Mountain Club (AMC).

A patch—that is all I need to hear. "Let's do it!" I say. Now I don't know what I am thinking. We are two fifty-plus year old non-hikers. But, in fact, I'm not thinking. I'm just feeling the energy of the grace wave starting to vibrate with vitality within, as if to say, *This is what you are supposed to do!*

THE WIND BLOWS HARDER; THE RIPPLE BECOMES A WAVE . . .

It seems the commitment to climb the sixty-seven four thousand footers in New England puts us on the crest of the grace wave.

Our first four-thousand-footer hike is Mounts Whiteface and Passaconaway in the White Mountains on May 6, 2006. We think we are just going out for a hike when we climb our first mountain. We are wrong. We are beginning the journey of a lifetime.

RIDING THE WAVE . . .

On the way down Passaconaway, Pat tells me she is going to write a hike report and post it on an online hiking community website. "Huh? Who would want to read about our hike?" I ask her. She assures me that people read these hike reports. I can't imagine writing or reading such a report. How much is there to say? We climbed up and then we climbed down. And I really can't fathom anyone caring. Pat also talks about designing our own website and posting our hike reports and pictures. I think she's crazy. She writes the first hike report and sends me the draft and I love reading about our experience. It makes it last longer. It makes it more memorable, more real. She posts it on the hiking forum and people respond, wishing us well on our quest. Within a month or two, Pat creates our website. She e-mails each new hike report to her family and friends. I still can't imagine anyone being interested in what I have to say.

We keep hiking and Pat keeps writing hike reports. After each hike, Pat asks me if I want to write the report. I say no, over and over again. Pat writes the first five, holding the experience open for me, until I am ready. To me, writing the reports feels like such a risk. I risk being seen.

I finally follow the nudge from with-in and write about our hike up Mt. Moosilauke. After that, Pat and I take turns writing the reports. My first hike reports make fun of myself and my inexperience. But it doesn't take long before they take on a more personal tone as I realize something much deeper is happening to me in the mountains. The progression of my hike report writing, from superficial to much deeper, and from hike-focused to me-focused, mirrors my journey. Hiking is putting me in touch with parts of myself that have been buried deep inside for years. In the mountains, childhood fears and memories are coming out to be seen.

Writing the reports after the hikes allows me to explore the experiences. I search for the right words, substituting one after another until I light on the exact word that reflects my genuine experience, deepening my understanding. Writing helps me see why a hike feels so big or intense or difficult. It helps me put the feelings into words so I can share the experience with others. Once I'm done writing, I e-mail the link, sending the essay out to our ever-growing list of followers and supporters. I often get beautiful feedback, saying my sharing has touched someone, which in turn touches me.

The grace wave gets credit for the words and pictures you are holding in your hands. So many people said to me, *Write a book.* I am grateful to every one of them for encouraging me. Even after writing this manuscript, many questions remain. Will I find a publisher to turn it into a book? Bookstores to stock it? Readers to buy it and then to turn the pages? I'm leaving that up to the grace wave. I know I am supposed to share this experience. So, I am showing up for my part. Here are my hike reports.

FINDING YOUR OWN GRACE WAVE . . .

You don't have to be a hiker to appreciate these reports. You only have to have your own mountains to climb. And we all have our own mountains: jobs, projects, raising kids, illness, taking care of aging parents, finances, finding meaning in our lives, overcoming personal obstacles. My hope is that by reading about the hikes and what I learn about myself, you will see yourself, feel the ripple within you, and hop on the grace wave.

THE MOUNTAINS AND OUR GOALS . . .

There are sixty-seven mountains in New England that are four thousand feet or higher and count toward the official AMC mountain list. The very first goal we set is to climb all of them. Of the sixty-seven four thousand footers, forty-eight are in New Hampshire. You can also get a patch for reaching each of these forty-eight peaks.

Once we start hiking and realize there are other official mountain lists that award patches, we add them to our list of goals, of course! So, we are also working on climbing the White Mountain Four Thousand Footers in Winter, and the New England Hundred Highest peaks. We also decide to climb the New Hampshire 52 With-A-View, a list developed by the Over The Hill Hik-

ers, a group from Sandwich, N.H. These mountains are under four thousand feet and offer great vistas. Having these additional mountain lists to draw from allows us flexibility; so if we want a shorter climb with great views, we climb a 52 With-A-View. If we want challenge, we climb a four thousand footer.

This book covers a five-year period from 2006 to 2010, with each year reflecting a different stage of our journey. The hike reports are in chronological order. Because we are hiking from a number of different mountain lists simultaneously, you will find hike reports about the forty-eight four thousand footers in New Hampshire mixed in with hike reports about other mountains and adventures. As I hike and then write about the experience, I grow more into myself, and my writing reflects this. So, the order becomes more important than the mountains and the lists. In the end, it is not about the number of mountains we summit or the patches we earn. It's about the journey and who we are becoming as we climb.

When you are inspired by some great purpose, some extraordinary project, all of your thoughts break their bond: your mind transcends limitations, your consciousness expands in every direction, and you find yourself in a new, great, and wonderful world. Dormant forces, faculties and talents become alive, and you discover yourself to be a greater person by far than you ever dreamed yourself to be.

Patanjali

Pat and I commit to the quest of climbing the sixty-seven mountains in New England over four thousand feet high before we know what we are getting into. Surprised and challenged by weather, steep trails, and trying circumstances, I learn that hiking is hard, that accepting help is even harder, and that there is a lot more to hiking than the hike. Back home on my computer, I nervously write my first few hike reports and share them with trepidation.

1. POWER BAR UP MOOSILAUKE

July 14, 2006, Glencliff, New Hampshire

Never let the fear of striking out get in your way.

Babe Ruth

On our way up to Moosilauke, we stop in Meredith at our favorite convenience store to smell the warm muffins, revel in the smile of the friendly woman baking them, and check out the supply of power bars. I lost my legs hiking Tecumseh a week ago. Tecumseh is one of the shortest of the four thousand footers, and the hike is only six miles—but my legs felt like lead and each step I took verged on being my last. I think it was a result of over-exercise and having a bad day, but it scared me. I am determined not to lose my legs again. My answer? Power bars!

The convenience store has a wide assortment and Pat and I pick out four bars and buy them all. I know, we probably don't need four. But I do need my legs and if it's going to take four power bars to ensure I have them mentally as well as physically, then $3.96 is a small price to pay. We buy a Reese's Sweet & Salty bar, a Hershey's Sweet & Salty bar, a Luna bar and a Nature Valley Sweet & Salty Nut Almond Granola bar.

We arrive at the Moosilauke Ravine Lodge at 8:52 a.m. As we start up the Asquam-Ridge Trail, my mind takes me back to Tecumseh. About halfway up the mountain, when my legs were almost totally gone, we met a young woman who looked very athletic and fit, who had already climbed the majority of New Hampshire's four thousand footers. While chatting about our hikes, she mentioned that Moosilauke was "hard, very hard," compared to Tecumseh, which was "nothing." Great. I lost my legs on the easy hike. What's going to happen today on the hard hike?

A quarter of the way up the trail, Pat, perhaps reading my anxiety, suggests we try the Nature Valley Granola bar. Great idea! I get to rest, breathe, mop the sweat dripping from every inch of my body, and eat while feeling the sun on my face. The power bar is okay but difficult to rate (on a power bar tasty scale of 1 to 5, 5 being the best) since it is our first and we have nothing to compare it to. So we decide to wait until we have tried the others.

Hey, I think the bar works! Or maybe it's my mental determination to make it up the mountain. Or maybe I am just having a better day. But I have legs and they seem to be working properly, no lead, just my regular Nancy legs that feel strong and ready for each step up. What a relief!

The trail is beautiful, littered with sweet white and pink flowers, covered with moss, and highlighted with sunlight. The climb is gradual, more gradual than Tecumseh and, of course, I have my newfound legs. We see lots of moose

tracks and are hoping to see their owner, but no such luck. After four miles, we join the Beaver Brook Trail, and in another two miles we clear the treeline. I love how that happens. I am climbing up and I notice, all of a sudden, that I see more sky than trees. There is more sunlight around me and then pow!—I am out of the trees and surrounded by nothing but blue.

I expect bald rock, but the summit of Moosilauke is a meadow, with the wind blowing the grasses that ripple across the green summit like ocean waves. When we clear the treeline, we are met by a blast of chilly wind that surprises us. It is a hot day, so the first minute feels great, but after that I don

my windbreaker. Pat, being better able to sustain her body temperature, is fine. All along the rock-lined trail to the summit and in between the boulders and along the sides of the meadow we see clumps of delicate white flowers. We walk to the summit sign for a picture. I love when there is a sign—it's absolute confirmation that we've made it. Summit: 12:20 p.m.

First lesson learned: take pictures of your moments of bliss. We experience two moments of sheer bliss on this hike and we don't take a picture of either of them. When we reach the summit, we find a large flat rock, out of the wind, to enjoy our lunch. Then, we take off our boots and socks—ahhhh, wiggle our toes in the breeze—ahhhh, and lie back on the warm rock to catch a few rays—ahhhhh. Bliss.

Time for power bar number two—a Reese's Sweet & Salty with Peanuts. We both take a bite and react simultaneously. Yummy. Oh, my God, this is a 5! We smack our lips and smile at each other. Reese's has set the bar!

After lunch and bliss and recharging with our power bar, we change into dry socks, reboot, and are off to the South Peak and then down the Carriage Road, which is wide and beautiful and offers glimpses of the mountains beyond. Pat has an incredible sense of distance and mentions that we should be seeing the Snapper Trail sign soon. Less than a minute later, there it is. Time for the third power bar, a Hershey's Sweet & Salty Pretzel bar, a 4 on the power bar yummy scale.

The three-mile trip back down to the Ravine Lodge is a cinch. The temperature is balmy, the breeze light and refreshing, and the distance short. We reach the bridge to the Lodge, but follow the parking sign, which turns out to be the long way back to our car. On the way up the last incline, we have a bite of the last power bar. I know we don't need it, but it has melted since I put it in the top of my pack (smart) so we might as well try it since it can't be saved for later. It is a Luna Bar for Women, Nutz over Chocolate. More like cardboard for women. It is a 1 on our rating scale and we manage only a bite each before putting it into our garbage baggie.

Time for our second moment of bliss, which also entails taking off our boots. This time we find bliss at the brook just below the Moosilauke Ravine Lodge. We sit on a flat rock, take off our boots and socks, and dangle our feet in the cold water: sssssssssss, ahhhhh. Nothing feels better than cold water on hot feet, knowing we've made it, and having a wet-wipe, a cold Snapple, and a congratulations burger and fries to look forward to.

What an awesome thing: hiking (with working legs) in the beauty of the White Mountains on a gorgeous day with a great friend, and checking off number ten on our four thousand footer list. Woo hoo!

STATS

MOUNTAIN: MT. MOOSILAUKE (4,802)

NEAREST CITY: GLENCLIFF, N.H.

DATE: JULY 14, 2006

TIME: 6 HOURS AND 40 MINUTES

WEATHER: SUNNY, WARMING INTO THE 80S, WINDY AND 60S ON THE SUMMIT

MILES: 10

ELEVATION GAIN: 2,484 FEET

TRAILS: ASQUAM-RIDGE TRAIL, BEAVER BROOK TRAIL, GLENCLIFF TRAIL, CARRIAGE ROAD, SNAPPER TRAIL

HOLY SHIT FACTOR: LOW, BUT SWEET AND SALTY

July 30, 2006, Sherburne, Vermont

> *We have stopped for a moment to encounter each other, to meet, to love, to share. This is a precious moment, but it is transient. It is a little parenthesis in eternity. If we share with caring, lightheartedness and love, we will create abundance and joy for each other. And then this moment will have been worthwhile.*
>
> Deepak Chopra

We set our sights on Killington, the second highest peak in Vermont. We invite two special guests—a mutual friend, Rob, and Don, my husband of twenty-nine years. I persuade Don to go on two hikes a year, if I'm lucky. He says he's a ball-sport guy and needs a ball to have fun. I consider bringing a ball on the hike, but decide he might not find that amusing. I'm hoping he'll climb Camel's Hump with us in October, so I behave.

During the ninety-minute drive, I worry that I forgot my hiking boots (wow, really stupid if that is the case). I am wearing flip-flops for comfort on the drive up. When we stop at a convenience store ten miles from the trailhead, Pat takes off for the portable toilet and I check the trunk. There they are with socks neatly tucked under the tongue. When Pat comes back, she asks me about my boots, clearly concerned.

"I forgot 'em," I tell her, straight-faced, then look down at my flip-flops. "I can hike in these."

Pat gasps. Her eyes get big. "Nancy, you can't . . . "

"Sure, I'll be fine," I say.

I can't help it. I start to laugh.

We arrive at the Bucklin trailhead and begin the usual futzing around with the gear, putting this here and that there, tying bandanas on our heads or hitching them to our packs.

"Oh no," I say. "Where are my boots?" They are no longer in the trunk. I know I saw them there. Pat, Don, and Rob are getting ready to hike and pay no attention to me. "Where are my boots?" I yell with a tinge of panic. I start throwing things around in the trunk. Pat turns around, laughing, holding out my boots.

Booted, packed, and watered, we are off at 10:02. The temps are in the 70s and it is a beautiful sunny day.

The trail is calm, level, and wooded, much of it along a brook. We talk and laugh, enjoying our guests and the new opportunities for conversation and connection.

We meet a woman coming down who tells us she hopes the summit clears before we get there; it had been totally socked in the clouds for her. Well, that's what you get when you start hiking at 5 a.m.!

About halfway to the peak, the carefree trail takes a turn for the worse—up—and stays that way for the remainder of the hike—wooded, and steep as hell.

Now, when you bring friends along to join you in your quest to summit the four thousand footers in New England, you make assumptions. At least we did. Neither Don nor Rob hike regularly so we'd prepared ourselves for what we thought that might mean. Pat and I brought extra water, Gatorade, and food in our packs in case the boys ran out. And we figured we might have to slow our pace. NBD (no big deal).

Slow our pace? We have to run to keep up with Rob. Now c'mon! He has a cold! He's sniffing and sneezing and hiking faster than I've ever hiked. My ego suffers a major blow. But I don't spend much time worrying about it, because I am too busy just trying to breathe. I pray for a bit of level ground so I can catch my breath. No such luck.

Pat keeps right up with Rob, making tracks up the mountain, putting me entirely to shame. (She later confides in me that she was really working hard to stick with him.) They leave Don and me in the dust, huffing and puffing, sweat dripping down our faces. Pat and Rob stop for a few short rest breaks, but I think that's because they hear us panting behind them and are concerned for our well-being.

We pass the Cooper Lodge, a backpacker's shelter, and climb the last steep two-tenths of a mile to the top. We reach the summit at 12:24 p.m. It is 63 degrees and windy, but cloudless, with a beautiful three-state view. The wind has a cold bite to it and we all put on extra clothing over our soaking wet Techwick tops.

The summit is packed with kids and families and adults all dressed in cute shorts, tank tops, and flip flops, laughing and giggling, acting like the wind isn't freezing cold. And more summer party people keep arriving. But from where? Why aren't they sweaty? Oh—the gondola ride from the base of the ski area to the top—that's where everyone is coming from. They haven't hiked up! They rode up on the gondola!

We settle on a warm rock in the sun, apart from the crowd, and chat with a fellow hiker. We enjoy our lunch and pose for a few pictures with the captivating view behind us. We start down the trail at 1:02 p.m.

Going down for me is easier than up; for Pat it is more difficult. So she and I switch places. I am the one struggling to keep up with Rob, and Pat and Don bring up the rear. Rob is jogging down the mountain. It takes everything I have to match his pace. I finally give up and ask him how the hell he is able to go so fast.

"Oh, I just let gravity do the work and I don't hold back," Rob says, smiling. If I did that, I would wet my pants.

We stop once on the way down, and we all lean over to stretch our backs. Mine is killing me because I am carrying a killer-pack filled with stuff we

don't need. We get down the steep section and I breathe a sigh of relief. This will be easier. Easier like hell! We sprint to the car! We make it down to the parking lot at 3:12 p.m. We enjoy cold sodas while we high five all around and take a few pictures in the parking lot; then it's homeward bound.

We make a rest stop at a convenience store on the way home. Don gets out very gingerly, kind of sideways. Might be a long night . . .

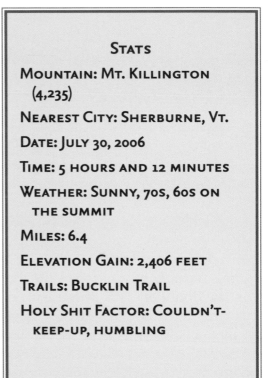

Stats

Mountain: Mt. Killington (4,235)

Nearest City: Sherburne, Vt.

Date: July 30, 2006

Time: 5 hours and 12 minutes

Weather: Sunny, 70s, 60s on the summit

Miles: 6.4

Elevation Gain: 2,406 feet

Trails: Bucklin Trail

Holy Shit Factor: Couldn't-keep-up, humbling

3. WITH HALE COMES BALANCE

August 26, 2006, Twin Mountain, New Hampshire

> *I always try to balance the light with the heavy—a few tears of human spirit in with the sequins and the fringes.*
>
> Bette Midler

Hale brings balance to our hiking. The 4,054-foot White Mountain is a reprieve from our last two hike-'til-you're-draggin', oh-my-God-are-we-almost-there hikes —Cannon and the Kinsmans, and Katahdin via the Knife Edge. Those two twelve-hour slogs left my knees halfway down the trail and my big toes numb. The Holy Shit Factors for each hike were way beyond anything I had ever imagined possible. Climbing Can-non and the Kinsmans I lost my full Nalgene water bottle only a quarter of the way into the hike. It fell out of my backpack pocket and rolled off a cliff, never to be seen again. The last hour of the hike, Pat and I entertained the thought we might not make it out. We had gone the wrong way around Lonesome Lake and wasted a precious hour of fading sunlight. We hiked the last mile and a half in the pitch black with one tiny penlight to help us find our

sand footer. No black-and-blues, no blood, not much mud, and no holy shit!

It's a partly cloudy day as we set out on the Hale Brook Trail at 10:06 a.m. with Dejah, a sweet, strong, energetic two-year-old yellow Lab who belongs to my daughter, Jess. This is our first time climbing a four thousand footer with her, so we are hoping fellow hikers on the trail will be dog-lovers and that Dejah will be a hiker-lover.

Wooded and running along a brook for the first half-mile, the Hale Brook Trail reminds me of the Bucklin Trail on Killington and the Tecumseh Trail on Tecumseh— wooded, with a pretty steep incline the entire way. Other than a few switchbacks thrown in around its mid-point, the trail is straight ahead and up. We arrive at the summit at 11:50 a.m. The summit is an open bare circle, but trees all around the periphery obscure the view. If you stand on the summit cairn, you can see the tops of the surrounding mountains; otherwise, no views.

We eat lunch, pleading with Dejah to lie down instead of begging for food. We take pictures and start down the mountain at 12:34 p.m. On our way down we

way over roots and around boulders and off the mountain. On Katahdin, the clouds rolled in so thick we couldn't see where we were going, the wind threatened to blow us off Knife Edge, we had to climb straight up and straight down two "chimneys," we needed every layer of clothing we had, and it was pouring rain the last few hours!

Hale, by comparison, is a breeze and gives us a much-needed break, an opportunity to rebuild confidence, and a chance to claim another four thou-

meet a fellow hiker on his way up.

"I thought this was supposed to be easy!" he whines. "That's what the guide book said." Hale is a four thousand footer with twenty-three hundred feet of elevation gain over 2.2 miles. Easy is relative.

Our descent is uneventful except for the awesome feeling of sharing the experience with a great friend, and with Dejah. Dejah is very well behaved. Who knows, we might bring her again. We arrive back at the parking lot at 1:59 p.m.

Balance. The killer hikes and the easy hikes—you need both.

Stats

Mountain: Mt. Hale (4,054)

Nearest City: Twin Mountain, N.H.

Date: August 26, 2006

Time: 2 hours and 53 minutes

Weather: Party cloudy, 60s

Miles: 5.3

Elevation Gain: 2,300 feet

Trails: Hale Brook Trail

Holy Shit Factor: Negligible, a reprieve from the hard hikes

4. SLUGS ON THE HANCOCKS

September 4, 2006, Lincoln, New Hampshire

Take nothing for granted. Not one blessed, cool mountain day or one hellish, desert day or one sweaty, stinky hiking companion. It is all a gift.

Cindy Ross, **Journey on the Crest**

The Hancocks: that is the plan. We leave Keene at 6 a.m. As we drive toward Concord, night becomes day, the sky turns blue, and the sun comes out, despite a forecasted twenty percent chance of rain. Our weather hopes are high until we stop in Meredith for our power bars, ice, and a bathroom break. A bank of clouds hangs over the Whites. "Get out of there," I whine, as I pretend to push the clouds away. We press on, sure they will dissipate.

The trailhead sits just after a hairpin turn on the Kancamagus Highway that could do major damage to you and your car if you're not careful. When we get there, the clouds are low and dense. I am disappointed, but at least we get to be out on the trail, together, hiking.

We set out on the Hancock Notch Trail, a wooded path that is incredibly gentle for the first few miles. I love that. Gentle gives me a chance to get my legs warmed up before the steep starts.

We have a number of easy stream crossings given the low level of water, and the path's gentle slope stays with us along the Cedar Brook Trail. As we approach the junction of the Hancock Loop Trail, I let out a woo hoo because we are now walking in the clouds, and whooping always lifts my spirits. And guess what? My woo hoo comes back to me. An echo. I stand there, thrilled, and woo hoo a few more times. I make Pat try it too. You know, hiking is chock full of life lessons. You get back what you give.

We set off toward South Hancock on the Hancock Loop Trail. No longer gentle, the trail takes a turn up and stays up for the rest of the climb, about a half mile. We are soaked from the inside out because we are sweating like crazy from working hard in the humid air. And we are also soaked from the outside in, from walking in the rain-mist-clouds. Yucky weather. You would think we would be miserable, but something happens. I turn around as we near the summit to see the clouds enshrouding us in their mist. I point out the I'm-sure-it's-there-somewhere view to Pat and we laugh. Then I decorate my hair with berries I find on the trail and we take a few pictures.

We reach the wooded top of South Hancock, we think, even though there is no summit sign. There is a sign for an overlook, but we figure there isn't much to over look, so we skip it.

The 1.4-mile ridge between the two peaks is surprisingly gentle. We've been on some killer ridges lately, so I am pleasantly surprised. There is one issue, though. The ridge trail is very narrow—narrower than a hiker's body—and lined with evergreen shrubs that are totally soaked with rain. They kindly share their abundance of wet with us as we pass between them. We are soaked and laughing. I now have rain-mist-clouds-water running down my legs on the inside of my pants, along with sweat, and probably a little pee from laughing so hard.

We make it to North Hancock, which also has no summit sign, soaked and happy. We start down, moving back into the trees for some protection where we break for lunch. Now that we've stopped moving, we're a bit cold so we stuff down our soggy sandwiches and get back on the trail. I really like my bliss moments. And for me, bliss usually involves sun, food, and a view. We have only one part of that equation today, food, which is a bit soppy. No sun, no hot rock on which to enjoy lunch, and certainly no view. So the bliss factor on this hike is disappointing.

We are on our way down from North Hancock on the Loop Trail, which is very steep, when we see them. Slugs. No, I'm not talking about me and Pat! I'm talking about those fleshy, slimy, oozing mollusks that love wet muck. Yuck. Gross. When they locate themselves shoulder-high on trees lining the

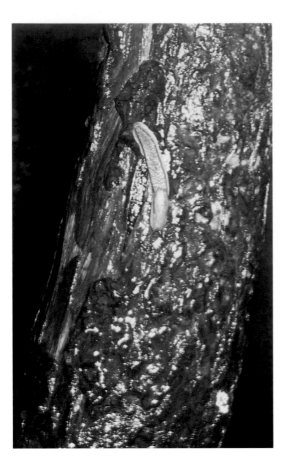

We make it to the junction of the Cedar Brook Trail, where I get to practice my echo again. Then, back on gentle ground, we eventually arrive in the parking lot for pictures of our we-bagged-two-more-peaks moment.

I learn a really important lesson on this hike. I learn that I can love living life, no matter what the circumstances, no matter what the weather. There is no better way to spend Labor Day than hiking, even in the rain-mist-clouds.

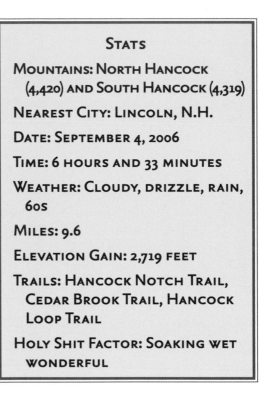

STATS

MOUNTAINS: NORTH HANCOCK (4,420) AND SOUTH HANCOCK (4,319)

NEAREST CITY: LINCOLN, N.H.

DATE: SEPTEMBER 4, 2006

TIME: 6 HOURS AND 33 MINUTES

WEATHER: CLOUDY, DRIZZLE, RAIN, 60S

MILES: 9.6

ELEVATION GAIN: 2,719 FEET

TRAILS: HANCOCK NOTCH TRAIL, CEDAR BROOK TRAIL, HANCOCK LOOP TRAIL

HOLY SHIT FACTOR: SOAKING WET WONDERFUL

trail it is bad news. Picture this: I am letting gravity take my body down toward the wet earth, my feet balanced on a rock. My plan to avoid a face-plant is to arrest my fall by landing with my left hand on the trunk of a tree down and to my left. Seconds before I land, while I am still falling, I see them. Two huge gross orange slugs. Right where my hand is heading. I don't really care if I fall, but I am not landing on those slugs! I shift my weight at the last second, uttering a gross noise as I register the yuck of it all, and land on another tree; thankfully a slugless one. I gather myself and move on.

5. WASHINGTON—THE PEAK EXPERIENCE

September 30, 2006, Bretton Woods, New Hampshire

> *"Human beings do not realize the extent to which their own sense of defeat prevents them from doing things they could do perfectly well. The peak experience induces the recognition that your own powers are far greater than you imagined them."*
>
> Colin Wilson

Do we think 4:30 a.m. is a sane time for the alarm to go off? Me neither. So I set it for 4:50, knowing I'm giving up gentle-wake-up snoozing for adrenalin-pumping get-the-hell-out-of-bed now! But my backpack's in the car and I'm ready.

Dejah is thrilled to be awake at 5 a.m., bounding down the stairs six at a time, her tail a wagging lethal weapon. Pat, Dejah, and I are on the road at 5:30 in the dark. Breakfast at daybreak with the happy peppy people at the Hillsboro Mickey D's. We stop in Meredith for power bars and a restroom break.

For the first time in months, there are no clouds over the Whites as we near Franconia Notch. The sun is out and the fall colors are fluorescent. Our euphoria is short-lived as we drive the last five miles to the Ammonoosuc Ravine trailhead. Washington, dead ahead, is one big mass of gray mist. The summit forecast is for clear skies by 11 a.m. We set out on the trail at 8:30 a.m., so the sun has a few hours to get her act together.

There are tons of cars in the parking lot, a forewarning of the number of hikers we'll see today, a Saturday during peak foliage. The trail starts out on a gentle incline, always my favorite way to wake up the legs.

After the first few miles, the "steep" starts. The trail resembles a stone stairway meandering up into the clouds, alongside Ammonoosuc River, which is dotted with breathtaking waterfalls. As we climb, the brilliant colors fade and, almost imperceptibly at first, turn to white. Frost laces the tree limbs and pine needles; ice covers the rocks. We meet a hiker coming down who says the trail from the Lakes of the Clouds Hut to the Washington summit is sheer ice and the mountaintops are shrouded in clouds. Thanks a lot, O Cheery One. Pat and I stay hopeful.

We reach the hut, now completely above the treeline, and take a right to bag Mt. Monroe. It is a short robust climb and I get colder every step I take, so I put on my fleece hat and gloves. "Nancy, turn around," Pat says. I spin and see the sparkling white summit of Mt. Washington framed in bright blue skies. No clouds. The sun comes through big time! We reach the Monroe summit at 11:40 a.m. and, wow, I'm not sure I can convey just how full I feel. The colors: gray rock, green and yellow grasses, and bright white frost in the foreground; orange, yellow, red, and green landscape; blue and purple mountains that fade in the far distance, backed by a brilliant blue sky. There is no end to how far I can see. So big, so vast, and only Pat and I on top.

We climb down and across the saddle, past the closed hut, and head toward Washington, joining a long line of hikers. The sun has melted any ice on the rocks, so footing is easy. The higher we go the more white the landscape, until we reach the summit, which is totally shrouded in rime ice.

Driving to the trailhead this morning I said to Pat, "Please may I be able to do this." It was as if I was pleading to God to grant me steel quads, iron calves, and the knees and heart of a tri-athlete just for this hike. I was nervous. I still consider myself a newbie hiker and Washington is the highest mountain on our sixty-seven four-thousand-footers list, fully a thousand feet higher than anything I've climbed. Yikes!

Arriving on the Washington summit at 1:15 p.m. in the windless sunshine, I take a huge breath of cold air and feel the pride fill my lungs. I made it! Woo hoo! We climbed Mt. Washington and it didn't kill us!

The summit of Washington is marred by buildings and train smoke and way too many people—lots of hikers from a dozen trails, Cog Railway riders, and Washington Auto Road drivers. We don't spend a long time on top. We wait in line for a summit sign picture (a summit sign—Hallelujah!) and then have lunch. Cold and soaked through, I change into dry clothes, and take a moment to warm up inside the cafeteria. Then we're off toward Mt. Clay, following a group of hikers from the summit of Washington all the way to the Clay Loop Trail. Before us is a stun-

ning view of the Northern Presidentials—Mts. Jefferson, Adams, and Madison, all in a row. We take the road less traveled, toward Mt. Clay, while everyone else continues down, thinking one summit is enough. Not for us.

Who exactly is Clay, anyway? I thought I knew all the presidents. But, it's a mountain and it counts, so let's go! We get to what we think is the peak and are about to celebrate, then have second thoughts. Do we high five here? Looking at the map, we decide maybe we haven't reached the summit and we'd better go over that next knob to see what we can see. Here is a case where a summit sign would be really handy. Did we bag the peak or not? And who the hell is Clay? We learn later that Mt. Clay, even though it is 5,533 feet high, doesn't count as a four thousand footer; it's just the northwest shoulder of Washington. And Henry

Clay wasn't a president either. Good old Henry ran five times and never made it. We bag the peak at 3:25 p.m. and the views are spectacular. We have no regrets. Clay may never have served in the Oval Office, and the mountain may not have made it onto the four thousand-footer list, but the experience of climbing Clay, along with Monroe and Washington, fills me with an I-can-do-anything euphoria.

Pat says, "Let's boogie." As we turn to head down, my tired feet trip on a rock and I almost do a face plant, landing in prayer position, laughing hysterically, trying like hell not to pee. We head out toward the Jewell Trail, back in a line of hikers, making our way down

est peak in the northeastern United States for the first time. In our quest to climb the sixty-seven highest mountains in New England, we just climbed the king. It's all downhill from here.

STATS

MOUNTAINS: MTS. MONROE (5,384), WASHINGTON (6,288) AND CLAY (5,533)

NEAREST CITY: BRETTON WOODS, N.H.

DATE: SEPTEMBER 30, 2006

TIME: 10 HOURS

WEATHER: CLOUDY IN THE MORNING, SUN WITH PASSING CLOUDS IN THE AFTERNOON, UPPER 30S, LOW 40S

MILES: 13.2

ELEVATION GAIN: 4,202 FEET

TRAILS: AMMONOOSUC RAVINE TRAIL, CRAWFORD PATH, TRINITY HEIGHTS CONNECTOR, GULFSIDE TRAIL, CLAY LOOP, JEWELL TRAIL

HOLY SHIT FACTOR: THIS SHOULD BE CALLED THE "OH MY GOD" FACTOR—INCREDIBLY HIGH WITH THE MOST ASTOUNDING VIEWS I'VE EVER SEEN

the mountain. The trail is a relatively graceful, gentle downhill that brings us to the parking lot in the fading light of day at 6:30 p.m.

This experience for me is the epitome of why I hike. On the trail, I feel full of wonder each time I look out into the world. Every second of the hike is filled with a kind of awe that could bring tears to my eyes if I pause too long. Getting into the car, Pat and I are jubilant. I'm happy tired, my toes are numb, knees are talking to me, and body is filled with the sensation of having worked really hard. I will always remember this sunny clear day we summited the high-

6. BLESSED BY WINTER IN OCTOBER— CAMEL'S HUMP

October 21, 2006, Huntington Center, Vermont

To recognize that everything is surprising is the first step toward recognizing that everything is a gift.

David Steidl-Rast

The plan: drive to Burlington, Vermont, on Friday night and climb Camel's Hump on Saturday. Weather forecast looks favorable—sunny with temperatures in the high 40s. Pat and I bring a special guest, my husband, Don.

We leave Keene at 5:30 p.m., have dinner in a steak house near Quechee, Vermont, and meet a snowstorm head-on along I-89 North. We're not talking about a little bit of snow here. We're talking about wind gusts threatening to blow the car into the other lane, snow pelting the windshield and sticking to the highway, and close to whiteout

conditions. There are cars off the road everywhere, and hazard lights blinking all around us; we are in a white-knuckle-oh-my-God-please-may-we-make-it blizzard. Pat is a hero and we arrive in Burlington safely. We all take a slow collective breath, bring our shoulders back down from kissing our ears, loosen our clenched teeth, take major pain relievers, and hit the sack.

We are at the trailhead at 9:37 a.m. Saturday morning. I have in mind a nice fall hike. Uh-uh. Four inches of snow blanket the ground at the trailhead. I expect it on the summit, but at the trailhead? It is 35 degrees when we start up. I am worried about Don, knowing he's already apprehensive about the hike and now

has snow to contend with.

We each make a mistake in judgment getting ready for this hike—keep in mind the sunny-with-temps-in-the-high-40s thing. Pat doesn't think she'll need ice cleats; why would you on leaves? So she doesn't bring them. I don't think I need my warm mittens so I bring a pair of light fleece gloves. Don, also believing the weather report, sports his mesh-topped Merrells—no need for heavy winter boots on a beautiful fall hike.

At the trailhead we plan to take the Burrows-Forest Connector to the Forrest City Trail to the Long Trail and do a loop. But no one has broken the trail yet and I know there is a steep section with a warning not to attempt it in winter without a compass because it is very hard to follow. We make a wise decision and take the Burrows Trail, which has already seen many boots before ours.

The trail is gentle, paralleling a brook for much of the way, then ascending more steeply as we near the summit. The trees are covered with snow and white is all around us—no color, no fall leaves, no blue sky, no bright sun—just white under us, around us, and over us. We are in a winter wonderland and it is breathtakingly beautiful.

I say something about the weather not being what I expected, with a negative spin to my words, and Don replies, "We are blessed." His words are a gift.

Every once in a while we come across a "Hi" written in the snow, a greeting from hikers before us. Pat replies with a "Hi" that she etches in the snow with her pole—hikers gracing each other's journeys, sharing in a way only winter permits. As we ascend, the temperatures go down to the low 30s, and the wind picks up and I start adding layers. About three-quarters of the way up, Don and I put on ice cleats while Pat puts on her rain pants (not that her rain pants will help her walk on ice, but they will keep her butt warm as she slides down the ice). I fool around with the cleats for what feels like forever, freezing my fingers in the process. Luckily Pat has hand warmers and I stick one in each glove, and give two to Don, whose hands are also freezing. Within five minutes I feel the icy hot pain of my fingers coming alive.

Although footing is pretty good much of the way, there are definitely icy spots where the cleats provide peace of mind. Pat makes her way along the trail carefully with the help of her pole.

Reaching treeline, we find ourselves in a cloud of white, rime ice on the tree branches on our left, snow covering all the shrubs on the right. We hit the summit at noon. The wind chill makes the air feel colder than the 23-degree temperature. My guess—the wind is a steady twenty-five miles per hour with gusts up to forty miles per hour. All I really know is it reminds me of when I was skydiving, free falling over Australia. (In 2003, I went to visit my daughter, Kelly, who was studying in a college semester abroad program. We bungee jumped and went sky diving on the same adrenalin-filled day.) The wind is roaring and my hood is furiously flapping around my face. It is difficult to find the summit because visibility is ten feet at the most. We see a cairn, but no summit sign, we don't see any more "up" and assume we're on the top. Pat sets up her camera and puts on the timer while I shiver and Don, loving the extremes, becomes one with the turbulence. We get a picture of all three of us in the freezer. We marvel at the force of nature all around us. It is freeze-your-ass-off cold and blow-you-off-the-mountain windy—a wild, exciting, exhilarating adventure.

We head off the summit back into the safety of treeline. Once in the cover of the white, rime-iced trees, Don says in a voice full of wonder, "That was great!"

By this time the trail has seen lots of

hikers and the path is a kind of ice and dirt stew with chunks of snow, rocks, and grit floating in the muddy slush. We are surprised to meet lots of people who are on their way up. Some are in short-sleeved shirts, others in jeans, and many are trying to keep their boots dry. Not going to happen; don't even bother.

Hiking down the mountain is anticlimactic, especially for Don, whose head is still in the thrill of the summit. As we near the car, he says, "That was easy!" He is a hiker after all.

We arrive back at the car at 2:16 p.m., change our soaked boots, and head off to Mirabelle's in Burlington for hot Cafe Latte's and whoopee pies. Woo hoo!

STATS

MOUNTAIN: CAMEL'S HUMP (4,083)

NEAREST CITY: HUNTINGTON CENTER, VT.

DATE: OCTOBER 21, 2006

TIME: 5 HOURS AND 30 MINUTES

WEATHER: COLD AND WINDY FOR OCTOBER

MILES: 4.8

ELEVATION GAIN: 2,562 FEET

TRAILS: BURROWS TRAIL, LONG TRAIL

HOLY SHIT FACTOR: HIGH, WITH THE SURPRISE OF WINTER

7. HEALING ON WILDCAT

November 18, 2006, Jackson, New Hampshire

Life's challenges are not supposed to paralyze you; they're supposed to help you discover who you are.

Bernice Johnson Reagon

Our intention is to hike Middle and South Carter. We leave Keene at 5:30 a.m., Dejah in the back seat happily sucking on her stuffed toy. We arrive in Pinkham Notch a little before 9, later than we had hoped. As we near the Visitor's Center, I suggest we hike Wildcat instead. The trailhead is closer and the hike is shorter—10.4 miles out-and-back compared to Carter's 12.4 loop. We are getting a late start, so a shorter hike feels more prudent. But, we are prepared for the Carters and do not know what Wildcat has in store for us. We know that Wildcat is a mini-range with five peaks, A, B, C, D, and E, and that only A and D qualify for the four thousand-footer list.

We park at the Pinkham Notch Visitor's Center and at 9:20 a.m. start off on the Long Pond Trail to avoid the river crossing on the Wildcat Ridge Trail, which proves to be a smart decision. We would have had to take off our boots and pants to cross the river and that would not have been fun. We hit the Wildcat Ridge Trail and up we go. Yes, up. Straight up. *The 4000-Footers of the White Mountains* by Steve Smith and Mike Dickerman calls it "an exceptionally steep rugged climb up." You got that right, boys! The highway stays below us as we hike up and up and up. Nothing gradual about this trail. The views of Washington are beautiful and we stop frequently to marvel at the Presidentials while sucking big wind. The trail is sparkling with mica.

The many ledges and very steep, tricky climbs lead to a problem. Dejah starts to cry, a high pitched whine, and her paws bounce up and down on the granite ledge in a panic. Something happens to me. Her cries transport me back to a time in my childhood when I was scared to death. All of a sudden I am not adult Nancy on the trail, but a young girl frightened for her life, escaping into the woods, cold and alone. It is a memory I have always had. My guess is I am five years old. I am wearing a dress. It is cold, dusk, in the fall around Halloween. I am running through the woods as fast as I can away from something terrifying. As a child I remembered my pursuer as a bear. But I know now I am running away from a person who is trying to bring me back. I am running so fast I am afraid that I will trip over a log or run into a branch or tree, and then he'll catch me. I have never run so fast. I escape. Although the memory is incomplete, what I do remember is shear terror. I am in it now.

It takes all I have to keep climbing. I feel vulnerable and cannot find a safety zone inside me. Each time we hit a particularly steep spot, Dejah cries. Pat encourages her until she gives it a try and makes it easily, while I struggle with the effect her panic has on me. At the ridgeline, having successfully negotiated the ledges, Dejah is wagging her tail, happy as can be. I am very upset, still back in time, trying to get a grip on the current moment and let go of past horror. I muster the courage to tell Pat what is happening. She understands. We have shared a lot as friends; this is another opportunity. So we hike on, with me struggling to re-enter the present, Pat encouraging, Dejah oblivious and happy.

At 12:17 p.m., we arrive on the summit of Wildcat E, which I understand was formerly a four thousand footer, according to Smith and Dickerman. (What does that mean—a former four thousand footer? E shrank? E doesn't cut the mustard? What?) We take a moment to re-assess. We know it will be dark on our way back down and both Pat and I are worried about descending that incredibly steep trail after dark. I have visions of Dejah flying off the side of the mountain, or me falling off the ledge, which makes me shudder. We

talk about our options and decide instead to go down the Nineteen-Mile Brook Trail from Wildcat A, at the other end of the ridge, and hitchhike the four to five miles back to our car. Sure, someone will pick up two backpackers and a dog at night! Perhaps it's not a great plan, but it's a plan nevertheless. We climb past the gondola station to the summit of Wildcat D, bagging our thirty-ninth four thousand footer at 1:15 p.m. High five.

On the way down from Wildcat D we meet a couple of hikers who tell us that the roughest and most difficult part of the trail lies ahead (thanks). They also share that the best way off the mountain is to take the Polecat Ski Trail, from the gondola station, down to the Wildcat ski area parking lot, which is only a mile from our car. They say it is gradual and well-packed-down because lots of hikers and ATVs use the trail. Now we have a feasible plan.

Although I am struggling emotionally and physically on this hike, I have not lost my humor. I mean, couldn't someone have come up with slightly more creative names than Wildcat A, B, C, D, and E? It sounds like kindergarten on the slopes—and there is nothing kindergarten about the Wildcats! How

about using other animals? Wild Fox, Wild Emus, Wild Kanga, Wild Porcupine—wild anything. Or stick to the cat family. There are plenty to choose from: cheetah, jaguar, leopard, lion, tiger, cougar, panther, and bobcat. Or we could name the peaks what they deserve—Mt. Hell-Of-A-Climb, Mt. Sucking Wind, Mt. O Holy Shit, Mt. What-the-Fuck or Straight-Up Mountain. Anything but A, B, C, D, and E!

And while I'm pissing and moaning, how about a few signs? Without signs on a ridge with five peaks it's difficult to figure out where we are. We go down, in this case straight down, and then we go up, in this case straight up. At the point where we are about to descend again I think this must be a peak. Let's

call it C. We start down again and then straight back up again and when we reach what feels like the height of land I figure we are on B. Of course it could be C. This continues ad nauseum until I have absolutely no idea if we have summited C or B, and, by the way, where the hell is A? We do another up and down and I am hoping we are on A, but no, we don't think so. The trail continues, so that must be B; could be C. We go down and back up—maybe this is A? Thankfully, Pat has read that you can see the Carter Notch Hut from the summit of Wildcat A. Thank God, there it is. We are on A. We bag number 40 at 3:30 p.m. Now we have to go all the way back.

I am still struggling with feeling un-

safe, so the hike takes a huge emotional and physical toll on me. Pat's reassurance and empathy help me continue to put one foot in front of the other. We retrace our steps along the ridge, going sharply up and down and up and down and up and down. I don't even try to figure out what peak we are on. About halfway along the ridge, at dusk, we stop to put on our headlamps. The mica sprinkled all along the trail reflects sparkles of light, glittering all the way back, making the trail look luminous.

Finally, after what feels like forever, we arrive at the gondola station at 5:32 p.m. and begin looking for the Polecat Ski Trail. At this point it is pitch dark and clouds are rolling over the summit, limiting our visibility considerably. I say

considerably because that sounds like what I should say in a hike report—but what I really mean is we can't see shit! How are we supposed to find the trail if we can't see more than twenty feet in front of us? It feels surreal and is totally disorienting. As we search for the trail marker, we see a pair of green eyes looking back at us and hear a strange high-pitched noise. *Yo, Pat, we've got company.* We don't know what it is but he definitely spooks us.

We can't find the trail and can see only the gondola station so we decide to hike down underneath the gondola cables, walking from pillar to pillar, thinking we might be able to see one to the next. Wrong! We start down and immediately find ourselves on jagged rocks, and in dense bushes. We can't see the next pillar and we can't see what we are walking on—we just know it isn't feeling good. At this point I have another flashback. I am a kid skiing. Riding up on the chair lift, often the ski trail is right below us and we try to spit on the skiers (Nice, huh? I promise I've grown up to be a decent human being but I had my moments as a kid.) Often the trail disappears and we are looking down at ledges and rock cliffs. I'm thinking hiking under the gondola might not be such a good idea. We decide to try and find a ski trail and hike back up to the summit. Surely my quads have a little bit left. Or not.

After some fifteen minutes of searching, Pat finds what looks like a trail and down we go. Ah, this feels better! We are on smooth ground, heading down, and can just barely make out ATV tracks in front of us. We are on the Polecat Ski Trail! As we descend, our knees start talking to us. Loudly. We are both done and announce it. The trail, however, is not done, but continues down for two-and-three-quarter miles. Dejah seems happy; her knees don't seem to be talking to her. As we descend, the clouds clear and the night emerges. Thousands of stars light the way, with the Big Dipper directly in front of us. We turn off our headlamps and gaze up at the starry sky, reorienting ourselves. I finally find safety. It takes the whole hike. But I am back to me.

We reach the ski area parking lot at 7:15 p.m. and walk the last veeeerrrrryyyyy looooooonng mile on Route 16 back to our car. We get to the car at 7:35 and head home.

Something very important happened to me today. I wasn't climbing Wildcat; I was back in the woods behind my childhood house, running for my life, feeling the terror. By realizing what was happening and sharing the secret I'd kept for my lifetime, I opened up a space inside to let healing begin. The little girl in me learned she is not alone, that she can trust the adult me to take care of her, and that we will be okay. We emerge at the bottom of the mountain, less separate, more whole.

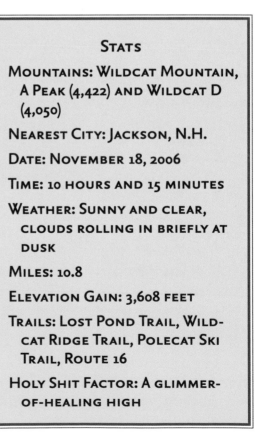

STATS

MOUNTAINS: WILDCAT MOUNTAIN, A PEAK (4,422) AND WILDCAT D (4,050)

NEAREST CITY: JACKSON, N.H.

DATE: NOVEMBER 18, 2006

TIME: 10 HOURS AND 15 MINUTES

WEATHER: SUNNY AND CLEAR, CLOUDS ROLLING IN BRIEFLY AT DUSK

MILES: 10.8

ELEVATION GAIN: 3,608 FEET

TRAILS: LOST POND TRAIL, WILDCAT RIDGE TRAIL, POLECAT SKI TRAIL, ROUTE 16

HOLY SHIT FACTOR: A GLIMMER-OF-HEALING HIGH

8. IT'S NOT ABOUT BAGGING THE PEAK —MT. MANSFIELD

December 9, 2006, Underhill Center, Vermont

Sometimes, accepting help is harder than offering it.
Star Wars: **The Clone Wars**

Mt. Mansfield, Vermont's highest peak, is the goal. Pat, Dejah, and I leave Keene at 5:30 a.m. and arrive at the trailhead at 8:30. Eight to nine inches of new snow grace the ground. We skid trying to park near the unplowed park entrance and decide to go back down the road to the plowed section. We gear up and set off.

It's surprising how much work snow adds to a steady climb. We trudge up the park road, finally reaching the trailhead. Given the conditions, we decide on a shorter loop than our original plan. With the trail snow-covered it is hard to tell what we're stepping on; it just looks like a bumpy white path. Sometimes we're surprised by good traction under the snow and other times our feet meet with ice and we lose our footing, slip, and try again. Winter hiking requires much more effort—a new lesson learned.

Pat and I have all the right gear for this winter hike. We have lots of extra layers, wind breakers, hard shells, soft shells, glove liners, heavy mittens, balaclavas, wind hats, ice cleats, gaiters. You name it, we have it.

Correction: we almost have all the right gear.

I am wearing my light-hiking boots that have taken me over 230 miles up and down four thousand footers since May 6. I bought winter hiking boots and wore them for ten minutes on a previous hike. They were stiff, heavy, and hot, and I couldn't stand them. I changed into my light hikers and was so happy, even in the snow we encountered at the top of the ridge. So, I figure I will be fine on Mansfield. Wrong.

From the beginning of the hike, my feet are cold. I ignore it and keep walking, sure they will warm up. Halfway up Mansfield, sweat pouring down my face, my feet are still cold. I start to concentrate on moving my toes as I climb, hoping they will warm up. By now, we are hiking in the clouds—no views today and that realization adds to my darkening mood.

"Pat, I'm not sure I like winter hiking," I say, overwrought with cold feet, discomfort, and disappointment. I have lost my perspective and can't recall any happy winter hiking moments.

We keep climbing. Pat is worried about my feet and suggests a few times that we stop and warm them up. I am determined to keep going, not to be a wimp, not to make this worse than it really is. But finally I am just too cold.

Pat helps me take off my frozen boots. We put hand warmers and extra socks on my feet and wait for the big warm-up. Pat and I take turns holding my feet. I am upset—ashamed that I need help and scared because I can't feel my feet, nor can I feel the warmers working at all. I am worried Pat will begin searching for a real hiker for her hiking partner.

Pat brings out a surprise—hot chocolate—and pours me a cup. It is meant for a summit celebration, but the circumstances call for it now. It feels so good going down, but I don't enjoy it because I am too overwhelmed by the

situation. The heat never reaches my toes. But the act of kindness does not go unnoticed.

"I think we should go back down," Pat says. I start to cry. I am never one to turn around, to give up. We've had lots of tough moments in our hiking adventures this year, and I've never considered turning around. But I know she is right and I don't even fight it. Pat gives me a hug full of warmth, and in spite

of my vulnerability, I let myself feel the friendship.

We start down. I had not realized the trail was so steep on the way up, but it feels sheer and slippery going down. I have no feeling in my feet so it is hard to place them carefully and I just don't care. I am in survival mode, taking a step at a time. I'm beating myself up mentally with every step I take. *Why can't I be stronger, like Pat?* I ask myself. *Why can't I just keep climbing?* I feel emotionally and physically weak. I stop on the trail and concentrate on moving my toes, trying to feel something.

"How do I know when it's time to stop and do something?" I ask Pat, grimacing.

"We need to stop now," Pat replies, calmly, clearly, with concern.

I sit down, we take off my boots and socks and Pat places my bare feet on her stomach—skin to skin.

"Pat, I'm angry, mad at myself, ashamed, embarrassed," I say through tears. I feel only concern and care from Pat, no judgment, no anger. I am touched by her kindness and ability to stay focused.

Dejah picks up on my anxiety and runs around frantically, licking our faces, getting all our gear snow-covered and wet. Pat comforts her with treats and she quiets down.

My feet feel nothing at first. And then I start to feel pin-pricks. My feet are tingling painfully back to life. I have no idea how long we stay like that, Pat kneeling in front of me with my feet against her stomach, her clothes wrapped around my feet, me struggling with my anxiety.

"Thank you, Pat," I say, my feet still embraced by her warmth. Thank you isn't adequate but it's all I can say. I pull my feet away, put on dry socks and my boots, and we start down again. My boots feel cold as ice, but my feet . . . my feet feel. They are mine again.

Hope is the only word for what is happening to me. I feel hope where before there was none. It feels like such a contrast from how I was feeling only half an hour ago, when anguish, despair, and misery were winning. I feel alive again. I notice the beauty around me and remember why I love hiking. I feel like I am back to Nancy and my whole world view has done a 360.

"Oh my God, Pat!" I say. "I can feel my feet! I'm okay! I feel like I can make it!" Pat smiles as relief floods through us both. We continue down, pensive and filled with the enormity of what has taken place today. We arrive back at the car at 1:30 p.m.

"We'll be back," I promise Pat. "We'll bag Mansfield and celebrate big time on top."

Three hours later we arrive at my house, much earlier than planned. Don, my husband, is thrilled to have me home. He worries about me hiking in winter.

Since May, I have been focused on bagging peaks—adding them up one by one, sometimes two and three at a time, always working toward our goal of climbing the sixty-seven New Eng-

land Four Thousand Footers. Yes, I love the views, the challenge, the exercise, and the laughs with Pat, but the purpose of our hiking is to add to the growing list of mountains scaled. Or so I thought.

We didn't add a peak today. But the hike is one of the more meaningful in my life.

I grew up in a violent household; my mother always angry, my father of-

ten absent. I sought help from teachers, ministers, nurses, and doctors. No one wanted to interfere. So I learned to trust no one, and learned that if I was going to make it, I'd have to take care of myself. My life's mantra became: I can do it; I don't need anyone's help.

Hiking Mansfield, it felt excruciating to admit my vulnerability, trust Pat, and accept her kindness and care. It deepened our friendship and put a kink in my I-don't-need-anybody armor. The experience shows there is help and friendship out there for me; I don't have to go it alone anymore.

I am human. I'm a fifty-two-year-old woman who wears the wrong hiking boots, always wants to succeed, hates to give up for any reason, and has a difficult time accepting help.

"Someday we'll laugh about this," Pat says.

She's right. But not yet. Until then, I know I have been blessed by this experience and by my friendship with Pat. Perhaps that is more important than bagging any peak.

STATS

Mountain Attempted: Mt. Mansfield

Nearest City: Underhill Center, Vt.

Date: December 9, 2006

Time: 4 hours and 30 minutes

Weather: Cloudy, temps in the 20s

Miles: 4.2

Trails: Halfway House Trail

Holy Shit Factor: Our first time turning around . . . really hard

My dear friend, clear your mind of can't.
Samuel Johnson

We dig deep and then reach in and dig even deeper to find the strength and courage to get ourselves up some of these mountains. We face freezing temperatures, battering winds, and snow up to our waists; each experience pushing our edges, expanding our comfort zones. We discover the thrill of being cheered and cheering others to a summit, and a sense of belonging to a larger community of hikers. We realize we are learning who we are and how to live richer, more meaningful lives as we tramp through the beauty of the woods to the never-ending views on the summits. In the midst of it all, we discover child-like joy.

9. TRAINING ROUND ON MADISON AND ADAMS

January 7, 2007, Randolph, New Hampshire

If you have the courage to step outside of your comfort zone, you will not only be amazed by the marvel and sights of the world, but also with the wonders that lay deep within yourself.

Rosanna Ienco

The original idea is to climb Madison, which expands to include Adams since Adams is only an inch away on our White Mountain map—why not?

We leave Keene at 5 a.m., Pat driving the three-plus hours to the trailhead. Pat has been fighting a debilitating depression that pushes her into a terrible black hole, unable to enjoy life or even our hikes. But today Pat is excited about the hike, smiling, sharing, and back to her old self. I have missed her. What a blessing it is to have my friend feeling good again.

Dejah, Pat, and I are on the Air Line Trail by 8:15 a.m. It is windy at the trailhead, which has me a bit worried, but I ignore the concern. There is no snow at the bottom and the footing is fine. It is a steady climb up and about halfway we put on cleats to make our way up the icy trail. I can hear the wind howling above us and comment to Pat that I hope the wind dies down before we get to the top. By the time we hit treeline, my feet are unhappy. I don't like my winter boots; they're too big—my heels move up and down no matter how many socks I wear or how tight I tie the laces. Add the weight of ice cleats to my boots and I am not a happy hiker. Plus, I fell on Mt. Monadnock a few weeks ago and hurt my knee. It's still sore—what's up with that?

We hit the famous sign: "STOP. The area ahead has the worst weather in America. Many have died there from exposure even in the summer. Turn back now if the weather is bad." The wind is howling. Pat and I look at each other and continue on.

We change our clothes just below treeline, put on down sweaters, wind hats, gloves, and balaclavas before heading out into the roaring wind. I am perfecting the art of changing into dry clothes in the freezing cold. My system includes a specific order of packing and a particular way of folding my clothes, having hand warmers warmed and ready, and saying "holy shit" over and over while moving fast and furiously.

Above treeline the mountain is stunningly beautiful: snow covers the ground, although most of the rocks are bare, and clouds move across the ridge tops, showing hopeful sections of blue. The temperature is in the 20s and the wind—well, the wind is the story. It is whipping around us, as if to say, *You are not welcome here—go away or I'll blow you away!* Although I've hiked in windy conditions, on Camel's Hump in Vermont, and Knife Edge on Katahdin in Maine, I have never experienced wind this strong. At first it feels exhilarating, but my feelings about the wind deteriorate from there.

Key question: Where the hell is Adams? Mt. Madison is on the left. A humongous pile of rocks to our right disappears into the clouds and I assume, silly me, that it's Mt. Adams. It looks far away but, according to the sign, we are eight tenths of a mile away, a distance I can handle. We begin our ascent. The trail starts out like a path but our climb quickly morphs into rock hopping and boulder scrambling. As we inch higher, the wind grows stronger, with bursts that force me to lean over and hold onto whatever is on the ground. *Is this safe? Should we be up here?* I move slowly and concentrate on holding my body upright against the wind, which works, until another wind gust forces me to hunker down and pay homage to the trail. The wind is so loud, it's hard to think, much less communicate with someone else. And if that's not enough, my clothes are flapping in my ears, increasing the level of distraction to an almost unbearable level.

I have all I can handle dealing with the wind when my clothes start beating me up. A strap attached to who-knows-what (there are straps attached to *everything* on hiking gear) whips around my face and smacks me directly in my right eye. Ouch, that really hurt! My eye waters, and for the moment I can't see. Pat comes over and tethers the strap to keep it in line. We start walking again and another strap attacks my left eye. Pat fixes it and we continue on, following the cairns. At some point we start to head around this massive cone. This has me concerned.

I scream at Pat over the wind, "Is that Adams?" pointing to the cone of rocks.

"I don't know," she yells.

Then I see it. I point to a peak on the horizon mostly shrouded in clouds and say, "Is *that* Adams?"

"I don't know," Pat yells back.

We get out the map. But just unfolding it in the gale to its full newspaper size is a challenge, let alone trying to figure out where we are, especially since I can't see squat without my reading glasses.

I yell, "Well, we're closer to Adams than Madison, right? So let's at least bag Adams." Translation: I'm in distress and I can't do both peaks.

Pat nods and up we go.

I look up at what-I-wish-is-Adams-but-I-bet-is-not and see clouds whizz across the summit propelled by the ex-

treme winds.

I look at Dejah. Her ears are furiously flapping back against her head, her eyes are slits, and frost crystals glint on her nose. *Is she okay in this wind and cold? Will she get frostbite?*

A gust almost knocks me over. Tears sting my eyes.

"Pat, I'm scared of the wind and I'm not sure I can get to Adams if it's that peak way the hell over there," my voice barely audible above the wind.

It's tough to admit I'm scared. But the simple fact is the wind puts me completely out of my comfort zone. We have been trudging up toward Mt. Adams for forty-five minutes in this wind, with gusts of forty-five to fifty-five miles per hour (Pat has a wind gauge and is brave enough to use it!) and I am done, finished, kaput. Bagging the peak is no longer important to me. I want out of this wind. I want to feel safe. Why don't I just say, *Pat, let's get out of here!* But I don't. I'm ashamed of

my fear. I don't want to take the summit away from Pat, and she is trudging forward.

My emotions kick in big time because I'm fighting a raging battle inside myself, as well as battling the wind and cold, and tears start to spill. Crying while wearing a balaclava, which is a combination hat and face mask, is not much fun. I immediately have nose problems. Where is all that moisture supposed to go? I pull the balaclava down and wipe my nose with the side of my mitten. My nose glides along a hard

rubber blade made to clear snow and rain from ski goggle lenses. Ouch! Bad idea to put that there, mitten manufacturers. The wind whips my tears away, tossing them toward Adams, wherever it is. I pull my balaclava back on, backwards, and struggle to turn it around so the holes expose my eyes, nose, and mouth. If I were not so far out of my comfort zone, I would be laughing hysterically.

Pat sees my state. We stop and scream over the wind and decide together to go to the Madison Hut and regroup. As we turn around on the trail and head down, the clouds clear. There, directly in front of us, is Mt. Madison, a bright white cone against a shocking blue sky. I don't let the sight into my heart. I am focused on getting down to the hut. The descent is long—I can't believe we climbed that high. We are starving, but I am determined not to eat until I am back in my comfort zone, which I feel sure will be at the hut, in the sun, protected from the wind.

We finally arrive and stand in the lee of the hut to eat lunch. Mt. Madison, our original destination, is just behind us, and it is only four-tenths of a mile to the summit. The winds are still ferocious and I am clear that I cannot brave them one extra minute. I am not up to bagging the peak, although that goal pesters me, pushing my brain to re-examine my heart's decision. Pat looks at my tears and says she has had enough as well. We head down Valley Way at 2:30 p.m.

The walk down is long! We put on and take off our cleats a number of times to deal with ice. I figure we have got to be at least halfway down the four-mile trail when we pass a sign saying we have three miles to go. You have got to be kidding! At dusk we slip on our headlamps and finally make it back to the parking lot at 6:30 p.m., both of us tired and sore.

Madison and Adams will always be there. We will be back.

STATS

MOUNTAINS ATTEMPTED: MTS. ADAMS (5,774) AND MADISON (5,367)

NEAREST CITY: RANDOLPH, N.H.

DATE: JANUARY 7, 2007

TIME: 10 HOURS AND 15 MINUTES

WEATHER: SUN AND CLOUDS, TEMPERATURES RANGING IN THE 20S WITH WIND CHILL BELOW THAT

MILES: 8

TRAILS: AIR LINE TRAIL, GULFSIDE TRAIL, VALLEY WAY

HOLY SHIT FACTOR: BLOW-US-AWAY HIGH

10. THE UPSIDE OF WINTER HIKING—SANDWICH DOME

January 21, 2007, Waterville Valley, New Hampshire

> *The great man is he who does not lose his childlike heart.*
>
> Mencius

I thought winter hiking was all seriousness, risk, and hard work—slogging up through the snow in heavy, clumsy boots, treading carefully over ice, staying warm in freezing temperatures and extreme wind, forcing myself to drink and eat even when my food and water freezes, and bearing the weight of a backpack stuffed with enough extra gear and warm layers to keep myself safe from hypothermia. These seem to be the downsides to winter hiking. But I have discovered an upside, too. Winter hiking is also silly-giddy-whoop-and-

hollering-child-like joy. Who knew?

"We're down, hon, safe and sound," I say to my husband, Don, having just reached the car after a six-hour winter hike up Sandwich Dome with Pat.

He breathes a sigh of relief. We had recently watched *Touching the Void* in which a rock climber barely makes it down the Peruvian Andes alive, and

48

had just heard about a twenty-four-year-old hiker lost for two days on Mt. Lafayette in New Hampshire's White Mountains. Don had visions of me being stuck on a mountaintop.

"I may not be there when you get home," he says. "I'm going to borrow a weed-whacker."

It's January in New Hampshire. "A weed whacker? You are a crazy man!"

His retort is strong. "You hike in the White Mountains in sub-zero weather and you call ME crazy? You're the one who's crazy!"

He has a point . . .

I'm a newbie hiker—just started in earnest last May when Pat and I decided to hike the sixty-seven mountains in New England over four thousand feet high. So far, we have bagged forty-three. This first winter hiking season has been tough. We've endured freezing cold, icy trails, deep snow, and below-zero chill factors. We've turned around twice before reaching the summits.

So, given the difficulty, why do it? It's a question I've been asking myself since the beginning of the season. In fact, when we turned around on Mt. Mansfield because of my frozen feet, I found myself admitting, through tears, that I didn't like winter hiking. And my husband, after hearing about our escapades, suggested that perhaps winter is not my hiking season. I hike in winter because it pushes me outside of my comfort zone and into the land of "aha" moments—a place that is rarely comfortable, always surprising, sometimes painful, and often emotional—where I learn who I really am.

We climb Sandwich Dome—a grueling three-and-a-half-hour trudge. It is steep and I huff and puff, sweat rolling down my back and chest, totally soaking my multiple layers of Techwicks and fleece. My heart pounds in my ears, and I have assumed the "steep" position—hands on hips and elbows pushed back, trying to maximize my lung capacity. Hopefully I am burning major fat cells. Of course, I complain about how steep it is as we climb. This is not a four thousand footer. We are taking it easy by doing one of the hundred highest mountains in New England; Sandwich Dome is *only* 3,980 feet high, twenty feet shy of the requirement. But in my mind, since it isn't a four thousand footer, I think it will be a gentle stroll up to a view. Nope. In addition to the steepness, there is no hot rock with a view to lounge on for lunch, my favorite part of our summer hikes. We keep trudging, gnawing on frozen power bars. The trail is wooded so we are protected from the wind until we reach the exposed peak. At the top, it is windy and very cold. No surprise since it was in the single digits at the trailhead. The chill factor is below zero and our cameras are on a collective strike—working conditions are much too cold. We freeze trying to take pictures of the amazing contrast between the white rime ice and the blue mountains on the horizon.

No time to celebrate bagging the peak; we turn around and head down fast before we freeze. On the return, gravity, my enemy going up, becomes

my friend going down. I move quickly with only the minimal effort it takes to put one foot in front of the other. Gravity does the rest while the snow cushions my steps. We come to a very steep section where we need to take it slow. Or do we? Pat sits down and slides on her butt. I follow suit. Yippee!

I laugh and whoop and holler as I lean from one side to the other to avoid rocks in the trail. I am going fast, my feet right in front of me, ready to brake if need be. Here's what I find: I can't do it seriously. I sound and feel like a six-year-old. Each steep section that elicited a swear word on our ascent becomes the thrilling bliss of our descent. I am loud. I feel free. I am no longer cold or even worried about the cold. I just let go and slide down the mountain. The experience floods my body with bubbly serotonin that infuses me with giddy energy. It is intoxicating. We get down ninety minutes faster, and much of that time is on our butts.

The payoff of the long, butt-busting, clothes-drenching hike up is the thrilling, butt-coasting, life-awakening ride down. You need the right pants—like wind pants, something with little resistance to them. Other than that, no previous experience, no training, no equipment is necessary!

The Sandwich Dome climb turns my view of winter hiking upside down and gives me a whole new perspective. The reward isn't in getting to the top—it's in the ride to the bottom! The upside of winter hiking is the down SLIDE! Steep? Bring it on!

As I look back on our hike yesterday, I realize I saw a part of who I really am that I love. Laughing with abandon and screaming with delight, I blissfully, gleefully slid down the trail on my butt! Sliding down the mountain released the excited happy child in me that had been shut in, not even thinking she could come out on a winter hike. As a result, the child inside is closer to the surface today. I feel her smiling just under my skin, behind my eyes, near my cheeks. She's looking for a chance to come out and play again now that she's been released by the responsible adult. I'm lighter, less serious, more effervescent and vital. And when I think about our next hike, I'm more hopeful of opportunities to play and have fun. I keep replaying a video in my mind of me sliding down Sandwich Dome. I can hear the little girl inside me giggling, whispering in my head, *Let's go sliding again. Can we? Huh? Can we?*

I start thinking about other ways I release my inner child-like spirit. I say child-like because children seem to have vast amounts of it naturally and then it is sucked out of us as we grow up. But if we had it as children, then we have it as adults. It's not a child quality; it's a human quality. Actually, I realize I search out opportunities to release the enthusiastic passion in me often— white water rafting in the Grand Canyon, skydiving and bungee jumping in Australia, Pictionary with friends and family. I love my cheerleader side. She's fun and her enthusiasm is contagious. It is a big part of who I am.

Hiking is a microcosm of how I live my life. How I hike is how I live. I work hard at hiking I push hard, challenge myself, set goals, work through the struggles, and focus on overcoming the difficulties and learning the lessons. I focus on the hard parts. The Sandwich Dome "aha" reminds me that not all of life, or hiking, is hard—life also abounds with ebullience and irrepressible joy.

Difficult circumstances bring out our true characters. Similarly, opportunities to truly enjoy life also reveal who we are. I know I have a survivor in me. But I also know I have a playful exuberant child in me as well. I'm thankful for both.

STATS

MOUNTAINS: SANDWICH DOME (3,957) AND JENNINGS PEAK (3,406)

NEAREST CITY: WATERVILLE VALLEY, N.H.

DATE: JANUARY 21, 2007

TIME: 5 HOURS AND 30 MINUTES

WEATHER: SUNNY, SINGLE DIGIT TEMPERATURES

MILES: 8

ELEVATION GAIN: 2,553 FEET

TRAILS: SANDWICH MOUNTAIN TRAIL

HOLY SHIT FACTOR: HIGH, ON A SLIDING SCALE

11. BUILDING GOOD KARMA ON WAUMBEK

February 16, 2007, Jefferson, New Hampshire

I've got a great ambition to die of exhaustion rather than boredom.

Thomas Carlyle

We climb Mt. Waumbek today. The name Waumbek comes from the Native American term "waumbekket-methna" meaning "white or snowy mountains." Fitting . . .

Buried in this snowy hike report are the following juicy tidbits:

- What to do when your mitten is stolen before you begin your winter hike
- The real reason trees are so important along the trail
- How high Pat and Nancy can lift their legs (maybe only dogs will care about this)
- How to keep your hiking partner motivated when she's pooped
- When to turn back on your snowshoeing hike
- How to earn good hiking karma

We leave Keene at 5 a.m. and arrive in Jefferson a bit before 9. On the drive up, Pat predicts 13 degrees, twenty to forty mile per hour winds, minus 21 degrees chill factor. Great wish I didn't hear *that*! We park in a roadside pull-off and walk up the road toward the trailhead. The walk from the car to Starr King Road is my first moment of truth. It is 8 degrees and the wind is assaulting us head on. My jaw is frozen in place and my eyes are watering, but I can't put my face down out of the wind because I need to see the cars speeding by us spraying slush. *We're hiking today because ... ?*

We walk up the Starr King Road and meet Pancho, a springer spaniel who clearly wants to play. His owner comes out and tries to lure him away from us, with no success. We are trying to adjust a hiking pole when Pancho steals Pat's mitten and trots down the road, ready for the excitement he is sure will fol-

low. He evades both of us for a good ten frustrating minutes. The owner brings out treats and a toy, but nothing deters Pancho from his mission of keeping himself the center of attention. The dog dodges by me and I make a flying leap, landing in a snow bank. Pat finally tries a more sensible approach and commands "STAY," holding up her hand. He stays! She continues to repeat the command as she approaches him and finally grabs her mitten.

Pat and I try in vain to adjust one of our hiking poles but no matter what we do, it does not tighten. So with three poles, snowshoes on, and Pancho finally on a leash being led away by his owner, we are ready.

I step over the snow bank, onto the trail, and sink into the untouched snow up to my knees. *What the hell are we doing?* This is not going to be a walk in the park—or anything close to it. It will be nothing short of grueling, breaking trail through three feet of heavy, new snow. We soon develop a system that keeps us trudging. We identify a tree up the trail as our goal and then the trailbreaker huffs and puffs her way to the tree while the other follows slowly behind, cheering her on.

The cheering helps.

Pat asks me, "Okay, where's your tree?"

"I'm going to that birch tree with the yellow blaze," I answer, and off I go.

My first steps are high, big, and full of energy. In my mind I'm saying, *yeah, I can do this!* I have pep at the beginning of my turns, but it fizzles and my strength fades as I move up the moun-

tain. About halfway to my goal, things get tough. I'm breathing heavily and my legs feel weighted and are burning. Pat hears me grunting and groaning, sees me slowing, and starts to cheer: "You're amazing. You're doing awesome. You're almost there. Five feet, three feet, two feet. Woo hoo! You are incredible, Nancy!"

I have barely enough strength to move off the trail so Pat can take the lead. I hand the two poles to Pat; she chooses her tree and leads the way while I try desperately to catch my breath. And so we slug up the mountain, cheering each other on.

For the person breaking trail, it is incredibly hard work. The snow feels like wet sand and our legs like Jell-O. When I finish my turn, I am incredibly thankful that I made it to my tree and can begin to rest and recover as I follow Pat. Watching Pat's snowshoes pounding up that mountain, I am grateful for her strength, long legs, vitality and her refusal to let the mountain win. As I follow slowly behind, it is hard to stay warm because I'm soaked with sweat but am no longer working hard. I'm not generating body heat; I'm just losing it. By the time I am cold, it's my turn to break trail again.

About two hours in, I am silently discouraged and thinking I can't go on. *What the hell am I doing?* I start talking to myself, knowing that physical activity is 90 percent attitude and I don't want to quit. I tell myself I can do this and, miraculously, I get a second wind. I fall a few times, and let me tell you, it's not easy getting up in all that snow.

As we hike up the mountain, the snow gets deeper. *How could it get any deeper?* This is not an excuse, but I am short. The snow starts at knee level and gradually moves up until it reaches my crotch. I can't raise my leg high enough to get my snowshoe over the snow. I start lifting my legs with my hands, thinking that with the extra pull I can clear the snow. Nope. Not even close. My legs just don't go that high. So both Pat and I resort to lifting one snowshoe a bit and kicking down the snow, then lifting it a bit higher and then a bit higher so that each step forward now takes three tamping steps. Our progress slows to a snail's pace. We take shorter and shorter turns breaking the trail.

We decide we've had enough after three-and-a-half hours of slogging up the mountain through thirty inches of snow. Our legs are toast, it's windy and bitterly cold, and we are moving so agonizingly slowly that we would not make it to the summit before 4 p.m. It is time to turn around.

As we walk back down, we are amazed at each step we took up. "I can't believe we got this far," Pat says. I add a smart "Holy shit" and we continue on. I don't spend much time in life being amazed at myself, or anything close to that, so it is freeing and even joyful to be pleased with our efforts.

We aren't the only ones who will be pleased. There is no doubt that Saturday morning a few peakbaggers will walk to the Starr King trailhead and jump for joy when they see that the trail has been broken out. If we were there, we might say to them, *ah, not so fast*, since the broken trail only goes half way. But we earn 1.5 miles of good karma points.

The walk back to the car from the trailhead is freezing, I am soaking wet with sweat, and the wind goes right through me. It takes me half an hour to warm up in the car, heat blasting.

Pat and I have had some pretty big adventures together. This one ranks right up there. We've hiked through rain and mud and ice and wind, and now through snow. Major snow. I'll never think of snowshoeing again in the same way. But I pray that the next time I have those damn things on my feet, Pat is right behind me cheering me on.

Waumbek, you have not beaten us. We will be back next Saturday.

STATS

MOUNTAIN: MT. WAUMBEK (4,006)

NEAREST CITY: JEFFERSON, N.H.

DATE: FEBRUARY 16, 2007

TIME: 4 HOURS AND 30 MINUTES

WEATHER: PARTLY CLOUDY, VERY WINDY AND VERY, VERY COLD

MILES: 3

TRAILS: STARR KING TRAIL

HOLY SHIT FACTOR: 30 INCHES OF SNOW PUSHES THE METER TO THE TOP

12. THE RAPTURE OF BEING ALIVE ON CARTER DOME

March 10, 2007, Jackson, New Hampshire

People say that we're searching for the meaning of life. I don't think that's it at all. I think that what we're seeking is an experience of being alive, so that our life experiences on the purely physical plane will have resonance within our own innermost being and reality, so that we actually feel the rapture of being alive.

Joseph Campbell, **The Power of Myth**

I am screaming down the mountain on my wind-pant covered butt, totally out of control. I have slid through the giggly, woo-hoo, this-is-incredibly-thrilling part to the oh-holy-shit-I-can't-stop moment of truth. I'm digging my elbows and snowshoes into the snow to slow what feels like a suicide slide down Carter Dome. The trail veers off to the right just ahead. Pat is standing at the turn, yelling "I'll stop you!" at the top of her lungs. I'm coming so fast I'm at the turn in seconds . . . oh my GOD . . .

I guess I'd better start at the beginning.

We get to the trailhead at 9:09 after leaving Keene at 5 a.m. We've got the drive to the Whites down. We know where to stop for breakfast (McDonald's in Tilton), where to stop for our first bathroom break (Irving Station in Meredith) and where to stop for our last bathroom-and-muffin break (the Mountain Bean off Route 3 in Twin Mountain).

The Nineteen Mile Brook Trail is hard packed and we bare-boot it up. Once we get to the Carter Dome Trail, the snow is less packed and we put on snowshoes. The climb is moderate but the temperature is warm and the snow is soft and wet and is sticking to the bottom of my snowshoes. It's not easy to walk up a mountain with huge, heavy, wet snowballs attached to the bottom of my snowshoes. I stop often and kick them off, but within seconds I am carrying new snow balls that grow as I climb.

We get to the Mt. Hight intersection and decide not to do the steep hike up to that peak today. The soft snow and snowshoes are giving our hamstrings, quads, and glutes a workout already.

The gusts of wind we experience going up are infrequent but mighty. Instead of delivering a cold bite, they bring a tinge of spring warmth. It feels so refreshing and helps keep my dripping sweat somewhat at bay.

We get to the top of Carter Dome at 12:50 p.m. and meet some nice guys who offer to take our summit picture. I will always remember the man we met on top of Whiteface, our first four thousand footer, who told me, "There are no assholes above four thousand feet." Our experience has proven that to be true.

The climb down the Carter-Moriah Trail starts off reasonably; it's not too steep. Pat has been talking about an opportunity to slide so I am anxious to get going.

We get to a section that looks steep enough to be slide-able. Pat doesn't have her wind pants on so decides to snowshoe down. She offers to carry my snowshoes so I can slide. Woo hoo; what fun! But I notice, with a trace of concern, that my wind pants provide absolutely no resistance to the snow's surface and I whizz along, much faster than my previous slide on Sandwich Dome. I file that important fact away in my "what the heck" folder and continue on.

Before long we arrive at what turns out to be an incredibly steep section that goes all the way down to the Carter Notch Hut. Pat tries sliding down in her regular pants, with snowshoes on, and down she goes. Her pants provide some friction so she is going at a good clip, but not whooshing down too fast.

Unlike me. My wind pants, despite being duct-taped together in the rear, provide a frictionless sliding surface and I take off, slip-sliding away. At first it is fun. I am giggling. Then it becomes exhilarating, and I am screaming. All of a sudden, I realize I'm out of control and can't stop. I try to brake with the snowshoes and my elbows with no luck. This reminds me of riding my brother Jim's go-cart down the Hurricane Road hill and realizing I had no brakes. Thanks, Jim. Anyway, the trail turns and I don't. I barrel into the woods, finally stopping myself with my shin against a tree trunk. Ouch! Climbing out of the woods in really deep snow is pretty funny and lots of work. Pat comes halfway and extends her hand.

The steepness continues. I slide a few more times with close to devastating results that awaken in me a healthy fear for my life. I decide to snowshoe down the rest of the way. Smart girl, yes?

It's too steep to walk straight down on snowshoes; I have to sidestep. So here I am, carefully sidestepping, when my snowshoe hits a branch, I lose my balance, fight to regain control, and fall down the trail, landing on—you guessed it—my frictionless-wind-pant-covered ass.

So here is where I started this story: screaming down the mountain at breakneck speed, totally out of control. I dig my elbows and snowshoes into the snow to slow my suicidal slide down the Carter Moriah Trail, but to no avail. The trail veers off to the right and Pat is standing at the turn yelling that

she is going to stop me. I have no time to really process this information, but if I had I would have been able to see what lay ahead for both of us. BAM! I hit her, fly off the trail, and continue down my merry way in spite of my friend's valiant effort. I'm flying through the woods toward a cluster of trees that one way or another will be my final resting

place. Luckily, my snowshoes catch on a branch before I get to them and I come to an unsteady, precarious stop.

Silence. I lie there assessing. I'm alive, I can move, nothing hurts. *Oh my God—where's Pat?*

"Pat! Pat! Pat!" I yell in panic.

Out of the top of my eye I see Pat's snowshoes sticking out of the snow. I hear her laugh. Relief floods through me and mixes with the adrenaline already coursing through my body. I join in the laughter and we just lie there laughing, picturing our predicament—way off the trail in deep, unpacked snow, Pat upside down and me barely clinging to my spot on the steep incline. My laughing makes me shift my body; I lose hold of the branch and continue sliding down to the cluster of trees where I stop for good.

Getting up is hilarious and hard at the same time. But we manage. Each time I put my weight on my snowshoes I sink down further into the snow. If I put my hand down and lean to get leverage, my whole arm disappears. When I finally succeed in standing I see that Pat is also upright.

We bushwhack our way back up the trail and check for damages. I have a cold rear end due to the fact that my wind pants collected half the snow on the trail on the way down. Pat hit her head on a tree and her butt on who-knows-what, but is smiling.

We arrive at the Carter Notch Hut at 2:15 p.m., ready to take a break from the steep climb down. The hut is very dark, packed with winter gear, coats, backpacks, and people. We manage to squeeze into a corner and gobble down our lunch, then it's back out into the wide open spaces of mountain and sun. From the hut, the four miles down to the parking lot are moderate (except for that hill coming out of the Notch. Who put that there? I am definitely done with up).

We are physically pooped, emotionally exhausted from the intensity of the slide down, and feeling blessed by our shared experience. Most of all, having risked the consequences of frictionless wind pants on steep downhill trails, and having felt the spine-tingling fear of flying down said trail totally out of control toward what could have been

my demise, I am reveling in the rapture of being truly alive.

We get back to the parking lot at 4:30 and change our clothes at the AMC Pinkham Notch Visitor center. As I walk into the lodge, I breathe a humongous sigh of relief. Several hikers dealing with sore feet hear me sigh and burst out laughing. They can relate.

We get back to Keene around 8:30 p.m. and Pat drops me off at home. Saying goodbye, I lose my balance on the icy driveway, and would be landing on my rear end again if not for Pat catching me. However, the effort causes me to lose control and expel a bit of gas, which sends both Pat and me into fits of laughter, which causes me to need to get into the house pretty darn quick. Too much information?

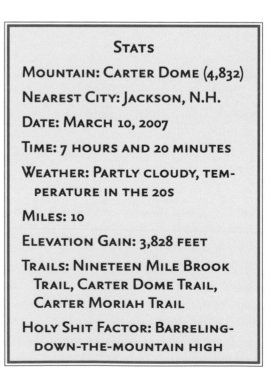

STATS

MOUNTAIN: CARTER DOME (4,832)

NEAREST CITY: JACKSON, N.H.

DATE: MARCH 10, 2007

TIME: 7 HOURS AND 20 MINUTES

WEATHER: PARTLY CLOUDY, TEMPERATURE IN THE 20S

MILES: 10

ELEVATION GAIN: 3,828 FEET

TRAILS: NINETEEN MILE BROOK TRAIL, CARTER DOME TRAIL, CARTER MORIAH TRAIL

HOLY SHIT FACTOR: BARRELING-DOWN-THE-MOUNTAIN HIGH

13.   A HIKE WITH HEART—MADISON

March 31, 2007, Randolph, New Hampshire

> *Let your heart guide you. It whispers, so listen carefully.*
> Little Foot's Mother, **The Land Before Time**

Pat, Dejah, and I hit the snow-encrusted trailhead at 8:37 a.m. I am talking with Pat as we huff and puff our way up Valley Way, and I'm not thinking; I'm just giving voice to what is in my heart. As I talk, I real-ize the past few weeks of intense confu-sion around a possible job change are evaporating into the cool crisp morn-ing air. Each deep breath releases some of the racket that's been reverberating inside of me, easing the struggle with

every step I take. Leave my job, stay, leave, stay. Until now, I've felt caught in the chaos of a massive class-five white-water rapid, unable to make this major decision in my life. But now, as I let my-self air-out hiking, I am released from the frothy white water and back in the calm of the wider river. I don't fit in my current job. I am not happy there. I know what I need to do: leave and take the job offer that's on the table.

Hiking brings clarity. It seems that while pushing my body up and down mountains surrounded by all that is naturally beautiful and true, and sup-ported in friendship by Pat, I uncon-sciously let go of all the inside noise and I'm able to listen.

"Wow," I say to Pat, "when I let my heart know what it knows, and stop fighting it, everything is so simple and clear." A few steps later I add, "The hardest part is believing in myself enough to follow my heart." Emotion fills my throat, confirming my truth.

By 9:30 I've hiked through the clutter filling my head into my heart's clarity and I feel lighter than I have in months.

Just in case I have any lingering doubts about listening to my heart, confirmation comes up the trail. I'm waiting for Pat, who is taking a body-function break, when a guy breezes up the path. We strike up a conversation.

I tell him this is our second attempt at Madison and that we had to turn back the first time because of frigid cold and high winds. He tells me he has been on many search and rescue teams in the Whites and has pulled thirteen bodies off these mountains. In my mind I nickname him Mr. White Mountains.

"The hikes where you turn around are worth much more than the hikes where you get to the summit," he says. "You have to listen to your heart and your body, not to your head. Your heart and body are aligned, and there is congruence between them that will keep you safe." As he says this, I feel a vibration of joy inside me; my heart is jumping up and down screaming, *Yippee! See, see—it's true! He knows it too! Listen to me!*

Mr. White Mountains disappears up the trail as quickly as he appeared.

Our original plan is to take Valley Way to Madison Hut, drop our packs at the hut (I love this part of the plan), and bag Mt. Madison, then come back to the hut for lunch. Pat suggests an alternate route: take the Watson Path to the summit because it's shorter, which might leave us more time to bag Mt. Adams too. I love Pat's plans. She adds an element of adventure that takes us to an edge I might not otherwise experience.

So up the Watson Path we hike. We expect the trail to be challenging. Madison is 5,367 feet high—the fifth highest mountain in New Hampshire. The trail is less than four miles to the summit, so it has to be steep. As it turns out, it's vertical! I've never seen anything like it. It is literally 1.5 miles of straight up. The snow, which has seen no one all winter, is hard-packed from time. With ice cleats on, we kick our boots hard into the snow's surface to break the slippery crust and get a foothold. I climb most of the way with hands grabbing onto tree trunks or limbs, cleats barely clinging to the snow. Below me all I can see is ice-crusted snow. The slope is a minefield of trees that would stop an out-of-control slide . . . painfully. One slip and . . . .

I can't think about that. I just keep digging my feet in and going relentlessly up. Climbing up Watson Path takes all our concentration and our conversation fades to heavy breathing and periodic checks on one another.

Once above the timberline, which, by the way, takes forever to reach, conditions change. The snow is gone. We are moving across a boulder field, rock hopping and scrambling hand over hand. The wind is fierce and has a freezing sting to it that gives me a cold headache. One thing remains the same:

we are still going up, mounting one discouraging false summit after another.

My quads are screaming, my lungs are struggling to get enough air, my pack feels so heavy the small of my back is aching, my body is wet from sweat and cold from the furious wind, and my energy is depleted. I am out of my comfort zone. I try to absorb the spectacular views, land disappearing into a blur of blues and grays as far as I can see, but fear blocks the euphoria of seeing the incredible expanse of earth that lies at my feet.

The voice in my head says, *Just get to the top and get down; keep going.* The rest of me wants a warm haven from the wind, where I can talk with Pat. Climbing in these conditions is isolating. You can't hear each other and you have to keep moving. The only goal becomes getting away from the exposure on the top and down to safer ground.

We get to the summit at 1:18 p.m. Pat

holds the camera at arm's distance and snaps a picture for our summit portrait. We immediately start down, following the cairns, when we see Mr. White Mountains approaching. I turn to Pat and yell, "Hey, we beat him!" and give her a low five so he won't see. He stops to acknowledge us and tells us he's just summited Jefferson and Adams. Okay, Nance, reality check! We are having trouble bagging one peak and he is on peak number three in the same amount of time! He heads off to bag Madison and we continue down.

Only one thought screams at me. *Get me off this mountain, NOW.* I heed the call. I am on a mission, moving as fast as I can, trying to get to the hut that is less than half a mile below us. I want to be back in my comfort zone, off the top of Madison, out of this biting cold and whipping wind. I'm making progress, but don't see Pat in my periphery. I yell back over the howling wind, "Pat, are you okay?"

"No!" she yells. "I'm having a really hard time."

Everything stops for me. My panic morphs into strength as I turn around and head back into the blast. My urgency melts into concern. In the calm waters of my heart, I am thankful for my friend's courageous vulnerability. I hug Pat. I look her in the eyes. I know exactly how she is feeling. I was in the same emotional space the first time we tried to summit Madison and we turned around as a result. Slowly we head down Madison's rock-strewn cone, linked by friendship and our efforts to descend.

We arrive at the Madison Hut around 2 p.m. and, standing in a protected corner outside the building, share a sandwich and a smile. We head down Valley Way, leaving Adams for another day.

We are both thoroughly used up and the steep 3.8 miles back down feels like an eternity. We arrive at the car nine grueling hours after we started. Sitting down sends electric pulses of relief through every worn-out cell of my body. And I just breathe. We made it.

I went out for a hike, rediscovered my heart, and remembered I have all I need within me.

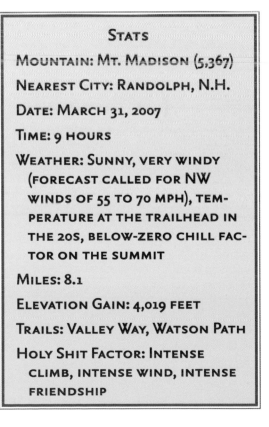

STATS

MOUNTAIN: MT. MADISON (5,367)

NEAREST CITY: RANDOLPH, N.H.

DATE: MARCH 31, 2007

TIME: 9 HOURS

WEATHER: SUNNY, VERY WINDY (FORECAST CALLED FOR NW WINDS OF 55 TO 70 MPH), TEMPERATURE AT THE TRAILHEAD IN THE 20S, BELOW-ZERO CHILL FACTOR ON THE SUMMIT

MILES: 8.1

ELEVATION GAIN: 4,019 FEET

TRAILS: VALLEY WAY, WATSON PATH

HOLY SHIT FACTOR: INTENSE CLIMB, INTENSE WIND, INTENSE FRIENDSHIP

14. A MAJOR MILESTONE ON ADAMS

May 5, 2007, Randolph, New Hampshire

> *Life doesn't require that we be the best, only that we try our best.*
>
> H. Jackson Brown Jr.

It's Sunday, May 6, exactly one year since Pat and I started hiking with the goal of bagging New England's sixty-seven highest mountains. And it's the day after we climbed Adams.

I'm sitting on my purple couch, a bag of ice on my knee. My body just wants to melt into the cushions. I don't want to move. I want to be still in the silence and slack off all day. My shoulders and back feel like they have been carrying the weight of the world, my calves are tighter than a pair of too-small control-top panty hose, my quads feel like they have been tenderized, my left hand is black and blue and sore, and my knee is swollen and stiff. And I am so happy.

Today's mountain is badass Adams, and the stakes are high—it will be our fiftieth peak. If we make it, we can say we've bagged fifty mountains in one year. The *if* in this case is a big *if*. This will be our fourth attempt to climb Mt. Adams.

The first time we tried, in January, the ferocious wind and cold scared the bejesus out of me and we turned around. In March we bagged Madison and were hoping to continue on to Adams, but Madison whipped our butts and we left Adams for another day. Just a few weeks ago, we attempted Adams via Lowe's Path. New snow and limited visibility made following the trail virtually impossible and we turned around.

Adams, Take four . . .

Pat, Dejah, and I leave Keene at 5 a.m., and my "climbing anxiety" kicks in on the drive north. *Will I make it?* I've had an emotional week—my last days at my old job, as a hospital development director, before starting my new one, as a development director at an arts and dance nonprofit organization. I am taking all that heavy emotional baggage up the mountain with me.

We hit Lowe's Path at 8:30 a.m. and set out. We start the climb in spring, temps in the 40s and a trail of thick soupy mud and lots of water. By the time we hike through the moderate rise and arrive at the steep section, we are climbing in winter snow. By steep, I mean perpendicular, almost ninety degrees, straight up. At 5,799 feet, Adams is the second highest mountain in New Hampshire. But as the four thousand-footer book by Smith and Dickerman says, "there is nothing else second-rate about this ruggedly spectacular mountain." Adams has the highest elevation gain of any of the White Mountains, 4,450 feet in 4.7 miles.

We make it part way up the steep section, past the Log Cabin, before putting on ice cleats to give us traction on the slippery surface. We arrive at treeline, always a welcome sight, around 11:30, and eat half the sandwich wraps we'd bought this morning at the Mountain Bean. Yummmm.

The wind is tolerable, unlike other times we have ventured above timberline in the Presidentials, and the trail has mellowed out a bit. The path is bare in most places, with pockets of snow here and there, and shimmers with flecks of mica. I've been collecting mica chips on our hikes in hopes of using them for our New England sixty-seven four-thousand-footer ceremony. We have only four mountains left to climb!

The steep section takes its toll, or maybe it's all the emotion I'm lugging with me; I am pooped. But, miraculously, I can see the summit and am sure I can get there. Whoops—not so fast. That is NOT the summit. Oh shit, is that Adams all the way over there? It looks like Adams is a galaxy away and I am dragging. Pat tells me not to look so I put my head down and keep moving.

We climb up and over the false summit, known as Adams 4 (that's imaginative), through the now snow-covered trails of Thunderstorm Junction and across Gulfside Trail. The snowfields are so slippery we have to dig our toes into the crust to avoid sliding down the mountain. Why we don't put on our cleats, I do not know. I think we are both done for and don't have enough energy to make the switch. In my heart, I know we are going to make it, but boy, oh boy, my body isn't so sure. On the last snowfield I lose my footing and start to slide. I use every last morsel of energy to dig my toes and fingers into the hard-crusted snow to stop slipping and hold panic at bay. I am on my hands and knees, barely holding on, and the anger I feel toward my current employer erupts from within. Kneeling on a snowfield on Adams, I finally let myself feel the frustration of having my gifts pushed aside and my suggestions ignored for years. I rest my forehead on the snow, and let the tears glide down my face and onto the slope.

I gather myself and stand. *This goddamned mountain is not going to beat me. I will stand on that summit.* The hike becomes a rite of passage—the mountaintop representing the transition from old job to new. Pat and I have attempted to summit Adams three times before and, similarly, for three years I have struggled to find satisfaction in my work, trying in vain to make a difference and share my talents with this organization. Until now, Pat and I

have been thwarted in our summit bids of Adams. But today will be different. Today we will make it.

Pat sees that I am overcome with emotion. She's been a witness to my job struggle and she is my climbing partner, a witness to the hiker I've become. One hundred feet from the summit, she asks me to sit down on a rock to regroup. She puts her arm around me, helps me to center myself, find my heart, feel my power, regain my strength.

We reach the summit minutes later at 1:48 p.m. The wind is fierce and it is cold on the pinnacle. We hunker down among rocks and take a movie of summiting our fiftieth peak. It is an emotional moment. We are tired, proud of what we have accomplished, and

linked together in a friendship that has changed us both.

To the south, Washington's towers are clearly visible atop a massive mound of foreboding dark gray rock, partially swept clean by the ferocious wind, with snow filling in the more protected areas. Madison and the peaks we once thought were Adams stand in a majestic line-up to the north, no longer taunting us.

Both of us are in good spirits as we slide down the snowfield on our butts, our hearts lighter having reached the summit. We pass three snowboarders and I think they are crazy to be up here. Then it occurs to me that I am up here too.

We are really tired so we know going

down is going to be a long haul. As we climb back up to Adams 4, Pat postholes, her foot crashing through the soft snow next to a boulder, and falls in up to her hip, in obvious pain. I am scared to death she has broken a foot or ankle and begin digging the snow out around her leg with newfound energy. She eventually is able to pull her foot out and after a few moments stands. Thank God! We take a needed breather and enjoy the second half of our wraps for a late lunch.

The panorama heading down is spectacular, mountains dissolving into the blues of the distance, the trail clearly marked by white-quartz-topped cairns that appear smaller and smaller as they stretch down the mountain. I love the cairns, markers that reassure me I am going in the right direction, starting a new life in a new job where the staff is anticipating my arrival with excitement.

We reach treeline and our anxiety heightens. The incredibly steep trail is covered with soft snow, actually more like ice crystals or tiny glass beads that are very slippery. Three weeks ago we slid down the trail on our butts, but not today. The snow is far too fast and we know we would kill ourselves. Pat falls and slides twice, trees stopping her each time, and she has the bruises to prove it. I'm slow, sidestepping down, and am relieved when the grade turns more moderate, and we can relax.

But we are so tired. I fall twice during our descent. Once I wrap myself around a sapling, my feet in running water and my butt two inches from a river of mud. I do a backbend to avoid a mud bath, which almost causes some pee control problems for both of us as I try to unwind myself from this precarious predicament. Once I land on my knee on a rock in the water. Ouch! It is not surprising there are painful moments when we push ourselves this hard. Pat and I are quiet for the last mile or so, reserving our dwindling energy to keep walking. We make it back to Lowe's store at 6:50 p.m. and I lean against the car, taking a moment to soak in the re-

lief. We made it. And that brings tears. It wasn't easy and we made it—maybe not as quickly or with as much dexterity or ease as other hikers, but perhaps that's the point. It wasn't easy and we made it.

Sometimes I can't believe I'm writing about myself, an ordinary, non-athletic over-fifty-year-old woman giving my best at summiting one New England mountain at a time. Pat and I stand on the peaks of fifty four-thousand-foot mountains in 365 days. As I sit on my purple couch the day after Adams, one of our toughest hikes, ice on my knee, I am exhausted and profoundly proud

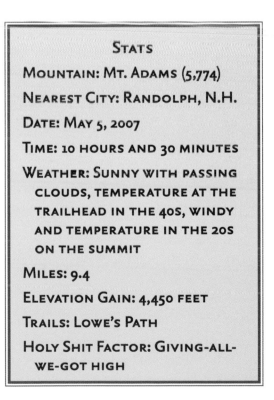

STATS

MOUNTAIN: MT. ADAMS (5,774)

NEAREST CITY: RANDOLPH, N.H.

DATE: MAY 5, 2007

TIME: 10 HOURS AND 30 MINUTES

WEATHER: SUNNY WITH PASSING CLOUDS, TEMPERATURE AT THE TRAILHEAD IN THE 40S, WINDY AND TEMPERATURE IN THE 20S ON THE SUMMIT

MILES: 9.4

ELEVATION GAIN: 4,450 FEET

TRAILS: LOWE'S PATH

HOLY SHIT FACTOR: GIVING-ALL-WE-GOT HIGH

15. THE ALMOST-SUMMIT OF JEFFERSON

May 22, 2007, Bretton Woods, New Hampshire

> *The hikes where you turn around are worth much more than the hikes where you get to the summit.*
>
> A former member of the
> White Mountain Search and Rescue Team

Striving to reach our potential and taking care of ourselves—are they mutually exclusive? Can we do one and still do the other? If so, it's a balancing act I haven't mastered.

It seems there is a point people reach when striving becomes pushing and they are no longer taking care of themselves. I crossed that line on this hike. When I should have turned around, I convinced Pat I was okay and we hiked on.

When I met Pat, I met my match. We are both strivers, goal-oriented, if-we-say-we're-gonna-do-it-get-out-of-the-way types of gals. That's why we picked Jefferson to hike. In my heart, I knew I needed an "easy freebie" hike after a string of killer climbs through the winter, but the lure of perfect weather and bagging a peak that counted toward our four thousand-footer goal was too much for me to resist.

Was hiking Jefferson a good decision?

Here is the part I don't get. Most inspirational leaders seem to push far beyond striving, enduring huge personal sacrifices while making the world a better place. Think of Nelson Mandela, Paul Farmer, Greg Mortenson, Mother Teresa. Do you have to reach their level of sacrifice to make a difference?

When is enough enough? How hard do you push? When does striving to reach your potential become not taking care of yourself?

Did we push too hard on this hike?

By now you are wondering what happened.

Pat, Dejah, and I start out as usual from Keene at 5 a.m. and from the Castle Trail trailhead at 8:30. Unlike our last hike, we easily forge the river because we are armed with a plan—don't be anxious, know it's coming, take off your boots and socks, put on water sandals, and just walk across—which is exactly what we do. Wow, that water is frigid! Then up the trail we climb. We are enjoying the wildflowers that line the path—trout lilies and trillium and common wood sorrels by the hundreds. Pat is clearing the trail of fallen limbs,

as usual—a gift she gives to those who come after us. After a mile and a half we hit snow and the hiking gets more difficult. In places the trail consists of a three-foot ridge of soft crystallized snow running down the trail, the pinnacle in the center and tapering sharply off toward the sides. It occurs because the snow on the center of the trail has been packed down by hikers and melts less quickly than the snow in the woods. It is called the monorail and it is not easy to walk on. We are able to bare-boot it and the snow supports us, except for a few post-holes where one of our legs plummets straight down into the soft cold white stuff.

The Castellated Ridge we are climbing narrows into a rock formation known as the Castles, made up of some high ledges that require scrambling. Scrambling is the hiking term. My way of saying it is, *Oh holy shit, how am I going to get up there?* Pat, on the other hand, loves this stuff.

I am halfway up a wall of rock, trying to figure out how I am going to get to the top because I see no footholds or handholds. Dejah is crying because she can't figure out a way up either. Her distress upsets me so I abandon my own struggle to find a way to help her. I think that if she jumps toward the ledge, I can use her momentum to push her up. I'm not sure what I'm thinking, she weighs seventy pounds and I'm already precariously balanced on a rock shelf wearing a heavy backpack. Her leap isn't high enough to give me the leverage I need. She falls back into

my arms and I lose my balance. For a very long agonizing instant I realize my mistake. We fall. I don't tumble the whole way down, or I wouldn't be writing this report. I land on my butt and side on a lower ledge that juts out just enough. I hear Pat yell as I fall and she is there when I realize I am alive and barely balancing on a granite slab. She tries to help me remove my backpack, but I fight her off. Together we scooch down to safe ground. I am shaking, discombobulated, emotional, trying to get my bearings. I sit for a while as Pat does her best to comfort me. I know places on my body hurt, but as each second goes by, I also realize I am in one piece. Dejah, thank God, is okay too.

Moment of truth: do I listen to my heart and body or to my head?

"I'm okay," I say. "Let's just get to the top of this thing and see where we go from there." I move into buck-up you-can-do-this mode, no longer connected to heart and body. I feel numb. I just want to get away from this hellacious ledge and leave it behind me. Unsteadily, with all the courage I have left, I struggle to the top of the shelf. Pat hoists Dejah up to me and then follows. We still have a mile and a half of climbing to get to the summit and that is what we have come for, right? To reach the summit?

I am jittery, my balance is off, and I am juiced up with adrenaline. It feels like I have had ten cups of coffee mixed with a bottle of booze and haven't slept for two days. Pat is worried about me. I focus on not falling as we walk this trail

that is very rough and narrow with lots of rock hopping. We reach the Cornice Trail intersection at 2:45. Pat turns to me and I say, in tears, "I'm done."

We sit back-to-back, supporting each other on our perch above the world, feeling the sun on our bodies, letting the exhaustion dissipate, and taking a moment to absorb the beauty. I am back in my heart. It is a glorious day up on the almost-summit of Jefferson. We turn around only half a mile from the summit, at 3 p.m.

The slog down the mountain is excruciating. By now all the aches and pains from the fall come out of hiding and every step aggravates a bruise somewhere. My balance never really returns. I'm not me, and haven't been since the fall.

I know Pat is concerned and I keep trying to reassure her that I am okay. But, the bottom line is, I am not okay and we both know it. The walk down is quiet. Only encouraging words are spoken as we check on one another. Pat gives me her arm or hand when the terrain requires a big step down. I lean on her, hold my breath, step and grunt, balance myself, and then do it again.

When we get back to the river, we just walk across, boots, socks, pants and all. Neither one of us has the energy to agonize over the crossing or to put on our water sandals, and we have only half a mile to go. We get back to the car at 9 p.m. and are back in Keene at midnight. Long, exhausting day.

I wonder if I have it in me to make a difference in the world given my personal limitations and my tolerance levels that are evident on this hike. I am ashamed of my weakness, mad at myself that I couldn't push harder and farther, and sad that my fall completely overshadowed our hike. It scares me that I don't have what it takes; that who I am is not enough to get me to who I want to be.

Maybe that's my head talking.

My body is craving rest, ice and ibuprofen.

If I listen to the still, small voice that is my heart, I know that turning around was an act of loving myself and that the summit will be there for another day. I know I can't make a difference in the world by being anyone other than who I am, with all my striving and pushing, my limits and my struggles. Who I am has to be enough.

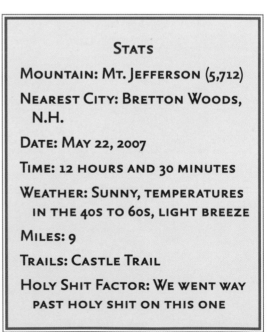

STATS

MOUNTAIN: MT. JEFFERSON (5,712)

NEAREST CITY: BRETTON WOODS, N.H.

DATE: MAY 22, 2007

TIME: 12 HOURS AND 30 MINUTES

WEATHER: SUNNY, TEMPERATURES IN THE 40S TO 60S, LIGHT BREEZE

MILES: 9

TRAILS: CASTLE TRAIL

HOLY SHIT FACTOR: WE WENT WAY PAST HOLY SHIT ON THIS ONE

16. CELEBRATION ON MT. ISOLATION

June 30, 2007, Jackson, New Hampshire

There is a living to give instead of to get. As you concentrate on the giving, you discover that just as you cannot receive without giving, so neither can you give without receiving—even the most wonderful things like health and happiness and inner peace.

Peace Pilgrim

Mt. Isolation doesn't sound like a likely place to encounter other hikers. Just the name implies a mountain set off by itself, remote, cold, a stay-away-I-want-to-be-alone type of place. Mt. Isolation is located in the Dry River Wilderness in the middle of the Presidential Range, with no hint of civilization anywhere. We assume "isolation" will also describe our experience, like many of our hikes when we see no one.

But we could be wrong. In their four thousand–footer book, Smith and Dickerman report: "Because of its remoteness, many peakbaggers put this one off, and the Four Thousand-Footer Club records indicate that this is the most common 'finishing peak' of the 48." I wonder if we will see any peakbaggers today.

Pat, Dejah, and I set out from Keene at 5 a.m. and from the trailhead at 8:40 a.m. The trail starts out with a moderate 1.8-mile climb then the grade lessens and remains fairly easy for the rest of the hike, although we gain over 3,000 feet in elevation. But Isolation makes up for its failure to live up to some of the other four thousand footers in steepness with lots of rock-hopping, suck-your-boots-off mud, blow-downs, and five river crossings over the very long 14.6-mile trek through the beautiful Sandwich Range Wilderness Area. The trail is lined with bunchberries, small white flowers, making it look like we are walking along a special path set up for a celebratory occasion.

We almost miss the sign to the summit of Isolation because we are looking down and the sign is above our heads. Luckily, hikers had built a cairn so we would not miss the right hand turn. We reach the very windy summit at 1:30 and are rewarded with panoramic views of Washington and the southern Presidentials with not a road, house, or telephone pole in sight.

On the hike down, Pat and I are sure AMC trail workers have added a few miles of trail while we were on top, not looking. The trail goes on forever and Pat and I are both dealing with knee pain as we make our way down the mountain. We arrive back at the car for Snapple and Diet Pepsi at 7:07 p.m.

Usually the climax of our hike reports is that we make it to the summit and back, earning the right to check off another mountain on our four thousand–footer list. But on this hike, reaching the summit is not the peak experience. The most exciting part of this hike is sharing it. On the majority of our hikes, Pat and Dejah are my only companions. But this hike is extraordinary in that we share it with lots of other folks on the trail, thirty-one to be exact—more than on any other hike except for Washington. This hiking trail, in the middle of nowhere, is a thoroughfare for peakbaggers.

In the parking lot before we set out, we meet a group of two men and a woman. One of the men tells us this will be his forty-eighth and final New Hampshire peak, and that he hiked the others twenty years ago, but never got to Isolation. We hope we will be on the summit with him.

From mile four on we start meeting hikers sporadically. One man tells us there is a group of eight women celebrating one member's forty-eighth peak with champagne on the top. Soon after, we see a line of women hiking toward us; they are full of smiles, strength, and solidarity. We clap and cheer for the person bagging number forty-eight. They are a happy lot and we feel fortunate to have that brief but exciting moment to recognize a fellow woman hiker who just accomplished the extraordinary.

Soon after, as we near the summit, we meet the man we'd first encountered in the parking lot. As soon as I spot him, I start to clap and let out a rousing woo hoo! I give him a high five. He has tears in his eyes; we do too.

We meet a couple on the summit. They are peakbagging, on their forty-second mountain. We share that this is our forty-sixth peak. As we say it out loud, it hits us that we have only two more mountains to climb to finish the New Hampshire forty-eight. They ask what summits are left and we tell them Owl's Head and Jefferson. We wish each other luck with our remaining peaks and start down Isolation, not feeling isolated in the least.

As we pass lots of hikers on our descent, I ask them if they are peakbaggers and, if so, how many they've completed. Everyone smiles and immediately recites a number, enjoying the opportunity to talk about something close to their hearts, as if I'd just invited them to tell me about the moments they're most proud of. Quite a few hikers respond with a number in the forties! What a bonding experience. We are all like-minded, engaged in, and committed to the same endeavor.

Kudos go to Nathaniel Goodrich, librarian at Dartmouth College, hiker, trailblazer, and founder of the Four Thousand Footer Club in New Hampshire. The club has encouraged thousands of hikers from throughout New England to take on the four thousand–foot challenge, sending them into the woods to climb all of New Hampshire's highest peaks, the well-known as well as the trails less traveled. It has also inspired many with something to strive for that is doable and challenging. It is a goal that, when accomplished, brings pride and strong emotion to the peak celebration, leaving hikers with a feeling they've accomplished something worthwhile, meaningful, and amazing.

To me, it feels like I belong there on Isolation, amid this elite group of people whom I don't even know. We are linked by what we share—a commitment to journey up and down each of New Hampshire's four thousand–foot mountains. I'm sure we have many of the same accoutrements—a collection of maps of the White Mountains, AMC membership windshield sticker, backpack, CamelBak, boots, Nalgene bottles, bug dope, Techwick shirts, poles, and a list of New Hampshire's forty eight—complete with check marks, dates, stories, and photographs. I belong. What a feeling! And what a statement coming from me. A year ago I didn't even consider myself a real hiker. Today, I have something important to share with everyone on the mountain. We are bonded by the experience of peakbagging Isolation together on this beautiful blue-sky day, by our common goal, and by the celebration to come.

Perhaps Mt. Isolation is a misnomer. Perhaps it should be called Mt. Celebration.

STATS

MOUNTAIN: MT. ISOLATION (4,003)

NEAREST CITY: JACKSON, N.H.

DATE: JUNE 30, 2007

TIME: 9 HOURS AND 30 MINUTES

WEATHER: MOSTLY SUNNY, TEMPERATURE IN THE 60S

MILES: 14.6

ELEVATION GAIN: 3,204 FEET

TRAILS: ROCKY BRANCH TRAIL, ISOLATION TRAIL, DAVIS PATH

HOLY SHIT FACTOR: CELEBRATORY HIGH!

17. SHARING OUR FORTY-EIGHTH SUMMIT ON JEFFERSON

July 22, 2007, Bretton Woods, New Hampshire

> *To become fully alive a person must have goals*
> *and aims that transcend himself.*
>
> Herbert A. Otto

We want a BFS (big fat sun) to light up our final New Hampshire mountain. So when the weekend weather forecast turns favorable, Pat and I plead with our friends and loved ones and wheedle our way out of commitments and into a free Sunday to hike our forty-eighth New Hampshire peak. We receive no resistance, only blessings.

At 5 a.m. we are off to the Whites and we're on the trail by 8:20. The

Caps Ridge Trail up Jefferson is short, 2.5 miles, but steep. The trail takes us over three Caps—rocky, steep ledges that require hand-over-hand scrambling, praying for hand and footholds as we crawl up the rock face. We don't bring Dejah. She doesn't like ledges. Of course, neither do I. Pat loves them!

From the moment we set foot on the black-fly-infested trail, I tell everyone this is our forty-eighth New Hampshire peak, following the example set by other hikers on Mt. Isolation.

When I tell people this is our forty-eighth peak, some know what I am talking about and some do not. But every-

body congratulates us and cheers us on. They get a dose of our excitement and we feel their generosity of spirit and good wishes. Their responses make me feel happy and proud and pump both of us up—if it is possible to be more pumped than we already are. You can't make someone else feel great without some of that feeling rubbing off on you. It's that simple a two-way, win-win celebration moment made possible by sharing it!

After some serious huffing and puffing, we make it to the summit at 11:03 a.m. A friendly group of four hikers shares our summit moment with pictures, hugs, high fives, and woo hoos! I am giddy and overwhelmed with pride and psyched and serious all at the same time. I whip out the four thousand–footer list in my backpack and ceremoniously enter "July 22, 2007" next to Jefferson. Pat and I sign the bottom. There, it is official.

One of the women on top mentions that Chuck Roast in Conway has four thousand–footer T-shirts with the mountains listed on the back. Wow-serinoes. That sounds cool.

We have lunch close to the summit. Pat surprises me with a cold Snapple she lugged up in a cooler in her pack. She breaks out her cold Pepsi and we toast each other. Bliss! I take out two rocks I had collected from other hikes. I don't know which four thousand footers they came from, but it doesn't matter. We place the rocks on the cairn closest to the summit, leaving symbols of our forty-eight four thousand–footer journeys on the top.

On the way down, we meet a group of hikers. As soon as I hear they are AMCers, I know they will appreciate our feat and tell them we have just summited our forty-eighth New Hampshire peak. They burst into applause and cheers.

We continue to relay our news to people coming up as we hike down.

One person asks, "How long did it take you?"

After some quick figuring, Pat responds, "A little less than fifteen months."

"Wow, you are an inspiration!" the hiker says.

Sharing our joy up and down the mountain feels natural. Yet, years ago I would not have said a word for fear others would think I was bragging or, even worse, that they wouldn't be interested. I didn't know then that we all just want to be a part, to join in, to be invited into others' lives. Sharing our big day with fellow

hikers is an invitation to join in the joy. Expressing my excitement and seeing it received and reflected back to me in the faces of people on the trail fills me with delight that is too big to contain. I think this is what life is really all about.

Being the competitive girls we are, we gain momentum and speed below treeline. A young whippersnapper bears down on our heels and we are determined he won't reach us to pass. We arrive back at the parking lot at 2:29 and take a "we made it, we did it!" movie. Then we drive to Conway and purchase our four thousand–footer shirts. To buy them on the day we climb our final peak adds another level of meaning to the shirts and to the day.

On our drive home, as on the drive up, we continue to play "High / Low"—

replaying our highest and lowest hiking moments, reminiscing about each hike up those forty-eight peaks. What a blast we have remembering them. Some poignant moments and some new realizations come to us as we retrace our steps.

We arrive back in Keene at 7 p.m. and pull in my driveway to find a huge "Congratulations" banner hanging on the garage.

Pat, Don, and I go to Longhorn's and celebrate with steak, mashed potatoes, and chocolate stampede.

New Hampshire's four thousand footers—done!

On to New England's sixty-seven!

STATS

MOUNTAIN: MT. JEFFERSON (5,712)

NEAREST CITY: BRETTON WOODS, N.H.

DATE: JULY 22, 2007

TIME: 6 HOURS

WEATHER: SUNNY, PASSING CLOUDS, LIGHT BREEZE

MILES: 5

ELEVATION GAIN: 2,700 FEET

TRAILS: CAPS RIDGE TRAIL

HOLY SHIT FACTOR: ON A SCALE OF 1 TO 48—IT'S A 48!

18. LITTLE KIDS ON OLD SPECK

August 4, 2007, East Andover, Maine

> *If I had influence with the good fairy who is supposed to preside over the christening of all children, I should ask that her gift to each child in the world be a sense of wonder so indestructible that it would last throughout life.*

Rachel Carson

The magic just happens. It starts in the car about halfway there, two hours into the drive. Pat shares her research on the Old Speck trails we are going to climb today. There's this alternative route on the lower part of the mountain called the Eyebrow Trail, she explains to me, which passes along the edge of a cliff. Pat's eyes light up as she tells me there are rungs and ladders installed in the rock ledges to help climbers ascend the steep grade. She stays calm for my benefit because she knows this stuff scares the hell out of me, but her enthusiasm for steep is leaking out her edges. Inside Pat is psyched. I'm leery on the surface, but inside I'm up to the challenge.

We are on the Old Speck Trail by 8:50 a.m. and soon after take the turn-off for the Eyebrow Trail. The up starts right away. The steeper the trail, the happier Pat is. By the time we see the railing made of thick, wire cable, Pat is smiling and taking wow-this-is-awesome deep breaths of appreciation.

"I love this stuff," she says, grinning. Minutes later, "I just love it!"

Then we see the rungs and the ladders and Pat's excitement is bursting. She springs up the ladder and the iron rungs and disappears around the bend on what feels like a ninety-degree straight-up trail. Her enthusiasm fuels her step and I believe she could run up the mountain. I finally catch up.

"I love this trail!" she exclaims.

She doesn't need to tell me. If her chest were made of glass and I could peek in when she wasn't looking, I would see a kindergarten class out for recess playing on a jungle gym, swinging and climbing and shouting with glee.

It's not long, about 1.1 miles, before we reach the end of the Eyebrow Trail, and rejoin the Old Speck Trail. This is where my kid kicks in. The path is covered with mica—shiny pieces, big mirror-like flakes, thick hunks, and rocks laced with mica. I can't contain myself. I love mica. I love that it looks like fairy dust on the trail. I have been collecting it on all of our four thousand–footer hikes. But I have never seen anything like this. It is everywhere! Clear, silver, and black fragments, tons of them, like shells on a Sanibel beach. I spend most of the hike bent over picking up shiny gems.

"Wowsers, Pat, look at this!" I shout ahead to Pat.

"Wow, oh, wow! A huge piece!"

"Oh my God, it looks like it is just growing out of the ground!"

"There's tons of it! Pat, did you see this?"

By now Pat is laughing.

I put piece after piece in my shorts pocket. I stop every few minutes for the next find. I'm collecting treasure, blessed each time I come across another cache of these sparkling trail diamonds. Pat has caught on and has started her own collection, but she is more discriminating and picks up fewer specimens. She seems to be able to let some mica-covered trail pass by without needing to stoop down to see if there is an extra special prize in the midst of the shimmer. But I can't walk past any of it; I have to stop and exam-

ine nature's gifts and take what calls to me. Then I jog to catch up.

"Look at this piece, Pat! Look at this! Pat, look!" I say over and over. I am five years old and I want to share my find with my friend.

My pockets bulge even more now that I've decided to collect mica-glazed rocks as well. I start putting the larger ones in my pack.

By the time we get to the summit at 12:10 p.m., both our pockets are swollen with wealth from the mountain. I feel like I have a stash of prized possessions, rare finds, glittering jewels swelling both front pockets of my shorts. It's

Easter and I have a basket-full of chocolate eggs, more than I ever dreamed; or it's summer on Cape Cod and I come across a large, intact conch shell, smooth and colorful, near the water's edge; or I'm panning for gold in one of those silly fake Boom Town type places out West and there, glittering in my pan, is a hunk of real gold.

The summit sports a tower, but we choose to sit on a few hot rocks and enjoy the view from ground level. We take our boots off, spread our toes, and turn our faces toward the warm sun. Ahhhh. We eat our lunch side by side, two best friends simmering with the excitement of a fun adventure on a perfect day in August. We spend almost an hour of bliss on top before heading down at 12:58.

We continue adding to our mica collections on the way down one of the most beautiful trails we've ever hiked, when Pat sees two gray jays following us. We met gray jays for the first time on Mounts Jackson and Webster, where they ate out of our hands. Pat gets some trail mix, reaches out her hand and almost immediately a bird lands on her palm and grabs the raisins.

The kid in me is wide-eyed with wonder and excitement. *I want to try!* Pat gives me the trail mix. I hold my hand away from my body and the birds come. It feels like we are in some magical wooded land where birds come to share their spirits with you. I start talking to them when they alight on my fingers. I know it's really happening because their claws are sharp.

We leave our feathered friends full and happy and continue down the mica-decorated trail, me trying not to bend over for a closer inspection and possible collection every other step. We arrive back at the car at 4:15 p.m., change into dry, clean clothes, and sit in the parking lot enjoying a cold drink, the perfect temperature, soft breeze, warm sunshine, and our distended pockets.

Pat and I often have deep conversations when we hike, but today is light-hearted, treasure-hunting, bird-communing, jungle-gym-type climbing, young-at-heart fun. On this hike the sweat, heavy breathing, and hard effort are minimized by the sheer joy of experiencing the mountain through a child's eyes. What a blast!

STATS

MOUNTAIN: OLD SPECK (4,144)

NEAREST CITY: EAST ANDOVER, MAINE

DATE: AUGUST 4, 2007

TIME: 7 HOURS

WEATHER: ABSOLUTELY BEAUTIFUL, SUNNY LIGHT BREEZE, TEMPERATURE IN THE 70S

MILES: 7.6

ELEVATION GAIN: 2,800 FEET

TRAILS: OLD SPECK TRAIL, EYEBROW TRAIL, APPALACHIAN TRAIL

HOLY SHIT FACTOR: FULL OF WONDER AND DELIGHT

19. A DIFFERENT PERSPECTIVE—BALDFACE

September 16, 2007, Jackson, New Hampshire

Thousands of tired, nerve-shaken, over-civilized people are beginning to find out that going to the mountains is going home; that wildness is a necessity; and that mountain parks and reservations are useful not only as fountains of timber and irrigating rivers, but as fountains of life.

John Muir

It's Monday morning and I am dragging jelly legs around my office, wishing today was a rest day after hiking Baldface Mountain yesterday. Re-entry into the world at sea-level is tough. Sitting at my desk, computer screen full of e-mails, my view of the world is jagged and harsh, cluttered, busy, stressful, and linear. It is driven by the clock and calendar, my "To Do" list,

my responsibilities, and the bottom line. I see hour to hour and miss the whole day, see typos and backed-up traffic and miss the serenity and meaning found in the bigger picture. I feel small, constricted, and stuck. I reminisce about yesterday's hike, a difficult, nine-hour, ten-mile loop with over four miles above treeline. The memory is still close enough that I can beam myself up Star-Trek style to the open granite ledges. I am above the trees, in the sun, arms outstretched, trying to let it all in. I'm safe in the enormity and beauty. I've regained myself . . . for the moment.

Taking my first steps up the Baldface Circle Trail is the beginning of an unwinding process, a gradual move from one perspective to another, one step up at a time. I start at the bottom in the fray and frazzle of life. As I dedicate my body to the physical exercise of climbing the mountainside, my heart and leg muscles rise to the challenge and I start to feel more me. By the time we reach the first views, I'm centered in my heart. As I hike above treeline and look out at the expanse before me, I am transported to a different plane of living. Inspired by the colors and form of the earth below me, my view is immense, clear and peaceful, all encompassing, and never-ending. I can see the big picture and am reminded of how incredibly beautiful and utterly remarkable life really is. There are choices, possibilities, and opportunities that didn't exist earlier in the day. When I can see this far, how can my vision be anything but limitless? Soaking in the view, I take a spontaneous, deep breath, as if my body can't allow the expansiveness in without first expelling the stale air of small, negative thinking. Here, above it all, I am free to shed the weight of daily chaos and details, and just breathe in my surroundings. In that breath, I know that literally everything is possible.

I try to do a freeze-frame in my mind so I can take the moment home—the expanse from my hiking boots all the way to the horizon, peaks and valleys going on forever, from green and gold to darker purple where the clouds create shadow, to lighter and lighter blues until the colors melt into the sky. I am an insignificant witness. There's purpose and order out here, even though I don't understand it.

The hike has doses of difficulty that tug me back to reality. The elevation gain is 3,600 feet, only 200 feet less than a hike up Mt. Washington! The rock ledges are straight up, a 900-foot ascent in six-tenths of a mile. Dejah is scared she can't jump up to the next ledge and starts crying, which derails my concentrated effort to get myself up to the next rock ledge. Plus, I am getting a blister on each heel. Pat encourages both Dejah and me up the open rock face and helps me bandage my feet.

As I climb higher, the landscape seeps inside me and takes up residence in my heart. Eating my Lost Pilgrim sandwich wrap, sitting on a stone bench, looking up at the summit half a mile away, and gazing out at the panorama, I become part of it. I am the beauty. I am the peace. I wish I could hold onto this euphoric feeling when I am sitting in front of my computer screen, in crisis mode, struggling with the little stuff that doesn't really matter. In that frustration, I want to be able to mentally helicopter back up above the details to where the vista is sweeping and I can see the beauty and feel the serenity.

We reach South Baldface at 1:10 p.m. and hike the ridge that connects the two peaks. It is a series of five humps, each one larger than the last. The colorful fall scrub, off-white reindeer moss, and red mountain cranberries add depth to the scenery. I can't stop taking pictures.

On North Baldface summit, 2:12 p.m., surrounded by cool crisp air, bright sunlight, and sporadic clouds, my best friend and I are on top of the world, hugged by the sky, held up by the earth, warmed by the sun, surrounded by the beauty.

Walking the ridge back down the mountain, I expect to be quickly immersed in the woods as we descend. Baldface is different. We enter the trees and then minutes later re-emerge on another open expanse of rock ledge that stands above the vastness. I breathe deeply. Again and again the view re-emerges. It is as if I need to be reminded again and again that it is still there—that beautiful perspective above the chaos of life. The peace and the possibilities, all still there. It doesn't matter where I am, or whether I can see it or not. This view is always available.

Stats

Mountains: South Baldface (3,570) & North Baldface (3,610)

Nearest City: Jackson, N.H.

Date: September 16, 2007

Time: 9 hours

Weather: Cool, sun and clouds, little wind

Miles: 10.4

Elevation Gain: 3,600 feet

Trails: Baldface Circle Trail

Holy Shit Factor: Above-the-fray high

20. FROM FEAR TO JOY ON HAMLIN PEAK

September 23, 2007, Stacyville, Maine

Fear is the suppression of the excitement of life.

Marcus Daniels

My life is a constant search for meaning. Each day I am a bit more focused, clearer in my intentions, and more intense in my search for stuff that matters. I am less and less satisfied with surface con-versations, meaningless projects, and wasted time. I am unfulfilled when I cannot find some truth, some morsel that reverberates within my soul and makes me feel whole.

Hiking always holds meaning for me

because it helps me discover who I really am by challenging me. Often the challenge comes in the form of the elements—the freezing cold, driving rain, ice or deep snow on the trail. Or it is a physically demanding hike, where my muscles are screaming on a long steep root-and-boulder-infested trail. Or the challenge comes from facing my fears, like walking laterally along a smooth steep ledge. Being thrust out of my comfort zone is always good for a learning experience. But our Hamlin hike is about being in my comfort zone. It shows me how far I have come.

Pat and I climbed Katahdin last year. It was a complete and utter out-of-my-comfort-zone experience. We hiked across Knife Edge, the ridge between Pamola and Baxter Peaks that is made up of sharp serrated boulders, and drops thousands of feet on either side. Swirling clouds obscured our view, and the winds gusts were so strong we had to hunker down on the rocks to avoid being blown off the ridge. It took two hours and ten minutes to navigate along the Knife Edge's 1.1 mile. Then when we started down the slide on the Saddle Trail, the rains came. This trail unnerved me. I was cold and frightened in the rain and wind. I had not had a lot of experience with slides and the steepness and the wet, moving rocks under my feet sent my heart into my throat. I was out of my comfort zone from the treeline going up Pamola to the treeline coming down Baxter.

A year later, hiking Katahdin again, this time heading for Hamlin Peak, it's a totally different story. We hike up the Chimney Pond Trail, loving the fall colors, snapping pictures at every bend in the trail. We reach timberline and are immediately greeted by dark, foreboding skies. It looks like rain on the mountain summit, but sun is peeking out from the clouds behind us, illuminating the trail and the red, green, and gold groundcover in front of us. The sight of Knife Edge takes us aback. Last year, on our hike down, low clouds and rain concealed the view. But today we can see it clearly. We are amazed by its grandeur and impressed with our feat of a year ago.

Hiking up Hamlin reminds me of hiking Pamola. The trail above treeline seems to stretch on forever. The summit looks very far away—what appears to be a person on the peak is a tiny speck. But the sight does not overwhelm me as it did last year. I am excited to be out in the open, in the midst of the incredible scenery, loving how it changes as we progress up the mountain, fascinated by the perspective of distance as we inch closer to the summit. I don't gasp at the sight of the never-ending trail. I do not even dread the rain. If it comes, it comes.

Hamlin summit is alive with wind and color. Rust and red and burgundy grasses, yellow and gold leaves smattered with green, granite rock, clear sunlight, amidst light blue skies. The grasses of the tableland undulate in the wind.

As we walk, the wind increases and Pat gets out her wind gauge. When a

fierce gust comes, she holds the dial up high and we watch the digital numbers increase one by one. We start to cheer for a higher number, like auctioneers. We have 40; c'mon, 41, 41. Woo hoo 43! C'mon 44, 44! Oh, 45! 46! 47! Woo hoo! We are laughing, loving every minute of the wind's roar and force as it tries to push us back along the tablelands.

Last year on Knife Edge, the winds scared me to death. Since then we have had a few hikes above treeline in the Presidentials when the winds have been incredibly fierce and I have left the mountains feeling frightened. I remem-ber meeting a White Mountain rescuer on top of Madison. I shared with him that the winds scared me and he said, "Play with them." I remember thinking, *What the hell is he talking about?* Now I know. He was talking about Pat and me cheering, holding the wind gauge up, screaming above the wind's howl for another big gust to push the gauge higher.

The highest gust we record is 55 mph. On the Beaufort Wind Force Scale, 55 to 63 mph indicates gale force. Trees can be uprooted. On the tablelands, barely able to hold ourselves up, we laugh and play and measure and live the moment.

Reluctant to leave the sun and the thrill of the wind, we finally head down the Saddle Trail. Having encountered my fair share of slides over the past year, today I am comfortable making my way over slabs of rock and loose scree. I'm loving the beauty and breathing in each view as we descend. I am grateful for the opportunity to be back on Katahdin, climbing it again as a more experienced, stronger hiker.

We reach Chimney Pond and hike the last three miles out of the woods, still excited by what we have seen and experienced on top of Hamlin. It was exhilarating, thrilling, and immensely beautiful, yet fierce. It was not frightening. This time I loved the wind, the foliage, the sunlight and the endless ridge above treeline.

My experiences in the mountains have changed me. I have experimented with the fringe of my comfort zone, expanding my limits, becoming less afraid and more comfortable with each adventure. In my new-found margin of safety, I discover an awe and respect for the strength and harshness of the mountains and their weather. I can't control the trails or the elements, but, with experience, I can enjoy more and fear less.

On Hamlin, my fear turned to joy.

STATS

Mountain: Hamlin Peak (4,751)

Nearest City: Stacyville, Maine

Date: September 23, 2007

Time: 11 hours

Weather: Sun and clouds, windy, temperatures in the upper 70s to mid 60s

Miles: 11.9

Elevation Gain: 3,262 feet

Trails: Chimney Pond Trail, North Basin Cut Off, Hamlin Ridge, Saddle Trail

Holy Shit Factor: In-my-comfort-zone high

21. MANSFIELD—IT DOESN'T COUNT!

October 20, 2007, Underhill Center, Vermont

. . . the idea that some lives matter less is the root of all that's wrong with the world.

Tracey Kidder, **Mountains Beyond Mountains,** on Paul Farmer, working in Haiti

This hike isn't going to count because Pat and I have already hiked Mt. Mansfield. I'm not liking that it doesn't count. What's the point? I like stuff when it means something. When it matters.

This is easy to understand when you know my history. As a child, I tried to keep myself safe from my mother's wrath by being invisible. I grew up feeling like I didn't matter to anyone. As I reassemble my life in retrospect, I realize I have spent my adult years trying to ensure those around me never feel that way. I have spent thirty years finding ways to tell others they matter.

That's the message of the Pumpkin Festival, a community event I started in 1991 and ran for eight years. Each year we attempt to set a Guinness World Record for the largest number of lit jack-o'-lanterns in one place, at one time. The Pumpkin Festival issues an invitation to people everywhere to carve a pumpkin and bring it to downtown Keene. We need your pumpkin; everyone can help, every pumpkin carver matters, every jack-o'-lantern counts. And with everyone's participation, we create a spectacle of over twenty thousand lit jack-o'-lanterns shimmering from forty-foot-high scaffold pyramids that transforms our small community into the jack-o'-lantern capital of the world.

I love checking off a mountain on my sixty-seven four thousand footers list when I get home from hiking, tired and sore. Like the pumpkins, each mountain counts toward our goal. When we bag all sixty-seven peaks, we'll get a patch, proof positive we did it. But it's not really about the number of mountains we climb, or the number of pumpkins at the Keene Pumpkin Festival. What is important is that we are doing it. What we do in life matters, whether we discover our inner strength and beauty climbing mountains, or we become part of the spirit of community carving pumpkins at the Keene Pumpkin Festival. Whether or not we set a record, or check off a mountain, the experience changes us.

While the Pumpkin Festival spirit glows in Keene, we are hiking. I don't go to the festival—it is too difficult for

me. It's like bringing up my children. Don and I brought two daughters into the world, we cared for them and loved them and disciplined them until it was time to let them go. When they went off to college, I was left standing in the hallway sobbing as I stared at pictures of them sucking their thumbs. It's been painful to let go of the Pumpkin Festival, even though I left knowing it was time. I had done what I needed to do. Being the person creating, orchestrating, and delivering the "you matter" message to an entire community made me feel like I mattered, like I was mak-

ing a difference. I miss the hugeness of that feeling. I miss being the leader of something that magnificent and meaningful, that exciting and beautiful. It was such a high for me. Now I get the "high" in a more literal way—I climb mountains. Today we're climbing Mansfield in Underhill, Vermont.

We start out in Underhill State Park in the sunshine and warm breeze; Don, my life's partner, Pat, my hiking partner, and me. I love it when Don joins us once or twice a year, I feel more complete when he is with me.

Up we go. Don leads, and he's cranking up the mountain. Wowsers—racquetball, handball, and running sure put some speed on him since last year. It's hard to keep up!

The trail is steep and very wet and much of the time we are walking in a brook that runs down the middle of the trail. We have a few views of the sun reflecting on the brilliant leaves below us, but it's mostly gray above. We reach timberline and walk in clouds, the mist swirling around us.

We trek along the ridge or, I should say, the face. Mansfield resembles an elongated human face in repose, with a distinct forehead, nose, lips, and chin. We reach the ridge at the nose and eat lunch somewhere between the upper and lower lip.

I try not to wish for views and sun and just take what is. I know there is something in this for me that is important. What, though? I like views. I don't like rain! As I'm trying to talk myself out of my damp-and-dreary pity party, I look at Don and do a double take. He has taken off his new navy-blue bandana and his head is blue. He doesn't have a lot of hair so it's pretty easy to see. Blue! The bandana, coupled with the mist and drizzle and sweat, has dyed his skin!

This is bad timing. Don has a promising job interview the day after tomorrow. He's been looking for work since the beginning of the year when he courageously left his job because he was very unhappy.

He looks at me, eyes wide. "Nancy, what if this doesn't come off?"

I start to furiously scrub his forehead with my index finger and a bit of spit. I'm rubbing pretty hard. Eventually I see a red dot on his forehead where I've been scrubbing.

"It'll come off, honey," I say, trying not to crack up. I glance at Pat who is doubled over in laughter, out of Don's sight.

"Holy shit, Nancy, are you sure?" Don asks, showing me a blue hand. "I can't believe this. I can't go to an interview like this. Does it really look bad?"

By now Pat and I are laughing hysterically and Don, or should I say Hiker Smurf, begins taking himself less seriously and starts acting silly.

We resume our ridge walk, giggling to ourselves. We summit the chin and start down the Sunset Ridge Trail when the rain starts pelting us. Pat can't see because her glasses are fogged up and dripping with rain. Don twists his knee and is having trouble getting down the steep, wet rock trail. Our hiking pants are soaked through. I start to shiver, despite my hat and gloves. Don's blue head, now fully exposed to the driving rain, is getting a good scouring.

At this point our banter stops and we concentrate on getting down the slick rock face. Just keep moving, I say to myself, and for the next hour that is all we do—make our way carefully down the river of water, mud, and slick rock. The slippery conditions make us all more concerned for each other and the three of us help each other down the ridge.

When we reach treeline (a long way on this trail), the rain subsides and we emerge from the mist, drizzle, and clouds hanging over Mansfield summit back into the sun.

The last mile is boredom and agony for Don. He likes the intense stuff but can't handle the mundane. We're wet and chilled, looking forward to hot showers and a good dinner in Burlington. The trailhead can't come too soon!

Sunday dawns sunny and warm. I ask Don if he wishes yesterday's hike had had today's sun.

"No," he says. "I sometimes enjoy stuff more when there is misery involved. Anyone can hike in beautiful weather. But it takes something more to enjoy a hike like yesterday's in inclement weather. I am blessed that I can do that."

I take it all back—our hike up Mansfield counts.

We came back to the car enriched by the experience, and amazed at our ability to enjoy misery.

Writing this report of our Pumpkin Festival hike helps me understand myself. Hiking has taken the place of running the event. The challenge of planning the festival logistics, gathering volunteers, empowering and engaging a community, and marketing the Pumpkin Festival message has been replaced by the challenge of planning for and getting to the tops of mountains using steep trails, hiking in all kinds of weather. Instead of counting pumpkins, I'm counting mountains. Now, it is through hiking that I experience risk and fear, thrills and excitement.

It is seeing flowers and views instead of hundreds of orange gourds sitting cheek to cheek that brings beauty into my life. And it is through writing about the hiking experience that I find meaning. Each hike brings the fulfillment I long for, whether it counts or not.

Don, no longer blue, got the job on Monday!

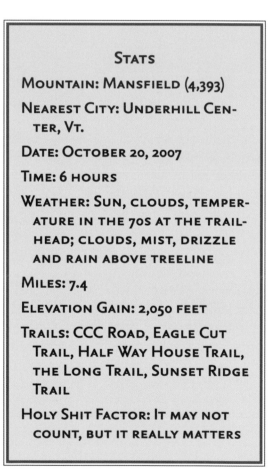

STATS

MOUNTAIN: MANSFIELD (4,393)

NEAREST CITY: UNDERHILL CENTER, VT.

DATE: OCTOBER 20, 2007

TIME: 6 HOURS

WEATHER: SUN, CLOUDS, TEMPERATURE IN THE 70S AT THE TRAILHEAD; CLOUDS, MIST, DRIZZLE AND RAIN ABOVE TREELINE

MILES: 7.4

ELEVATION GAIN: 2,050 FEET

TRAILS: CCC ROAD, EAGLE CUT TRAIL, HALF WAY HOUSE TRAIL, THE LONG TRAIL, SUNSET RIDGE TRAIL

HOLY SHIT FACTOR: IT MAY NOT COUNT, BUT IT REALLY MATTERS

22. GETTING COLD FEET ON SLEEPER

November 12, 2007, Waterville Valley, New Hampshire

Nothing is so fatiguing as the eternal hanging on of an uncompleted task.

William James

I'm emotionally and physically exhausted. How can that be? We climbed Welch-Dickey, two pimples in the White Mountains. The trail was 4.4 miles long and the elevation gain was only 1,819 feet.

Well, perhaps that's not the whole story. When Pat pulls into the driveway to

pick up Dejah and me at 5 a.m., I have my backpack full of necessary hiking paraphernalia and I have my inner physical reserves stashed for the climb—extra energy, fortitude, strength, and stamina. You know, all the extra physical "stuff" I need to help me get up a mountain that I don't necessarily need when I'm in the office working.

We decide to climb Sleeper, which is on the hundred highest list, but, oh, by the way, we need to climb the Tripyramids, a couple four thousand footers, to get to Sleeper. On the drive up we discuss routes. Pat wants to try a new trail, so we decide on the Sabbaday Brook Trail, a thirteen-miler that will take us over Middle Tripyramid and South Peak and then on to West Sleeper. It's a hefty hike and we are ready—we think.

We arrive at the Sabbaday Brook trailhead at 8 a.m. I'd read the trail description in the AMC White Mountain Guide, so we know what we will find—steep climbs and water crossings.

We pass Sabbaday Falls, a gushing,

thunderous waterfall. Did I say gushing and thunderous? Little do I know that pictures of water will be almost all I will take today.

We get to the first stream crossing and remember that the guidebook indicated we could bushwhack the one-tenth of a mile to meet the trail again, cutting out two water crossings. So we continue on the worn path that seems very well traveled—which makes sense to me since the stream is roaring and there do not seem to be places where one can easily cross. There is lots of cold water in that stream; the rocks are either glazed over with ice or covered with freezing, running whitewater—not very inviting. I'm not worried . . . yet. The bushwhack is easy and we arrive at the third water crossing, knowing that we have to cross this time to continue on the trail.

I begin to look for a place to cross. My inner dialogue goes something like this: *Huh—holy shit lots of white water. Doesn't look very good there. Let's go up a ways. Wowsers, look at all that ice, I'm not crossing there. Well, we could get halfway across there, but the rest of the way looks a little touch and go. Okay that rock to that rock, to that rock to . . . huh, not there. SHIT! Oh wait—what about there . . . .*

We move up the river, scout, shake our heads, mutter under our breath and hike up farther. About a half hour into the search for a place to cross we're still making our way up and down the banks of the stream. I scream in frustration.

Pat is doing the same thing, mentally hopping from rock to rock to see if she can find an easy crossing, or any crossing. We move along the banks of the river, tripping over leaf-covered rocks and roots, climbing over fallen trees, shoving branches away after they poke us in the eyes.

We are both annoyed. Pat tries to cross once, slips, almost falling in, and comes back. She decides to take off her boots and socks and walk across.

What? Are you kidding? That water's freezing! I am not doing that! I say to myself. I know, I know. It is just water and rocks, but all that ice makes me shiver with anticipation of the cold. My head is saying, *Now Nancy—it's only water, for heaven's sake. Take your damn boots off and cross!* But my gut is saying, *I don't want to do that!* and my heart is wishing I could find a place to cross that looks doable so I wouldn't be faced with this dilemma. Dejah keeps looking at us as if to say, *What are you girls doing? Let's go!* She certainly doesn't mind getting her feet wet. She goes partway across, looks back at us pleadingly as if to say, *you can do this,* and I know she is thoroughly disappointed when we don't follow.

I scream again.

I see a tree trunk angled across the river. It sits high, so a fall would not be fun, but I think I might be able to walk across it using poles. That thought sends Pat over the edge. Not her thing. So now an hour has gone by, we are freezing, and we are still on the wrong side of the river. We decide to give up. And believe me, we are not give-up girls. We head back down the trail toward our car when we pass the narrowest crossing we've seen all day. I say I think we can do it. We put our ice cleats on so we can get a good grip on the rocks and carefully make our way across. Phew—that's done! Ah, not so fast . . . . We walk a few steps and realize we are on an island in the middle of the river and have more water to cross to get to the trail.

We find a possible passage that features sharp rocks, water flowing over them, covered in ice. Pat bravely steps out, starts to slip and immediately, but very slowly and carefully, returns to the bank.

We retrace our steps and head back to the car, both of us fighting our demons. Pat says she feels defeated. I am angry with myself for not being willing to take my boots and socks off and wade across. We get up in the pitch dark to drive three hours to the White Mountains, all to be turned back by water.

"Well," I say, "maybe we weren't supposed to cross the river. Maybe this was not meant to be the day we bag Sleeper. Instead of fighting it why not just woo hoo?"

It is a "meant-to-be," we conclude.

We get back to the car at 10 a.m. and decide to climb nearby Welch-Dickey because it will count toward the 52-With-A-View list. Much of the hike we talk about our next attempt of West Sleeper. We plan on bringing neoprene boots to keep our feet warm and dry while walking in the freezing water and a towel to dry off. We should be all set!

Note: We attempt Sleeper again using the same Sabbaday Brook Trail the following Saturday. We cross the brook five times, taking off our hiking boots, putting on neoprene boots, walking across the brook, drying our feet, and changing back into hiking boots each time. We finally give into our freezing feet and head back to the car, having to cross the brook another five times!

STATS

MOUNTAIN ATTEMPTED: WEST SLEEPER

NEAREST CITY: WATERVILLE VALLEY, N.H.

DATE: NOVEMBER 12, 2007

TIME: 2 HOURS

WEATHER: MOSTLY SUNNY, TEMPERATURES IN THE 40S TO 30S

MILES: .5

TRAILS: SABBADAY BROOK TRAIL

HOLY SHIT FACTOR: HIGH FRUSTRATION LEVEL DUE TO WATER CROSSINGS

23. NEW YEAR'S RESOLUTION ON TECUMSEH

December 31, 2007, Waterville Valley, New Hampshire

In the quick, when it counts, you must have no doubt. Spit out all your doubt, breathe it out, pluck it from your heart, tear it loose from your mind, throw it away, be rid of it. We weren't born into this universe to doubt. We were born to hope, to love, to live, to learn, to know joy, to have faith that our lives have meaning . . . and to find the way.

Dean Koontz, **One Door Away From Heaven**

Today, as I hike, I become aware of how hard I make things.

We start out at Waterville Valley ski area, looking a bit out of place with snowshoes, backpacks, and a yellow Lab on leash. We find the trailhead easily and set out on the Mt. Tecumseh Trail at 9:35 a.m. After meandering through the woods for a mile, we take a right turn and see a path that goes up for as far as the eye can see. No turns, no level ground, no deviation from the steady steep climb. Wowsers. I can feel my anxiety heighten as soon as I register the challenging terrain. I immediately worry that I won't be able to get up this ferocious incline.

A wise inner voice comes to the rescue. *Don't look ahead,* it says. *What's up there is in the future. At this moment, right now, I am here and I am fine.*

The next moment finds me even higher up the trail and, incredibly, I am still fine! I glance up again. Holy shit! Wrong thing to do. The trail ahead hasn't changed a bit: it's still a very steep incline, still no turns, still no end in sight.

I realize that looking ahead—anticipating how difficult that steep climb up is going to be and worrying about whether I can make it or not—just makes the climb harder. While I'm worrying that I can't do it, I am doing it! And I have done it over and over again. In the past twenty months, I have successfully summited eighty-three mountains. Why would I think I couldn't do it today? I do the same in life. I choose not to believe in myself,

which leads to second-guessing myself, and I get stuck on a treadmill, not going anywhere, filled with self-doubt and self-recrimination.

I look down at my snowshoes, which collect snow as they shuffle up the mountain. I'm breathing heavily, sweating up a storm. It's snowing lightly, which provides no relief. I keep my head down and note what my body is doing. I do not feel like I am going to die. I feel strong and sure. I surprise myself when I live in the moment instead of anticipating what might happen. At this point I realize that I don't have to make things hard for myself. Instead of anticipating failure, I can believe in myself and trust that I can do it. I don't have to worry about what the summit of the mountain will bring until I get there. Right now, I can just be astonished that I feel fine slogging up the straight, steep trail. I don't have to go beyond the present.

I have decided to leave my job again. This one is not a good fit either, which is something I knew on day one, seven months ago. So I am leaving in order to make way for whatever is next in my life. I've been making this job departure an incredibly huge struggle, and it doesn't have to be. I can just leave. One foot in front of the other. Instead, I doubt my decision, worrying about money and what other people will think of me, and find myself in self-imposed turmoil. Why do I doubt my decision when each time I have left a job, it has been absolutely right? All I have to do is believe in myself and take the next step.

Dejah sets the example. She lives only in the moment. Her three-year-old-happy-peppy life is centered on food, exercise and, most important, on the people she loves. When we hike, Dejah likes to be the middle girl. She doesn't lead and she won't ever be last; she likes to be surrounded by those she loves. Smart dog. Every once in a while her exuberance gets the better of her and she runs on ahead. It usually happens at the beginning of hikes when she has too much energy to contain, or when she just can't stand how exciting the trail looks and she just has to check it out. This happens on Tecumseh. On that straight, steep, never-ending, oh-my-God section, Dejah can't stand our slow pace and she bounds up the mountain. Then she realizes what she's done—left her loved ones behind—and races back down at breakneck speed, skidding and sliding to a snow-spraying stop an inch from my snowshoes, smiling at me. *Here I am,* she seems to be saying as she tilts her golden head to the right. *Did you miss me? Got a treat in your pocket?* I love her and will miss her and my daughter dearly when they move to Texas in March.

We continue our ascent and I find myself thinking about the last time we climbed Tecumseh. So why are we climbing it again, you ask? Good question. Because it's on "the list." I love stuff when it matters. The lists help me focus on what is important, so life doesn't slip by with my dreams left undone.

The list I am referring to is the White Mountain Forty-Eight Four Thousand Footers in Winter. We've already climbed the New Hampshire forty-eight once; why not try them again in the treacherous ice, deep snow, and freezing cold? Are we nuts? Yes, I think so! But, in the spirit of living in the moment, we only have to climb one mountain at a time, one step at a time. If I focus on how difficult the hikes were in spring, summer, and fall, and imagine what they will be like in January, I won't hike in winter, ever. So I don't anticipate. I just celebrate each success as it happens.

Lists are a part of my life. I have my To Do List, my Life List of things to do before I die, Pat's and my Mountain Lists and my New Year's Resolution List. Climbing up Tecumseh, I announce to Pat my first New Year's resolution: To be completely, one hundred percent on my own side. If I were completely on my own side all the time, I wouldn't need any other resolutions. That one would take care of everything! If I were completely on my own side while climbing Tecumseh, I would have no doubt. I would be cheering for myself as I climb, blown away by my own strength, determination, and perseverance. Instead I'm worrying that I won't make it because it looks too steep. New moment, new choice. I choose to be completely, one hundred percent on my side. I choose to believe in myself. I choose not to worry about what anyone else thinks of me—only what I think of myself. I choose not to project failure into the future but only to react to my strong, beautiful self in the moment.

Finally the steep incline levels out a bit, but only for a few feet after which it again begins its relentless upward climb. This is supposedly the easiest winter four thousand footer. But I should clarify: the words "easy" and "four thousand footer" should never be used in the same sentence. There is nothing easy about climbing any of the four thousand footers.

We reach the summit at 11:54. Today is Pat's birthday and we are marking it by hiking. I have learned to mark important occasions. I try and find a way to put meaning into a special day, to make it stand out so I will remember it as a bookmark in my life's story. If I don't, time robs the memories and they drift away as years pass. So we mark Pat's fifty-third birthday with a high five on top of Tecumseh, our seventh four thousand footer in winter. Check it off the list, baby. Done!

We head down the mountain and the going is immediately easier. I let gravity take my body down the mountain quickly, the snow cushioning each snow-shoed step, getting an extra slide in at the end of each footfall. Woo hoo! The trees are beautiful covered with snow, and we can hear the whoops and hollers of skiers on the neighboring slopes. We meet a snowboarder hiking up and stop for a minute to chat. As we part, I step down and immediately take a header, falling ungracefully face-first in the snow—with Pat and the snowboarder watching. Nice timing. We all

laugh. I start to internally berate myself for falling in front of them. Wait a minute; that's not being on my side. New moment. New choice. I can choose to give myself a hard time or I can choose to know the fall and the laughter were gifts. I'll take the gift option.

By the time we reach the car at 1:50 p.m., I am back on my own side. I am right where I am supposed to be.

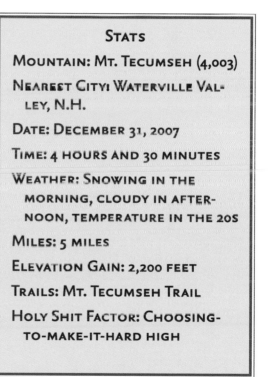

STATS

MOUNTAIN: MT. TECUMSEH (4,003)

NEAREST CITY: WATERVILLE VALLEY, N.H.

DATE: DECEMBER 31, 2007

TIME: 4 HOURS AND 30 MINUTES

WEATHER: SNOWING IN THE MORNING, CLOUDY IN AFTERNOON, TEMPERATURE IN THE 20S

MILES: 5 MILES

ELEVATION GAIN: 2,200 FEET

TRAILS: MT. TECUMSEH TRAIL

HOLY SHIT FACTOR: CHOOSING-TO-MAKE-IT-HARD HIGH

Many people today are looking outside themselves for well-being and happiness when what they're searching for has been inside them all along.

Sandra Magsamen

I discover who I am . . . frozen in fear, halfway up a mountain on an ice-slide; filled with grief, saying good-bye to my twelve-year-old golden retriever; heart racing, searching through adoption clues for my birth mother; afraid we're lost, in the middle of nowhere in the forests of the White Mountains. I realize I have all I need within me to summit these mountains and I begin to focus on the beauty around me and in me.

24. IT'S UP TO ME ON MOOSILAUKE

January 12, 2008, Glencliff Village, New Hampshire

The experience of overcoming fear is extraordinarily delightful.
Bertrand Arthur William Russell

You know what? Fear is a very elusive thing. So is pain. I was four thousand feet up a mountain afraid for my life, shoulder screaming in pain. Nine hours later I am warm and safe at home, sitting on my purple couch, when my husband, Don, asks, "So how was it?" I think about the an-

116

swer and realize the experience is still too intense to talk about. "Good," I say. He tells me about his day and then I drift off to sleep while he watches football.

The next morning over coffee I feel I've gained some safety in distance and time from the hike and I say to him, "It was really intense up there. We hit a very steep section, slick with ice, and I was so afraid." I look at him, pausing. "Like tears afraid."

There. I said it. I wait for his reaction.

"Wow, I wish you guys wouldn't hike in winter," he says.

I tell him more about how steep it was, how hard the ice was, how scared I was, but it all comes out sounding like a jumble of words. I labor to get them out and in less than a minute they are gone. He hears me, but doesn't get it. I can't bring back the fear or pain to help me explain. The feelings, along with the intensity, are gone. It's like having a baby. You go through this extreme experience with excruciating labor pains and, in time, you forget and are ready to have another.

We see Moosilauke, its rounded top obscured by a cloud, as we drive through Warren, to the trailhead. After all the warm weather and rain this week we are pretty sure the snow will be soft and we will not need crampons. (Ah, think again girls . . .) So with snowshoes dangling off our packs and cleats on our feet (at least we have something to help us cling to sheer ice), we head up the Glencliff Trail. I have just finished reading aloud Smith and Dickerman's description of the trail. They say it is a moderate climb with only one steep section.

At 8 in the morning, making our way through the soft snow at the base of the mountain is like walking on a beach close to the tide line. There is some give that requires extra work right away. (Could be a long day.) The first few miles are a steady, uphill climb. I pause often, adjusting the backpack I borrowed from a generous friend. My hips ache and we've been on the trail only twenty minutes. (I could be in trouble.) I keep pulling this strap and letting out that strap, tightening the waist belt, loosening it, leaning forward, backward, twisting and turning, trying to get comfortable. Pat gets into the act too, pulling a strap or two here and there, pushing the pack down then pulling it up while I fight to keep my balance. I've been hiking for twenty-one months and have yet to find a pack that fits me.

My struggle to find the perfect pack mirrors my continued attempts to find the perfect career. I have been struggling for years to find the job that fits me—a role where I can help make the world a better place and love doing it. I keep trying different jobs, and different positions, hoping to find the one made for me. In the beginning of our hiking journey, on Adams, I was in the throes of resigning my position as a hospital development director to become a development director for a dance and arts nonprofit. After less than a year, I realized I was not cut out to be a develop-

ment director. So, I resigned. I am an opportunity looking for a cause, and a hiker searching for the perfect pack.

About midway up the mountain I stop to take a break and notice the woods are sparkling, as if the trail is lined with enchanted Christmas trees! I look closer. On the ends of absolutely every evergreen branch is a droplet of ice. Together they look like miniature sets of white lights draped over the branches. It is absolutely wondrous! I would have missed these tiny glass teardrops completely had I been powering up the mountain, focused solely on getting to the summit. Luckily I'm old and need to catch my breath often. The magical crystal-bead forest halfway up Moosilauke is a reminder to slow down and take in the breath-taking details of life that are always all around me.

As we move higher up the mountain, the snow gets harder and harder. Soon it is ice. I wonder if we should have brought crampons. We talk about it, agree it would have been a good idea, but we are getting along fine at present.

We bank a right and the trail immediately takes a turn for the worse. The pitch steepens and right away I notice the difference in footing. Uh-oh! We are literally climbing up an ice slide. The ice is so solid my pole tip just slides off. I've got nothing to hold me onto this ice but the tiny screws on the bottom of my cleats. Right now I'm wishing for the sharp metal teeth on my crampons. I'm using one hand for a pole and the other hand to grab onto anything that might help me get up another step. My ice cleats are barely holding on and I can feel them slip each time I take a step, which scares the hell out of me.

Dejah clearly does not get the gravity of the situation. She is excited and runs up the slide. I can hear her nails scratching the ice, until she gets to a safe spot near a tree where she finds purchase. She innocently looks down at us, impatient for us to catch up. Of course we're incredibly slow because we're praying as we climb. Dejah tilts her yellow head and seems to say, *C'mon now, Gram. It's not that bad.* She gazes at me, registers the terror in my eyes and immediately bounds down to help. But, of course, she can't stop and starts skidding, trying to dig her nails into the ice so she can stay close to me. No chance. My heart is in my throat; I'm afraid she will lose control and slide down the mountain. She manages to stop just past me, turns around and heads back up, smiling. Dejah keeps sliding down and running up the mountain, back and forth, adding to my desperation, which by now is way off the stress meter.

The trail remains consistent—very steep, covered with thick, hard ice, and wide open with little to cling to. I am not sure of my footing and I know that if I slip and fall I will careen down the trail with nothing to stop me but trees. We are probably halfway up the steep section and I am so afraid. I lean my head on the top of my pole and let the fear in. It fills me. I take a deep breath and tell Pat I am scared. The truth sparks tears. Pat offers to turn around. I consider the offer, but am not sure if going down is the lesser of the two evils.

This is my edge. Right here, right now. I am on it. And I am not sure what is going to happen to me. I could lose my footing and slide down the mountain, surely sustaining severe injury. I could stand here and cry on the mountainside, paralyzed by fear. Or I could gather myself up and give it my very best shot. Without really making a conscious decision, I take one step up. I wedge my foot into the ice as securely as I can, shift my weight over that foot, and stand up. I search for and find the next best spot, put my foot on it, test its hold, then move my weight over that foot. Another breath. Another step up. No thinking, just concentration.

A hiker who came before us had climbed the trail when it was covered in soft snow and left snowshoe imprints that hardened overnight and give my foot a ridge to hold onto. The snowshoe imprints, now ice molds, have become reservoirs for icicles that have fallen from trees and slid down the trail, coming to rest in one of the figure eight cavities. They look like puddles of glass crystals. Dejah dislodges an icicle and it tinkles down the trail into a snowshoe reservoir near me. Even being so afraid, I am awed by the moment.

Finally, after about an hour, we reach the top of the steep section. All my pent-up feelings come spilling out, releasing the fear and tears in a powerful moment of relief. I did it.

As I come back to me, Pat asks, "Was this fear like the fear you experienced when you went bungee-jumping and skydiving in Australia?"

"No," I answer, still feeling relief flooding through me. "I was scared to death then, but I knew I'd be fine. But on this ice," I say, pointing to the steep section behind me, "I was not so sure. When I bungee-jumped, I relied on the system that had kept thousands of others safe before me. When I went skydiving I was harnessed to a professional skydiver. Climbing that ice slide, it was just me."

That intense, exhilarating-in-retrospect, desperately fearful hour on the ice slide is a snapshot of my life. I live it by myself, dependent on just me. No one else. Me alone. I am incredibly lucky to have a husband and children who love and support me, and a hiking partner who is strong, courageous, and wise. But in the end, I do it alone. My choices are my own. No one else can live my life but me. No one else can get me up the mountain but me.

I change my sweat-soaked clothes and Pat and I head off for the last eight-tenths of a mile to the summit. The landscape is monochrome and moon-like; the shrubs are covered with rime ice, the branches coated in inches of ice, and the trail is ice, covered by a thin coat of snow. The sun darts in and out of the clouds, revealing a view then taking it away. The walk to the summit is relatively easy, although the wind picks up as we near the cloud-enshrouded top. We arrive at the stone foundation on top of Moosilauke at noon. The visibility is very low and the wind is roaring. It is so cold I hold my hood down around my face, turning away from the force and bite of the gale. Five people are on the summit, surprisingly, and a

kind man whose face is covered entirely by goggles and a balaclava takes our picture. No dawdling; we quickly head back the way we came. I am dreading the ice slide, but push it out of my mind and try to stay centered in the moment.

It is not long before we are right back on top of the steep section. We don't even pause, but head straight down. The ice seems a tiny bit softer and I can just get the tip of my pole into it. Pat is first—brave girl. She kicks a heel in hard against the ice numerous times, gets a tenuous hold and takes a step. Then she kicks with the other heel. I am the beneficiary of the heel holes and believe me, I am thankful for every one. Near the top of the steep section,  we see two people sitting off the trail among the trees. They have bare-booted their way up to that point. Oh my God! They tell us they have decided to turn around. I can't believe they got as far as they did with no traction.

Unlike going up, I am nervous descending but not scared to death. I am very focused and determined to get

down safely. It is slow going and we are passed by a number of people wearing crampons. We stay to the side of the trail when possible, where there is more snow and less ice, sometimes falling into spruce traps with snow up to our hips.

Part way down, the worst happens. Pat loses her footing and falls on the ice slide. She starts coasting down the trail. Miraculously, she catches herself, hands around an ice-glazed tree trunk. I yell, "Pat!" If I can reach her, I can help her get back on her feet. But before I can get there, she loses her grip and begins a terrifying much-too-fast, out-of-control downward plummet. All I can do is watch helplessly, calling out her name. She barrels into a tree. After a terrible moment of silence, she yells back she is okay. She's banged up, but seems fine when I reach her.

We meet a guy who is amazed Dejah made it up the ice slide. He says he met a guy who turned around because his dog couldn't make it up.

It takes us about an hour to get down the steep section. For most of it I am holding my breath. My shoulders have become permanently attached to my ears. My right shoulder, bum since a car accident years ago, hurts like crazy because I have been leaning all my body weight on my right-hand pole. My mittens hold pine gum and scent, having grasped onto every pungent pine branch along the trail for dear life.

When we get off the steep section I take a deep breath, bring my shoulders down from my ears, and smile for the first time in hours. I look at Pat and watch the relief spread across her face. We are both in one piece. We're off the ice slide and back into the Christmas tree section of the trail. Whew!

By the time we get to the lower section of the mountain, the sun has warmed the trail and the snow is slop. We are walking in a giant slushy. We get back to the car, exhausted and totally done at 3:30, both of us knowing that something important happened today.

Our Moosilauke hike may be impossible to relive and frustrating to try to share with others. But the realization the experience inspires is life-defining. The remnants of the adventure leave me feeling both blessed and let down:

blessed to have lived so ferociously on Moosilauke, let down that the intensity of daily life is so much less, sitting at my computer writing this hike report. I was alive on that mountain, passionately, fearfully, alive every step of the way. I love the feeling of life coursing through my body, both the fear and the excitement. That is how I want to live. I want to live life big, on a grand scale, with enough fire and exuberance and love and inspiration to share. I want to look at life as a constant adventure and choose how high to climb. And I can do that, because I am the one making the choices. I'm the one getting myself up the mountain. It is totally up to me.

Stats

Mountain: Moosilauke (4,802)

Nearest City: Glencliff Village, N.H.

Date: January 12, 2008

Time: 7 hours and 30 minutes

Weather: Cloudy, clearing in the afternoon, temperature in the 20s, windy and cold on top

Miles: 7.5

Elevation Gain: 3,300 feet

Trails: Glencliff Trail, Carriage Road

Holy Shit Factor: Scared-to-death high

25. SAYING GOOD-BYE ON TOM AND FIELD

February 23, 2008, Bartlett, New Hampshire

> *People so seldom say I love you. And then it's either too late or love goes. So when I tell you I love you, it doesn't mean I know you'll never go, only that I wish you didn't have to.*
>
> Unknown

This hike report takes the form of a letter to my twenty-two-year-old daughter.

Dear Jess,
Today is my last hike with Dejah, your happy-peppy-three-year-old yellow Lab and my beloved trail dog.

It's 5 a.m. Dejah is awake and way too feisty as she hops in the back of Pat's RAV4 with her stuffed toy giraffe. We drive past the U-Haul trailer parked in

our driveway and head off to Mt. Tom in Crawford Notch, to put at least one, maybe two more notches in our winter hiking belts.

Dejah knows when we arrive at the Highland Center parking lot and immediately starts going crazy, crying and jumping, totally ready to get out of the car and start hiking. I am a bit less enthusiastic. Having just spent the last seventeen days in Chile, hiking, whitewater rafting, kayaking, and camping in the summer sun, I am not sure I can face winter. Did I really used to do this? Put myself deliberately out in the freezing cold and hike thousands of feet up a mountain? Was I sane? I have lost my winter hiking nerve and am no longer confident I can do this. My apprehension as I put on my hiking boots is just short of dread. But I certainly can't stay in the car listening to Dejah cry, so out of the warm car and into the cold outdoors we go at 9:30 a.m.

Dejah is so happy to be outside she hops and skips with joy, bounding toward the trail ahead of us, impatiently turning around every so often to make sure we are following. How can I not feel happy seeing her so euphoric and clearly wanting to include me in her jubilance? Her joy rubs off on me the way her hairs rub off on all our furniture at home.

We start up the gentle slope of the Avalon Trail, which is covered in hard-packed snow and ice with a couple of inches of new, light powder on top. As my snowshoes flick the soft snow off the trail, you are on my mind, Jess. In ten days, you and Dejah will move to El Paso, Texas, to be with your fiancé Sean, who is stationed at Fort Bliss. By the time I get home today, Sean's dad will have picked up your U-Haul, jam-packed with your treasured possessions, to drive to Texas so your stuff will be there when your flight arrives. So while you are packing, Dejah and I are out for one last adventure.

Knowing our hiking moments together are limited, I watch Dejah more closely today, trying to collect for my memory banks all the cute, quirky, sweet things she does on the trail.

Dejah, as usual, gets out her initial spurt of frenzied puppy energy in the first fifteen minutes and then remembers who she really is at her core, a dog who likes to be as close as possible to those she loves. So she runs back down the trail toward us and gets behind the leader. Nose to calves. She is the middle girl, right between us, just where she wants to be. And there she remains throughout the rest of the hike. Every once in a while, when she steps on my snowshoes, I stop and encourage her to get in front of me, which she does because she wants to appear obedient. And she stays there for, oh, maybe ten seconds before she turns around, glances up at me, and gets right back behind me.

Dejah reminds me of you, Jess. She knows her mind and she does what she wants to do. And she is so darn cute doing it, that although it may not be what I want her to do, I can't help but love her. Dejah also reminds me of me. She knows whom she loves and she wants us close. If I had my way, both you and your sister would always live close to Dad and me. I miss Kelly terribly so far away in Florida.

An hour on the trail and I am beginning to get reacquainted with winter hiking. I can do this. It's not so bad. Actually it is beautiful. The snowflakes on the tree limbs are so big and fluffy you can see the individual crystals. This is why I hike. I feel centered again in my heart and home. I've successfully transitioned back to winter hiking in New Hampshire. I turn around and check on Pat, who smiles back at me.

We stop for a water and breathing break and Dejah bounds down and sits opposite me, looking at me intently, praying in doggy language that this is also a treat break. Her tail wags sporadically, swinging back and forth wildly when her hopes are high, and becoming sluggish when they dip. She tilts her head to the right, looking optimistic. I stand there and look at her and she tilts her head to the left, continuing to look as endearing as possible. She is just too adorable for me to resist and I reach for the treats. Her tail wags frantically with glee, already telling me how grateful she is as she patiently waits for her reward.

On the way up we meet a large group of backpackers who exclaim when they see Dejah. She's a pretty dog. She is strong and fit, a soft cream color, big brown eyes, and bright white teeth, and she's sporting a new turquoise collar today. She returns the group's excitement and goes off to greet the hikers, taking a quick whiff of each as they pat

her. But she doesn't stay around for the extra attention. It is as if she realizes her heart belongs with Pat and me and she is back by our sides in no time.

We hit the junction with the A-Z Trail and head up to Tom. By 11:30 the trail has gone from moderate to pretty steep, our pace has slowed, and we slog up the headwall. I guess I should speak for myself. I slog up the headwall. Dejah never slogs—she trots, runs, slides, bounds with glee, jumps with abandon, but never slogs. Dejah is much like you, Jess. She is so full of life she sometimes can't contain herself. When I look at your smiling face, Jess, I can't help but feel proud of the beautiful, capable, strong woman you have become. It is a gift to have had you living with Dad and me over the past two years, while Sean has been in Iraq. We have loved sharing your life, being on the sidelines watching you live, work, and play. Your joy has been our joy. Like Dejah, whose nose is an inch from my calves, I love having you near me.

We make it to the top of Mt. Tom at noon, take some summit photos, and head down. I dread what lies ahead—I am going to have to change my sweat-soaked clothes into dry warm ones. And when I am already freezing, the thought of standing near the top of a four thousand–foot mountain and taking my clothes off is, well, crazy. But I know it is my only hope of getting warm, and Pat and I have a system that ensures the process is quick. So off come my hat, gloves, jacket, and shirts, until I am standing in the frigid cold with my bra

on. Then piece by piece I don my second set of clothes. Dry polyester shirt, warm fleece, zip up the jacket, hand warmers, another pair of gloves, a dry hat, then I stand there for a few minutes and let the warmth very slowly seep into my body. My muscles let go; I start to breathe again. Dejah is jumping, anxious to get started. I begin to move and realize I am going to be fine.

The switch from wet clothes to dry clothes on top of Tom, and from summer hiking in Chile back to winter hiking in New Hampshire, are transitions—moving through an ending to a new beginning. I find transitions difficult. Especially the one that is imminent. On March 5 we will take you, Jess, and Dejah to the airport. I dread saying goodbye. I know I will cry. Although this is an ending for both of us, it is the beginning of a new and exciting life for you. And maybe this will be like other transitions for me—the anticipation being the worst, the change difficult but fast, and then I will adjust to a much quieter, less furry, emptier home.

The hike along the ridge to the top of Field is a pretty steady incline and we take it slow. We get to the summit at 1:15 and set the camera timer to take our pictures. Dejah won't pose with us, but ends up in most of our pictures because she is never far away. There are tiny flecks of snow in the air swirling around us, sparkling, as if we are in a snow globe.

We start down the mountain on the Avalon Trail. Even when I am leading and I can't see Dejah, I know her warm loving self is right behind me. I feel her presence, her joy, her trust and innocent, full-on love. How can I not savor the time Dejah is with me when she is so filled with delight and passion for the moment, for the mountains, and for me? I turn around to catch a glimpse of her and she looks up at me, confused as to why I have paused, but thrilled that I am paying attention to her. She has been on so many of our four thousand–footer and hundred highest hikes. I remember her on Adams. She was so pooped she almost fell asleep during a break on the hike down. On Wildcat she tried out her new packs, but they confused her because she kept getting jammed between rocks that she thought she could fit through. She took a mud bath on the Sharon Ledges and she made it up the ice slide on Moosilauke six weeks ago when another dog had to turn around. Her spirit is indomitable.

The Avalon Trail is steep and we slide down on our butts much of the way, sometimes going too fast and getting a bit out of control. Dejah slides and skids right along behind the leader, her entire back end furiously wiggling as fast as we are flying. She gets very excited when we slide, her nose inches from my backpack until I come to a halt and she bounds around me, jumping with excitement. *Please, Grammy, can we do that again? Please?*

We survive the sliding and finally reach the Mt. Avalon spur. The sign says the Avalon summit is only one hundred yards up, but we decide to leave it for the day we come back to bag Willey.

We head down, reaching the car at 3:30. We put our backpacks in the back of the car and let Dejah spread out on the rear seat, as a treat. With her back legs straight out behind her, she stretches from door to door. She is asleep before we pull out of the parking lot.

I am home. My body is hiking tired. Your dad is in his reclining chair to my left. I am curled up on one side of the purple couch, and Dejah is where she always is in the early evenings: curled up beside me, her head lying on my blanketed feet. Jess, you are upstairs packing. And I, I do not take this scene for granted. I know in life it is only the relationships we have with others that really matter. I cherish this moment surrounded by those I love.

Good-bye, Jess and Dejah—I will miss you.

Love, Mom

STATS

MOUNTAINS: TOM (4,051) AND FIELD (4,340)

NEAREST CITY: BARTLETT, N.H.

DATE: FEBRUARY 23, 2008

TIME: 6 HOURS

WEATHER: CLOUDS, SUN, TEMPERATURE IN THE TEENS

MILES: 7.2

ELEVATION GAIN: 2,800 FEET

TRAILS: AVALON TRAIL, A-Z TRAIL, MT. TOM SPUR, WILLEY RANGE TRAIL

HOLY SHIT FACTOR: GOOD-BYE HARD

26. EXPECTATIONS ON HALE

March 15, 2008, Twin Mountain, New Hampshire

When I hear somebody sigh, "Life is hard," I am always tempted to ask, "Compared to what?"

Sydney J. Harris

Pat and I have one more Saturday to try and bag a winter peak before the official end of winter at the Vernal Equinox on March 20, even though winter will hold on in the New Hampshire Whites well past March. I pick Hale because I'm hoping for relatively easy. Our last hike, Mt. Washington, involved steep sidestepping in a refrigerator, and we turned around just short of Monroe's summit. I remember Hale as one of the easier four thousand footers when we hiked it in the summer. So my expectation is easy.

On the slow, slippery drive up to Twin Mountain through beautiful falling snow, I take out my Smith and Dickerman four thousand footer book and read up on Mt. Hale. You have to love those guys for this book, which makes peakbagging New Hampshire's forty-eight easy, but could they get working on the sixty-seven four thousand –footers in New England? We could use some help with Maine. Reading the "Hale in Winter" entry I come to this paragraph:

"While the hike up Hale is considered among the easiest in summer and fall, it is a different story in winter. Because Zealand Road is closed to motor vehicle traffic in winter, any effort to reach the mountain by the Hale Brook Trail means an additional 2.8 miles of road walking each way. The cushy 2.2 mile one-way summer jaunt is stretched to 5 miles. The round trip hike is suddenly an epic 10 mile battle."

Epic 10 mile battle being the key words here.

I pay no mind to the facts on the page. "Easy" is still my expectation as we set out on Zealand Road at 9:45 a.m.

The road to the trail is hefty, but we walk it quickly and by 11 a.m. we are on the Hale Brook Trail. The trail kicks off at a decent, moderate grade, but Pat and I have been exercising all week, starting with Washington on Monday, so I can feel my legs already. Not a good

sign, but this is an easy four thousand footer so I am not worried. Up we go through a few inches of new snow, crusty hard pack underneath. As we hit the steeper parts, it gets slippery, and we put on our snowshoes, which immediately start to grow snow clumps on the bottoms. I feel like I am walking in high heels made for Bozo the Clown. Great. My tired legs are dragging snowshoes with two-pound snowballs hanging off them. Easy is looking less likely. Whose idea was this, anyway? Is any four thousand footer easy in winter?

We arrive at a neat little stretch along a steep side slope that requires having ankles of flexible rubber. In the summer and fall, this is probably a cinch, but the snow has filled in any hope of a trail and we walk at a precarious angle, trying not to tumble down into the ravine—which, by the way, is so far down that we can't see the bottom. I throw "easy" out the window and now, secretly, I hope I can make it. Angry that I'm struggling, I consider making the universal wimp sign—holding three fingers, index, middle, and ring, up to my forehead, but I have mittens on, so I don't.

Making our way along the traverse is agonizingly slow and tough on our right quadriceps. No worries—Pat reminds me that we will get to work the other side coming back! All of a sudden I hear crunching snow and look up from my sideways slogging to see Pat take a tumble and head toward the ravine. Luckily, a tree stops her slide. She's okay, gets up like a trooper, and

plows her way back up to the trail.

We take a number of breaks on this sweet side traverse and notice a cool thing. As our snowshoes break the new snow surface, they send little snowballs careening down the slope into the ravine. I can feel my child within sparkle as I say, "Wow!" Each snowshoe fall releases a team of snowballs, which race down to their demise in the ravine. Some break apart, some are too big and can't get up the necessary momentum, but the small, round ones roll down the slope, leaving an imprint of their journeys, a track we trace to see how far they make it before smashing into a tree. But we have this God-awful traverse to finish, so we keep plodding. My ankles start up a conversation, asking me what the heck I think I'm doing trying to bend them toward the side of my foot. They tell me they are not made to do that, and they would like me to adjust my stance. Sorry, no can do.

We finally finish the traverse, after which the trail heads up, steeply. That's okay, I say to myself, this is a four thousand footer. We have to gain some altitude. So up we go. Up and up and up. After a good bit of trudging, Pat and I

are sure we are almost at the summit, which is only 2.3 miles up from the trailhead—we must have hiked that far. We keep going up. My legs are finished. I decide a bit of positive thinking might help. I tell Pat that we are five "sees" from the top. One see is as far as the eye can see in one seeing. We both feel better. We rest our hope in my omnipotent knowing. Yeah, right . . . .

But that's wishful thinking. We keep slogging up. Five sees, seven sees, ten sees. I stop counting. The trees turn white with rime ice, and then they turn to ice covered with rime ice. And we continue slogging up. *In winter there is no such thing as an easy four thousand footer.* I repeat that as I climb so I won't ever have that expectation again. I look up at the trail. Surely we are almost to the top. We continue to watch snowballs, loosened by our snowshoes, tumble down the slopes. We start cheering for the snowballs. We're getting a bit slap-happy.

The trail continues up, and every so often we hit another tilting slope so we are going up sideways. "Who made this trail, anyway?" I shout into the woods. I stop and chomp on a few icicles, buying breathing time. I want to blame someone, maybe Smith and Dickerman, for the difficulty of this climb, but they told the truth—which just leaves me and my "easy" expectations.

My legs ache. I stop, bend over, and stretch my hamstrings and lower back, while drawing a star in the snow. This star marks the spot where I feel I can't go any further. I stare at it, zone out for a moment. Pat stops and looks back at me with a what-are-you-doing look and I continue on . . . and on and on. In the privacy of my soul, I decide I'm throwing away my snowshoes and winter hiking boots when I get home. We turn a corner and I see that the trail continues. I decide I am going to give all my winter hiking clothes to the Salvation Army.

We stop taking breaks because we know if we don't get up there soon, we will never make it. So we put our heads down and we go up. We don't talk. Laughing has ceased for the moment. This is serious business. Get up this mountain, now. Minutes pass; they feel like hours. My legs burn. Then Pat yells with what sounds like glee. The summit is in sight, thank God.

We arrive there to see trees drizzled with ice and shrouded in white mist. We take pictures of us sitting on the summit cairn and then offer a primal yelling of a very bad word as loud as we possibly can. That feels good!

The hike down is much easier than the hike up, and we wonder what we were complaining about. But we know what to expect going down. Even the traverse isn't so bad. Like little kids, we laugh as we cheer on the tiny snowballs running rampant down the slopes. We

are lighthearted, though our legs are toast.

The walk along Zealand Road goes on forever. We get back to the car at 5:06, totally done and ready for a warm car and a relaxing three-hour-ride back home.

Rubber ankles and cheering for mini-snowballs and hollering swear-words and aching muscles are our hallmarks on Hale. We are two fifty-plus-year-old women having a blast, even when we are slogging through the unexpected, not knowing when we will reach the summit. I guess I'll keep my winter hiking gear.

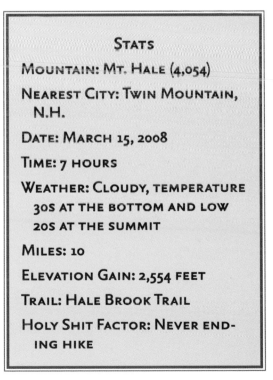

STATS

MOUNTAIN: MT. HALE (4,054)

NEAREST CITY: TWIN MOUNTAIN, N.H.

DATE: MARCH 15, 2008

TIME: 7 HOURS

WEATHER: CLOUDY, TEMPERATURE 30S AT THE BOTTOM AND LOW 20S AT THE SUMMIT

MILES: 10

ELEVATION GAIN: 2,554 FEET

TRAIL: HALE BROOK TRAIL

HOLY SHIT FACTOR: NEVER ENDING HIKE

March 29, 2008, Lyme Center, New Hampshire

When you are sorrowful look again in your heart, and you shall see that in truth you are weeping for that which has been your delight.

Kahlil Gibran

I anticipate Smarts Mountain may be a hard hike for me emotionally.

Pat and I leave Keene at 7 a.m., which is a leisurely morning for us. We arrive at the Smarts Mountain trail-head in Lyme, New Hampshire, and start up the steep beginning of the Lambert Ridge Trail at 9:30.

Hiking always seems to bring to the surface whatever is lying deep within me. I just can't get up the mountain if I am carrying extra baggage, so I shed it as I climb. In the shedding, I learn something. Today I am carrying a heart full of grief.

The snow is sparkling in the bright sunlight and the sky is a deep blue. Although the trail was packed out some time ago, the most recent snow covers it untouched, leaving a slight dip that marks the way. Thank goodness we have something to follow as the blazes are few and far between. Our journey into the woods and up the mountain seems somehow more sacred because we are alone: no other cars in the parking area, not a soul on the trail.

We reach our first view and I am surprised how high we've climbed so quickly. The wind along the ridge reminds us it is winter, sending the snow crystals into a swirling plume of sparkles and sending both Pat and I into our packs for an extra layer of clothing.

As we ascend, I find myself holding on to the last moment of Rajah's life, as if I were still there, two days ago at 3 in the afternoon, lying on the floor next to my ninety-six-pound golden retriever, stroking his head, telling him I loved him, that I would miss him, that he had been a perfect dog.

Perfect. Really. Rajah showed me how perfect life is. He was pure exuberance chasing tennis balls in the backyard and dredging up rocks in Charley's Brook, his head underwater so long I often worried. He was in ecstasy swimming in Goose Pond, running on the beach at the inlet on Cape Cod, drooling for a piece of cheese at night and rolling in smelly gross stuff in the woods. His joy was contagious when he bounded through deep snow or ran in the rain, or walked with me to the beaver pond in the summer. He loved car rides and would sit in the back seat, his head out the window, ears blowing back in the wind. I loved it when he stole my mittens, hoping for a game of tag (which I always lost) or he grabbed the end of the dishtowel for tug of war. I would start to pull and he would choke up on the towel. I'd laugh, call him a cheater, and he'd yank the towel out of my hands.

Whenever I was upset or needed advice or comfort, I would lie down on the floor of my office next to Rajah and talk to him, my tears soaking into the rug. He would always lift his front paw and put it on my shoulder. Those were the times I felt closest to Rajah. We knew each other's hearts. There is no doubt that in those moments he loved me and he knew I loved him.

Rajah was too old to join me when I started hiking, so I brought Dejah, until she moved to Texas last month with Jess. Rajah would always greet us at the door with a happy growl of welcome when we came home from our hike— no jealousy, just sheer joy that we were home.

Even after two knee operations and a series of health problems, Rajah dealt with each setback with an acceptance that this was life, still at its best. He struggled to stand and walk, but always managed to get outside to do his business and then come back inside to relax on his bed while we watched TV.

No matter how sore or lame he was he would always chase a tennis ball.

The Lambert Ridge Trail evens out and I am enjoying the white beauty around me and the sight of Pat's backpack in front of me. Even though I am alone in my thoughts, I know Pat is with me in my grief.

She called me yesterday afternoon to see how I was the day after we put Rajah down. I answered the phone, but could barely speak, my voice high with choked sorrow, tears rolling onto the phone. She asked me if I wanted to do something and I told her I couldn't seem to make any decisions. "I'll be right there," she said. We drove to EMS, our favorite store, then to Panera Bread with my laptop to research a mountain to hike.

As Pat and I climb Smarts, I let the thoughts of Rajah move through me, but I keep coming back to the moment he left me. As we approach an opening in the trail, I say, "Let's make a memorial to Rajah." Walking with our snowshoes, we form the letter R surrounded by a heart in the new snow. I hope he can see it. I hope he is okay wherever he is. I hope he knows how much I still love him.

Experience tells me this beautiful flat trail will eventually turn upward. And sure enough, it does. We leave Rajah's heart to melt in the sun and head up. Although our pace slows, the trail's not too steep.

As I slog, I find myself not in tears of sorrow as I expected, but filled with an overwhelming appreciation of how

lucky I am that Rajah blessed my life with his gentle wisdom and playful, radiant spirit. How could I, for the past twelve years, have been so lucky to have this noble, quiet creature who taught

me about unconditional love, pure joy, tug-of-war cheating, and graceful aging?

Before I know it we are on the summit and it's 1 p.m. Pat gives me a high five and a beautiful smile. Check Smarts Mountain off the 52 With-a-View list. The ice-covered stairs on the mountain-top tower keep me on the ground, but Pat goes up halfway for a picture.

Then we head down the mountain. We get to the intersection of the Lambert Ridge Trail and the Ranger Trail. I ask Pat which she would like to take and she says, right off, the Ranger Trail. Loops are great because they enable the adventure to continue—we never know what the trail will be like or what we will see because we haven't been there before.

Unfortunately, the Ranger Trail is unmarked. There are no blazes that we can see. We follow the eroded trail as best we can, but the footing is difficult on the path where the snow has melted and left muddy, leafy soup. Whenever

possible, we bushwhack through the woods or along the narrow snow bank that lines the trail. We arrive at the garage marked on our map, relieved we are actually following a trail and not just a river. We continue along what looks to be a snowmobile trail. It feels like we are walking for miles and miles. As I negotiate my way, I continued to flash back to Rajah's last hours.

I was in Florida visiting our daughter when Don called to say that something was very wrong with Rajah. A trip to the vet determined that he had herniated a disk in his spine and lost all control of his back end. He couldn't walk or stand or go to the bathroom. Don continued calling, giving me sad updates, the news getting worse with each call, until it was clear we had a decision to make. And the decision was easy. Rajah was telling us it was time. He had shut down, hadn't moved, wouldn't even eat cheese, and could barely lift his head.

I came home from Florida to say goodbye. Leaving my suitcase in the car, I ran into the house and lay down with Rajah on the floor. "I'm here, Raj," I said. He immediately put his paw on my shoulder and looked into my eyes. I sobbed.

And then we eased his passing. I held him as the vet gave him the shot and then I watched as his life slipped away, my tears rolling down his cheeks.

How could life be there one minute and be gone the next? Where did his exuberance, his spirit, his love for me go?

As I snowshoe along the never-ending trail, I wish Rajah's life had been never-ending. The stuff you want to end never does. The awesome moments are gone in a flash. As I plod the last mile, I remember gazing into Rajah's big brown eyes, knowing at that last moment I still had him. Even though I knew we were doing the right thing, I couldn't help but not want it to happen. Even as he was dying, I wanted to hold onto him and not let him go.

But in my sorrow, as I hike, there is an acceptance inside that could only come from having watched Rajah live.

The trail continues. There are still no blazes and Pat and I start thinking we might be lost, that somehow we might have gotten turned around and wandered off the unmarked trail. Pat finally gets out her compass and we determine we are walking in the right direction and that eventually we should come to the road. We keep walking. I cross a gully, fall down on my hands and knees, and hear Pat laughing. I think she is laughing at me, but when I stand up I see it too. The parking lot.

Ah, the end. Maybe that is what Rajah was saying.

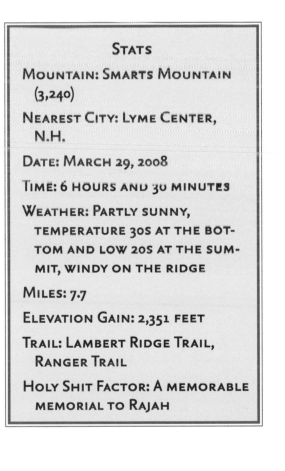

STATS

MOUNTAIN: SMARTS MOUNTAIN (3,240)

NEAREST CITY: LYME CENTER, N.H.

DATE: MARCH 29, 2008

TIME: 6 HOURS AND 30 MINUTES

WEATHER: PARTLY SUNNY, TEMPERATURE 30S AT THE BOTTOM AND LOW 20S AT THE SUMMIT, WINDY ON THE RIDGE

MILES: 7.7

ELEVATION GAIN: 2,351 FEET

TRAIL: LAMBERT RIDGE TRAIL, RANGER TRAIL

HOLY SHIT FACTOR: A MEMORABLE MEMORIAL TO RAJAH

28. UP, AROUND, DOWN, AND BACK UP MONADNOCK

April 23, 2008, Jaffrey Center, New Hampshire

To be nobody-but-yourself in a world which is doing its best, night and day, to make you everybody but yourself—means to fight the hardest battle which any human being can fight—and never stop fighting.

E.E. Cummings

"How do you know?" I taunt Pat, hands on my hips, frustration seething out my pores, incredibly exasperated that we are going the wrong way and have been for an hour. There is only a second of silence before she responds.

Okay, first I'd better set the stage for this . . .

Pat offers to take an afternoon off work to hike Monadnock. I jump at the chance. We haven't hiked in over a month and I am having withdrawal symptoms. What if I can't do it anymore? What if my body has forgotten how? Maybe it's like riding a bike and my body will remember how to climb without dying . . . I hope, I pray.

When I arrive at her house at 1 p.m., Pat has already picked out a route. She is as psyched as I am.

"I want to show you the Spellman Trail," she says. "It's the steepest trail on Monadnock."

I glance at the map, but really don't care what trail we take. It is such a beautiful day; we are together, doing what we love. Who could ask for more?

So up the Halfway House Trail we climb. After the first one hundred feet we joke that we've had enough uphill. We talk. We have such a powerful friendship that having a chance to really be with Pat and talk with her is a great gift to me. But this afternoon Pat seems distant. As we leave the Halfway House Trail and head up the Do Drop Trail, I ask her if she is in her heart.

It's my way of asking if she is feeling emotionally present, if she is with me. When I am not in my heart, I am thinking about something, or I'm critiquing myself or worrying about something, all ways of keeping myself separate from others. I am disconnected from my feelings and from my true self. To find my heart, I have to literally stop and focus inward and find me, find my kindness, my love, my tenderness, my vulnerability. When I am in my heart I feel an experience and I am truly connected to myself and others. That's how I want to live.

Pat stops on the trail ahead of me and we stand in silence. I know what she is doing— searching for Pat. It is such a powerful moment in that she is willing to be so vulnerable, to find her heart,

as I stand breathing behind her. After a bit, she turns and smiles, and I know she is back with me on Monadnock. I am touched to witness that moment.

We continue up, getting lost for a while on the Cliff Walk Trail, and find ourselves heading the wrong way— down.

Now a word about going down when we are supposed to be going up. I hate it! On all ninety-one hikes over the past two years, whenever the slope has turned downward on our ascent, I say something. I don't mind going up, but let's really go up! None of this down stuff when we will just have to recover all that altitude to get where we are going.

We realize our mistake, turn around, and arrive at Bald Rock for beautiful views. The trees are below us and the world is laid out in front of us, going on forever. We continue up and before we know it the summit is off to our left and we see lots of people milling about on top. When I finally see the summit I always breathe a sigh of relief because I know I am going to make it. Uh, not so fast. Not in this case.

Pat's plan is to go down the Red Spot Trail to get to the Spellman Trail. Okay, I'm game. And down we go. Within the first twenty minutes I am fuming, feeling like I am going to explode with frustration. We are still descending after forty minutes. I can't get a grip. Every step downward pushes me into a higher octave of annoyance. I can't hold it in any longer and start to vomit aggravation all over the mountain. "I hate going down, Pat. Holy shit! We are going down the whole friggin' mountain!"

We pass a couple on their way up. The woman is having a hard time and confides in us that she is exhausted. Pat is very sweet and encourages her to keep going. Silent, I give Pat a look that probably would have turned her to stone had we made eye contact. She asks me why I didn't say anything to the woman, commenting it was so unlike me.

"Do you want to know what I would have said to that woman had I opened my mouth? I would have said: Hey! At least you're going in the right direction! Up! We're going to the summit too, but you would never know it because we are heading down! We have been going down for more than an hour. As a matter of fact, we were almost at the summit when we turned around! Honey, you have no friggin' idea how lucky you are to be going up—which happens to be the right direction to get to the top!"

"It won't be much farther. I'm sure the trail is right around the corner," Pat says with a combination of hope and encouragement.

I stop and glare at her. Who is she kidding? She has no idea how far we have to go! With my hands on my hips, frustration seething from my pores, I say, "How do you know?"

Silence. We're looking at each other, each of us replaying that moment in our heads. I sound exactly like a ten-year-old totally fed up with the hike, and with life in general.

We burst out laughing. Real, honest, doubled-over, hands-on-our-knees, laughing. What a gift. We both feel

better.

We continue down and I lose my humor quickly. I notice that the bodies of water, the ones that an hour ago looked like silver dollars, now look like large lakes that I will be able to dive into in only moments. I just can't seem to unearth a positive attitude about this. For a while I am quiet and then I burst out in a bitching frenzy. "Holy shit, Pat. We are climbing down the whole damn mountain just to go back up again. We were within spitting distance of the summit and now we are so low there is absolutely no view. We are back in the trees, almost at the park headquarters!"

At this point there is nothing Pat can say, and she chooses to keep walking, probably praying that the cut off to the trail comes soon before I completely lose it.

We finally arrive at Cascade Link and soon after the Spellman Trail. Oh, thank God! I am sure Pat is thinking the same thing. The trail heads straight

up and I am thrilled. We are going up. Hallelujah! I don't give a shit how steep it is—we are finally going up. And that is really the only way we are ever going to reach the summit.

The combination of the fact that we are finally going in the right direction and the physical exertion required to get up the almost perpendicular trail takes me out of my cranky ten-year-old and plunks me back in my heart.

I am flooded with emotion. Looking back over the past hour or so, I realize I was fully me, at my crankiest, and nothing terrible happened. I didn't hurt anyone and I didn't lose my friend. Pat didn't get mad or leave or tell me to buck up. She laughed. And she was quiet. She offered to turn around. When I said no, she kept hiking. She loved me, even though I was not being perfect. I am touched by Pat's reaction, and by my truthful this-is-where-I-am moment. Normally I hide my frustration, which, I see now, is like hiding myself. Or I only show what I think people around me can handle. But today I am just me—no control, nothing held back. Maybe experiencing the real Nancy, as cranky as I was, is better than hiking with a fake Nancy holding in her feelings. At least it is genuine.

Now in a full lather of sweat and sucking pretty hefty wind, we finally reach the intersection with the Pumpelly Trail. We are on a beautiful ridge with gorgeous views. We are still heading up and I am so thankful. The trail at one point takes us down into a snow-filled ravine and I almost lose it. But it is a decline of only a minute, not an hour. I am able to hold on.

We left at about 1:30 from Pat's nearby house and we arrive on the summit at 5 p.m. What normally takes one and a half to two hours took us three and a half. Of course it did—because we went up, around, down, and back up.

On the way down we talk about what we learned from my pout-burst. I am a summit seeker. I don't like to dilly-dally around going here and there. I want a goal and I want to get there. We can take trails that are harder or easier, more direct or less direct, but I like to be headed in the right direction. I don't like going down and around when our ultimate goal is to go up. Pat is with me on this, but not quite as intensely. I also know that each step was my choice. We could have turned around; we could have taken a different trail. My choice, my learning. I am a peakbagger at heart.

And what we are in our hearts is really what matters.

STATS

Mountain: Mt. Monadnock (3,165)

Nearest City: Jaffrey Center, N.H.

Date: April 23, 2008

Time: 5 hours

Weather: Sunny, temperatures in the 70s and 80s, light breeze

Miles: 6

Elevation Gain: 2,517 feet

Trails: Old Toll Road, Do Drop Trail, Cliff Walk Trail, Bald Rock, Smith Connecting Trail, White Dot Trail, Red Spot Trail, Cascade Link, Spellman Trail, Pumpelly Trail, Smith Summit Trail, Fairy Spring, White Arrow

Holy Shit Factor: Up-around-down-and-back-up high

29. COMING FULL CIRCLE

April 27, 2008, Four Thousand–Footer Awards Ceremony, Stratham, New Hampshire

Life is all about timing . . . the unreachable becomes reachable, the unavailable becomes available, the unattainable . . . attainable.

Stacey Charter

Pat and I walk to the front of the school auditorium amid the applause of my husband, Don, and many fellow hikers. We receive our four thousand–footer awards, officially becoming members of the AMC Four Thousand Footer Club and acknowledging the new world borne of our friendship. We have climbed all forty-eight mountains in New Hampshire over four thousand feet high, from Tecumseh at 4,003 feet to Mt. Washington, the highest point in New England, at 6,288 feet. It's hard for me to believe.

Not too long ago I weighed over two hundred pounds, and was so filled with shame I could barely take part in life. I fought every day just to stay on an even keel, centered on loving my family, even though I hated myself. How could anyone love a two hundred–pound, five-foot-tall person? I couldn't look in the mirror, hated buying clothes, and had a closet filled with every size imaginable from 12 petite to women's 1X. I dreaded being in public and was embarrassed when people saw me as the fat person I was. Shame encompassed me, hung over me like low cloud cover, infiltrated every thought and tinged it with deep sadness and revulsion. It was hard to move, but I didn't notice. It took every ounce of courage I had to put on a bathing suit and play in the pool with my kids when we were on vacation in the Florida Keys. The only way to continue on was to push the reality of my size and looks far away, and stay entirely disconnected from my body.

I tried every diet imaginable, from fasting to drinking pre-digested protein. Then Lori, a dear friend, and I drove to the mall and bought the Atkins Diet book. I was ready. I followed the diet literally, every word, every food choice, lost forty pounds, and reached a plateau. I switched to Weight Watchers and started losing again. Another dear friend, Marty, talked me into going to an exercise class. I sat in the car for fifteen minutes, fighting sobs of shame that I would be the largest person in the class and would make a fool of myself. I forced myself out of the car and into the gym. One whole side of the room was a huge mirror. I held back the tears and walked to the very back where I could hide. I stayed for the whole class and then another and another until I was going four times a week.

Life is all about timing.

I met Pat two years later, after I had lost sixty pounds and was exercising regularly, lifting weights, and doing aerobics weekly. My children were grown, no longer needing my undivided attention. My husband had his own pursuits of golf, racquetball, and handball. It was time for me.

A new world being born . . . .

My friendship with Pat opened up this new world of exercise and adventure so gradually and naturally we didn't really notice it happening. We started out walking, and that turned into climbing mountains. We climbed all forty-eight four thousand footers in New Hampshire, ending in high spirits on Mt. Jefferson in just fourteen months. We hiked through all four seasons and endured hot sun, heavy humidity, deep snow, cold rain, sheer ice, steep slides, ledges with few hand or foot holds, and straight-down trails that made our knees ache. I have never been so afraid, elated, cold, hot, proud, or determined in my life. I spent years pretending I didn't have a body and now my body is doing incredible things, giving me unbelievable gifts, gracefully, and I am so grateful. Did I just say that? I am grateful for my body? Yes, I am grateful to my body for getting me up the mountains to see the unimaginable grandeur of the vistas from the mountaintops. I am blown away by the beauty I have seen and by my effort to get there. I have traveled from the lowest low, totally detached from an overweight body, to the top of the White Mountains, my body having lifted me up all those thousands of feet. It is hard for me to comprehend my own transformation.

I guess this is a reclaiming of sorts. I've hated my body most of my life and now, finally, we are beginning to make peace. It's no longer a tug of war; it's a more friendly game of give and take. I have changed how I eat and move and my body has rewarded me with strength, endurance, and the ability to get me where I want to go. It hasn't been easy. I still struggle with weight, and food, and feeling okay in my own skin. But when I am on top of a mountain, I never cease to be amazed that I got there under my own power. I am discovering my strength and my feelings through the effort of climbing, and that in itself is healing. The effort required to climb up and down pushes me not only physically, but mentally as I shed old, negative thoughts, replacing them with tentative moments when I acknowledge my body with kindness.

And there's more.

Pat has her own version of my story. Pat's struggle was with alcohol. As we got to know each other, Pat shared with me that drinking was part of her nightly ritual and had been for most of her adult life. It was a way to relax, to fit in, and to connect with others. I could see how difficult it was for her to talk about it, the guts it took for her to share this truth and trust I would hear it without judging her. One day we were hiking on the Wapack Trail and Pat was talking about the cycle of self-hate tied to her alcohol abuse, how much she wanted to quit and just didn't know how. I asked her, as compassionately as I could, knowing it would be hard to hear, "So why don't you just stop?" A moment of silence, but I could see she had heard me. Pat was ready. Timing is everything. She stopped on that day, June 10, 2006, and hasn't had a drop since. Talk about strength and courage! What I love most is that taking the alcohol away left just Pat, beautiful Pat without any veneer or false layer of protection, leaving her very vulnerable. I am sure that was very scary for Pat, but truly beautiful to see.

What's next?

We still have plenty of mountains to check off on our mountain lists: the sixty-seven New England Four Thousand Footers, the New England Hundred Highest Peaks, the 52 With-a-View and the White Mountain Four Thousand Footers in Winter.

But it's not what we do that matters most; it is how we do it and how it changes us. Who really cares how many miles we have hiked, run, walked, and talked together? What moves me most

4000-FOOTER CLUB OF THE WHITE MOUNTAINS
APPALACHIAN MOUNTAIN CLUB

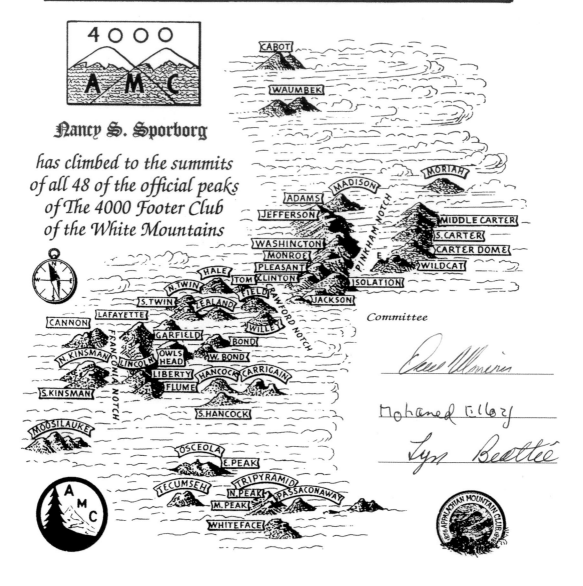

Nancy S. Sporborg

has climbed to the summits
of all 48 of the official peaks
of The 4000 Footer Club
of the White Mountains

Committee

is that every mile has been filled with moments of self-discovery within a growing friendship. There are tears and fears, celebrations, anger, laughter—it all comes into the world between us where we are safe enough to explore who we really are. We push, support, and inspire each other. Pat and I often marvel at the journey we are on, unable to believe our luck.

Here's an "aha" moment, right here, right now.

You know, it's easier crediting luck and serendipity for where Pat and I are today than stating the truth. But as I write this, I realize I am missing a chance to see Pat and myself more clearly, to honor us both more deeply. Yes, we had perfect timing and incredible luck. But I can't write it off to just luck. I am on this incredible adventure because I said yes to the journey, one step at a time, every step of the way. I made a choice, over and over again, for me. Pat has done the same. We both said yes—yes to the grace wave, yes to life.

30. MOTHER'S DAY ON CHOCORUA

May 11, 2008, Albany, New Hampshire

Promise me you'll always remember: you're braver than you believe, and stronger than you seem, and smarter than you think.

A.A. Milne (Christopher Robin to Pooh)

It's 5 a.m. and I'm so happy to be heading north I don't even make a crack about getting up before dawn or whimper, *it's kinda early, Pat.* As we approach the White Mountains, I am used to seeing clouds clinging to the highest summits. But today there is nothing but blue overhead. We arrive at the trailhead and hoist our packs onto our backs. Clearly I have forgotten that it is spring, not winter—I brought everything imaginable and my pack weighs a ton. Instead of having to choose a fleece to leave behind, Pat offers to share the load. Aware there is still some of the white stuff above three thousand feet, we hitch snowshoes to our packs.

We start up the Piper Trail at 8:30. As we climb we can see two of the Three Sisters and Chocorua standing proud in the sunlight. Our hike up features lots of ledges, steep pitches, beautiful views, crystal blue sky, light breezes, and new life bursting forth all around us. It's wonderful to see the budding trees and delicate flowers—nature springing into action after a tough winter. It is a perfect hiking day and we are both reveling in the beauty of the scene below us, the lakes getting smaller and smaller as we climb higher and higher, the horizon filling in with bluish-purple mountains.

I worried that my body had atrophied during our spring hiatus from hiking while we waited for the snow to melt. But I'm chugging right along; even the ledges aren't sending me over the edge into angst. We reach the top of the Third Sister at 12:15 p.m., and I am filled with relief and joy that I can get myself up the mountains. We have lunch, then hike a brief dipsy-doodle and arrive on the summit of the Middle Sister, where we find the remains of an old, stone fire tower. We can see snow-covered Mt. Washington in the distance. As a matter of fact, we can see everything there is to see; the 360-degree view includes

many of the four thousand footers we have climbed over the past two years. We continue on to the top of First Sister and head over to Chocorua, six-tenths of a mile away. Some of the trail is covered with easily negotiable snow, from which I make a snowball to throw at Pat, amazingly hitting my target. The last half of the trail to the top is open ledge surrounded by blue sky and an-chored by gorgeous scenery. The top is crowded when we arrive at 2:15, but thins out quickly.

As we stand on the summit of Cho-corua, seeing the foreverness of the world spread out like a patchwork pic-nic blanket before us, my problems seem smaller, the gifts of life feel larger, and a sense of well-being settles in.

Pat and I find a semi-flat ledge and lay our bodies down on the warm rock for a bliss moment in the sun. Ahhhhh. This is the perfect way to spend Mother's Day. After all, becoming a mother gave me the impetus to look for my birth mother. That search was the beginning of a separation process away from my family of origin to me. It was a monu-mental step toward knowing myself and living life to its fullest, which is exactly what is happening as I hike to the sum-mits of the mountains.

After fifteen or twenty minutes on top of the world, Pat and I reluctantly stand up. Before heading down, we chat with a young man on the summit.

"What trail did you take?" he asks.

"We came up over the Three Sisters," Pat says.

"Wow, that's the hardest trail!" he says. "How many miles is that?"

"Oh, probably nine or ten," she answers.

"When did you guys start?"

"8:30 this morning," Pat says.

"Wow," he says.

As we make our way back down on Pat's namesake trail, I find myself thinking about his last word: Wow! Wow is right. I have been profoundly changed by my hiking experiences. It all started twenty years ago on a search for my birth mother. It was on that journey that I found all I would need to climb mountains.

My parents adopted four children, including my twin brother, John, and me. I grew up having no resemblance, in any way, to my siblings or to my mother and father. My parents told us we were adopted and were very clear that we should never need to know more.

In 1988 Don and I were raising Kelly, age five, and Jess, age three. Watching the miracle of my children unfold and blossom, like the flowers along the hiking trails, was amazing. And it was even more astonishing for me because Kelly and Jessie were mine. As they grew, I saw how they looked like me, smiled like me and used their hands like me. Watching their personalities develop and seeing pieces of Don and myself in them both made me want to know more about my birth parents.

My life was profoundly changing at that time. I had started to remember my childhood and was coming to terms with difficult memories. My mother was a very unhappy woman who was angry all the time. I tiptoed around her, tried to be invisible, and generally stayed out of her way while growing up. For thirty-four years I had been praying that someday she might tell me she loved me. But, knowing what I had finally allowed myself to know, it didn't look promising. Maybe if I could find my birth mother, I would have a second chance at having a mother who would love me. It felt very scary. But I took it one step at a time, just like climbing a mountain.

I knew I was adopted through a state agency and, from my years volunteering for the United Way, knew of only one: Child and Family Services of New Hampshire in Manchester. I called on May 27, 1988, and asked if they had facilitated my adoption. It took a few phone calls on my part and some searching by the agency staff, but the answer came back: yes. I had formally started the search and I felt alive with anticipation and fear, not unlike how I feel climbing over ice on a windy day in the Presidentials.

My adoption, I learned, was a closed procedure; the agency could give me only a summary with all the names, dates, and places crossed off. To contact my birth mother, I would have to petition the court to find her and then, if she wanted contact with me, the agency would assist in that process. I never considered going this route. I knew I would find my birth mother my own way.

I received the adoption summary, an eight-page typed document with dark black splotches covering all the important information. It was emotional reading, learning about my mother and her family and a bit about my father. It took me weeks to assimilate the information, and months to let it in. Tears came often in those days.

Through the summary, I started to find myself.

Mother is 5'2" with green eyes and brown hair. She uses her face and hands in an expressive way for indicating her feelings. She verbalizes easily and well, thinking through her feelings as she talks. She has been a stimulating person to work with.

There I am, I thought, in my mother.

After months of reading and re-reading the document I had a few clues. First there was this sentence: "Miss _____ is a high school graduate and has completed two years of Teachers' Normal at Keene, New Hampshire, where she hopes to return in September 1954."

I also knew that my mother had to live in New Hampshire in order to put us up for adoption in a state agency. And I knew that Keene Normal School later became Keene State College.

I noticed something very interesting about the adoption summary. It was typed using an old pica typewriter, so each letter was exactly the same width. I could draw vertical lines through the document and count the number of letters in the crossed-off words. I knew my mother had a seven letter last name and a seventeen-letter hometown. I also knew I had a seven-letter first name, and John had a five-letter first name. When I figured this out, a memory surfaced from childhood. I remembered finding a piece of paper in a baby book in my parents' library. On top of the paper were the words "David and Debbie." David, five letters, and Deborah, seven letters. It fit. I had been named Debbie.

On a hot August day, during my lunch hour, I climbed a spiral staircase to the third floor of Elliot Hall, where Keene State College kept a collection of old yearbooks. I settled down on the couch with my yellow-lined pad. I knew my mother returned for her junior year in 1954, so would have graduated in '56. I pulled out the 1956 yearbook and started writing down the names of every

SHERMAN, MARJORIE ANNE
Northwood Narrows, N. H.
"Margie"
Elementary
S.C.A. 2, 3, 4; F.T.A. 3, 4; W.A.A.
3, 4; Dining Room 3, 4; Monad-
nock 2; Bowling Leader 3, 4; Bad-
minton 3, 4.

graduating senior with a seven-letter last name who lived in the state of New Hampshire. I had almost filled an 8.5-by-11 piece of paper, and was in the S's. I turned the page and froze. There she was! I was sure of it. She looked like me. Marjorie Anne Sherman from North-wood Narrows, New Hampshire. Looking at her picture I finally felt like there was a reason for how I look, for who I am. I checked the number of letters. Her name fit; the hometown North-wood Narrows, sixteen letters and a space, fit. I was shaking. I forced myself to breathe deeply, while tears stung my eyes and rolled onto the yearbook page. I slowly got up and gathered the '55, '54, '53 and '52 yearbooks to make sure she appeared in all except in 1954, when she

was having me. It all fit.

I had found my mother: Marjorie Anne Sherman.

I went downstairs to the Alumni Office, trying to look normal and casual, and asked for a current address for Marjorie Sherman. No luck. The staffer said she was either dead or married. I asked her to check the records for a married name.

"Here she is," the woman said. "Marjorie Lawton in Dover, New Hampshire." Oh my God! She could be anywhere in the world and she was still in New Hampshire. I thanked the woman as calmly as I could and walked to my car, talking to myself the whole way. *Oh my God! I found her!*

The insurance company I worked for

at the time had phone books for all of New Hampshire. I looked up Lawton in the Dover book and there she was. I had found her in one day!

It took me two months to take the next step. Two months of holding on to the fact that I had been Deborah Sherman. That I had a natural mother who was alive and living an hour away. Would she want to hear from me? Would she be angry with me for finding her? Did she want to have contact with me? Would she acknowledge me? Although I was afraid to write, I never questioned whether I would—I knew it was something I had to do.

In October 1988, I wrote her a letter.

Please read this when you have some quiet time alone. My name is Nancy Sporborg. I am a 34-year-old, brown-eyed, brown-haired woman with a twin brother and I'm looking for my biological mother.... I want to tell you how sorry I am that you went through the pain and trauma of an unwanted pregnancy in the '50s. I can only imagine how hard that must have been. But I want you to know that all you went through was a gift to me. You gave me life. And now I owe it to you, and to myself, to make the most of this wonderful opportunity you've given me.... I hope this letter has not caused you pain but perhaps has touched your heart—maybe enough for you to take the risk to write back.

A month later she responded:

Since I received your letter I have and am still examining and processing my pain and all those feelings I squelched for 34 plus years. I have never told any-one including my ex-husband and my children.... Do you think we could meet somewhere? I long to see you.

On January 15, 1989, I drove to Dover to meet Marge. As I got closer, I could feel my heart pounding so hard I was afraid it would come right out of my chest or that I would have a heart attack. The noise and pressure of the pounding made me feel my head was going to explode. I was talking to myself, trying to calm myself down. *It's okay, Nancy. You're okay. You can do this.* I drove in the driveway where a woman around my age, who looked like me, was shoveling snow. I parked, opened the door, and she came over to me. She took my hands in hers and said, "Hi, I'm Martha, Marge's daughter, and I want you to know how happy I am that you are here. Go on in, Mom's waiting."

Already in tears, I rang the doorbell. The door opened and I found myself eye-to-eye with a white-haired woman with a big warm smile. She folded me in her arms saying, "Oh, Nancy, I am so glad you are here." Then she pushed me gently away from her to get a good look at me, then pulled me to her again for an embrace. Over the next few hours she shared the story of my birth and I shared the story of my life. I felt found, reclaimed, loved, and wanted.

Only days later I told John I had found our mother.

"Why the hell did you go and do that?" he asked angrily.

"If you ever want to meet her, let me know," I told him.

A few months later he was ready. He

came to my house and nervously awaited Marge's arrival. When her car drove in the driveway, my heart was racing, this time for John. He walked toward her tentatively as she entered the house.

"Oh John, John, I am so glad to meet you," Marge said as she wrapped John in her arms.

"I'm glad to meet you, too," he said, wiping away tears.

We took a picture that day of the three of us. I never thought I looked like John, and always questioned if he was really my twin. But looking at that picture I know for sure. Marge and John and me—we are family.

Fast-forward almost twenty years. A few weeks ago we had a wedding shower for my daughter Kelly. Marge and Martha came. They were my family. I

was touched to the core by their presence. And, I let it in. I knew they were there because they love me.

I cannot imagine the strength it took for Marge to weather the difficulties, discomfort, and loneliness of an unwanted pregnancy in the '50s. I cannot begin to understand the suffering and devastation of being sent away by furious parents to a home for unwed mothers in Boston, or the courage it must have taken Marge to deliver twins alone, with no visitors and no contact from family or friends. Only days later in the hospital, a woman came and took her babies away while Marge sobbed. And then Marge lived her life as if it never happened. It took tremendous fortitude for Marge to acknowledge me, and tell

her children and her family about her firstborn son and daughter.

There have been many times on the trails when I have been challenged and afraid, and I have had to dig deep to find the strength and courage to take the next step. I know where I get my strength and courage, along with my brown hair and short stature—I get it from my mother, Marge.

As we descend into the woods on this Mother's Day hike, my knees start to hurt, the three-mile trail back to the parking lot feels more like six miles, and I am filled with gratitude. I am grateful that I am the mother of two beautiful daughters who look like me, laugh like me, love life like me. And I am so incredibly grateful to my mother, Marge, and my sisters, Martha and Anne (above, from left to right). They opened up their hearts and their families and welcomed me home.

STATS

MOUNTAINS: CHOCORUA (3,500) AND MIDDLE SISTER (3,340)

NEAREST CITY: ALBANY, N.H.

DATE: MAY 11, 2008

TIME: 9 HOURS AND 30 MINUTES

WEATHER: SUNNY, TEMPERATURES IN THE 70S AND 80S, LIGHT BREEZE

MILES: 9.2

ELEVATION GAIN: 2,851 FEET

TRAILS: PIPER TRAIL, NICKERSON LEDGE TRAIL, CARTER LEDGE TRAIL, MIDDLE SISTER TRAIL

HOLY SHIT FACTOR: THE HIKE AND THE STORY THAT GOES WITH IT, OFF-THE-CHARTS

31. SHARED JOY ON WEST SLEEPER

May 17, 2008, Wonalancet, New Hampshire

People from a planet without flowers would think we must be mad with joy the whole time to have such things about us.

Iris Murdoch

Today we are going to bag Sleeper. We've checked off sixty-nine of the hundred highest mountains in New England. Today we'll check off number seventy. But not so fast.

This is our third attempt on Sleeper. Back in November we tried two Saturdays in a row to bag the peak but turned around because of difficult water crossings on the Sabbaday Brook Trail—both incredibly frustrating experiences. But no doubt about it, today

is the day! We have chosen a different route so we won't have to worry about water. We are climbing the Livermore Trail to the Tripyramid's South Slide.

We leave Keene at 7—a luxuriously late morning for us—and set out on the Livermore Trail at 9:30. Not more than ten steps on the trail and we are exclaiming to each other.

"Pat, look at the flowers!"

"Oh, look at the trillium!"

"Hey, wow—look, they are everywhere!"

"Oh, they're beautiful!"

"I gotta get a picture."

"Oh, look at these!"

"Look at the hobblebush."

"Hey, what are these?"

"Beautiful!"

"Wowsers!"

We are completely dazzled by the wildflowers gracing the trailside. We see painted trillium, wake robin trillium, trout lily, red-stemmed violet, common blue violet, common strawberry, wood anemone, woody blue violet, and hobblebush, all in bloom. Our eyes wander back and forth from one side of the trail to the other. Cameras at the ready, we spot one beautiful flower after another, and point them out to each other. We look like little kids on a chocolate Easter egg hunt, spying the next treat and running over to get a picture. It's just that we're saying "Beautiful!" instead of "Yummy!"

I have found the more I hike, the more I notice the details—the finer, smaller features in nature that make me say, "Oh, look at these!" When I first started hiking, I was blown away by the big stuff—the views. Now I also love the baby pink and lavender color of blueberries before they become blue, the drops of water on the leaves twinkling in the sun, the delicate reindeer moss, the beautiful deep blue of the blue bead lilies, and the patterns and ripples in the granite beneath our feet.

Yet, if I were alone, I wouldn't be exclaiming out loud about the beautiful wildflowers, getting more and more excited by each one. I wouldn't let it out; I'd hold my enthusiasm a prisoner inside. I would miss out on the fun and wonder of saying it out loud, hearing the excitement in my own voice. And I would miss seeing Pat's face as she receives my enthusiasm and lets it expand her own. Sharing the experience makes it bigger; it multiplies the joy in an exponential way. We feed off each other's reactions and before we know it we are filled with delight.

The wildflowers lead to a conversation about how we are blooming, too. Both Pat and I are sticking our feet out and testing the waters of life in new and different ways, and like the wildflowers, slowly opening to the world. In my last trip report I shared the story of finding my birth mother, a story I have held inside for twenty years. But I realize there is a gift in the sharing. If I hold it inside, no one really knows me. I am a secret. If I share, I am visible; I am out there for the world to see. It's scary. But I have been so touched by people's responses to the story. And in their responses, I have felt seen, seen for who I really am. And there is just no greater gift than that. Being seen makes me want to open more, to let my light shine more freely, to bloom more fully.

Now, I'm in my fifties, so you'd think I would have already bloomed and am on the way out. But maybe Pat and I are perennials in a constant growing, blooming, and dying cycle. Ahhhhh,

that feels right. Each time I bloom, I am more fully me.

Once over the initial wonder of being surrounded by wildflowers, we start noticing that some of the clintonia have sprouted, but dead leaves from the fall encapsulate the new growth. The plants are growing right up through the brown dried leaves, but the new leaves are bound together, unable to open and bloom properly.

"Save me! Save me!" Pat squeaks, speaking for the clintonia.

We start pulling the dead leaves off the plants, freeing the green blades, allowing them to relax into their natural state.

It's like Pat and me. In order to bloom we have to first rid ourselves of old patterns or thoughts from the past that are getting in the way of living today. I call it baggage and my husband is always saying to me, "Let's unpack that bag, Nance." My baggage is the way I learned to cope as a child—I tried to be invisible. It worked then, but trying to be invisible doesn't serve me anymore. The day came when the risk to stay invisible was more painful than the risk to be seen, and so I shared the story of finding my birth mother publicly.

Ah, thank you, the clintonia seems to be saying as I strip away the dry dead matter and the plant's leaves unfold and unclench, allowing the sunlight to enter its center.

It would be easy to hike by and not notice the clintonia trapped by dead leaves. But we're engaged with the world when we're hiking and it feels like a two-way trail. Freeing the flowers is a way to give back and say thank you to Mother Nature who showers us with beauty every time we step out of the car and into the woods.

As we de-leaf we look at each other and laugh. We're sharing the joy of saving clintonia. I don't think I would be taking dead leaves off of plants if I were alone. Having a co-conspirator helps me take myself less seriously. Having someone to play with brings the kid out in me. I am happy. So is Pat.

As we take a right onto the Tripyramid Trail we have a blue-sky moment. The forecast for today is cloudy with a chance of showers before 8 a.m., a chance of rain between 8 and 2 p.m., and then cloudy the rest of the day. But, desperate to be in the mountains, we decide to hike anyway.

"Look! Blue sky!"

"It has turned into such a beautiful day!"

"I was prepared to walk in the rain."

"So was I."

"We are so lucky!"

As we start up the south slide, we meet Marty, a man who posts on the same hiking forum that we do. He recognizes our names. How cool is that! We ask him, just to be sure, which Sleeper is the one that counts toward the hundred highest, east or west.

"East Sleeper" he says. (We thought it was West Sleeper.)

"That's where we are headed," Pat says.

"Well, then, let me tell you two things," Marty says. "There's a lot of deep snow up there and I got turned around, lost the trail and ended up adding two miles to the hike. So be careful."

"Did you do a lot of post-holing?" I ask.

"No, I've got snowshoes." he says.

Pat and I look at each other.

Uh oh. We decided not to bring snowshoes because we lugged them up Chocorua last weekend and they stayed on our packs all day. So we figured we wouldn't need them. Whoops. It looks like we are in for an adventure.

We get to the junction of the Kate Sleeper Trail around noon and have lunch. While we are enjoying our sun-and-sandwich bliss moment, we talk about our destination. Pat thinks West Sleeper is the mountain on the hundred highest list. I check the map and agree. West Sleeper is 3,881 feet high, whereas East Sleeper is only 3,840. This is important because East Sleeper is another three quarters of a mile beyond West Sleeper along a snow-filled ridge. We decide Marty is wrong, and we head up to West Sleeper.

First we have to go down a slide, and I hate going down when I am supposed to be going up. But I manage to control myself and before I know it we are ascending again. Then we hit the snow.

At first it is passable, but soon we are post-holing through one to two feet of rotten snow. The second we take a step, down we go, plummeting into the freezing cold, filling our boots with ice crystals. But we've come this far, so we keep going. Here's the good part: We are laughing at ourselves. Shorts on, bare legs, wet boots, soaking socks, we struggle to extricate ourselves from one hole after another without falling and plunging our bare hands into the snow. What else can we do but laugh? Yet, had I been alone, I might have been swearing to myself. With Pat there, I find humor more easily and laughter feels like a bonus. We reach the un-marked summit of West Sleeper and gratefully turn around.

Back at the slide we find a hot rock in the sun. We take off our boots, wring out our socks, and air out our feet while we enjoy the second half of our sandwiches. We are surrounded by mountain peaks rising up in the clear blue sky. Pat points out the mountains we've climbed and we relive our hikes on each of them as we rest in the sun.

"There's Welch-Dickey. We hiked Welch-Dickey the same day we turned around on our first Sleeper attempt. Remember I thought we had summited both mountains and then realized we had another mountain to go?" I ask.

"There's Sandwich Dome," says Pat, pointing. "Wasn't Sandwich Dome our first winter sliding hike? We laughed and woo hooed all the way down the mountain!"

"Remember Tecumseh?" I say. "I barely made it up in the summer and in the winter I took a header while we were talking to a guy on the trail." We laugh.

Both of us are smiling, nodding, remembering. Life is pretty cool the way it works. First we get to share the experience and the joy when it happens and then we get to hold it in our hearts, where it is available for reminiscing anytime we want. And, oh! Even before the experience, we get to anticipate it.

We finally put on dry socks and wet boots and head down the slide and out Livermore Trail. We walk down in what we have termed a "Passaconaway." A what, you ask? A Passaconaway. On our very first four thousand–footer hike, coming down Mt. Passaconaway, we were blessed with a beautiful afternoon just like this, perfect temperatures, sparkling sunlight, and a warm soft breeze that stirs the air around us. I remember I was exclaiming most of the way down, "Oh, this is so beautiful!" We have always remembered it. We are reveling in the "Passaconaway" even as we are losing a bit of the spring in our step. It seems trail workers have added a few extra miles to the end of the trail when we were post-holing on Sleeper!

We get back to the car at 5:45 and to my house in Keene at 8:30. I immediately sit down at my computer and pull up the New England Hundred Highest peaks list. It's East Sleeper. Marty was right. We climbed the wrong mountain!

We'll be back . . .

You know, there's no failure in our attempts. They give us a chance to try again. And climbing another mountain is an opportunity to bloom more fully. It is another invitation to follow the examples set by the trailside trillium and let more of my beauty emerge by sharing more of myself. The wildflowers remind all of us to allow ourselves to be more easily seen by shining our lights a bit brighter. When we do, we make it easier for others to bloom around us.

And the best part—Pat and I get to share our wonder and joy. I radiate it out into the world. Pat catches it, feels it, and mixes it with her own. I see it emanating from her face as she smiles and it comes back to me.

Shared joy!

STATS

MOUNTAIN: WEST SLEEPER (3,881)

NEAREST CITY: WONALANCET, N.H.

DATE: MAY 17, 2008

TIME: 8 HOURS

WEATHER: SUNNY, TEMPERATURE IN THE 70S, LIGHT BREEZE

MILES: 11.2

ELEVATION GAIN: 2,328 FEET

TRAILS: LIVERMORE TRAIL, MT. TRIPYRAMID TRAIL, KATE SLEEPER TRAIL

HOLY SHIT FACTOR: BLOOMING AWESOME

32. BEING SEEN ON EAST SLEEPER

May 24, 2008, Wonalancet, New Hampshire

Intimacy is being seen and known as the person you truly are.

Amy Bloom

I am lucky enough to have had the experience of really being seen. Pat and I are driving up to Wonalancet, to bag East Sleeper on our fourth attempt when she says to me, "You are all about shared joy. That's who you are."

I feel my resistance, but my heart

wins. Tears sting my eyes and I let them be. I flash on a few of my most treasured life moments.

2006: I am in the Grand Canyon with my husband on a 225-mile rafting trip down the Colorado River. We have just gone through Lava Falls, one of the largest and most-feared rapids in the canyon. "Right here, everyone!" Kent, our paddle guide, says. Holding on to the paddle's T-grip, he lifts his blade high above the center of the raft. We follow suit. Our paddles clap overhead against each other's as we whoop and holler, celebrating our protected passage through Lava Falls and the sheer relief we feel at being right-side-up and alive.

2007: Pat and I arrive on the South rim of the Grand Canyon, completing a rim-to-rim hike, and we are thrilled. But the fun isn't over. Being the first to arrive, we wait for the rest of our group. As soon as we see some of our members on the zigzag trails below, we shout out their names and encourage them on. We celebrate each arrival with high fives, hugs and celebratory woo hoos. Many reach the rim in tears, overwhelmed with joy and pride at accomplishing the goal. It is such a privilege to share that glorious moment with each of them.

It fits. I nod my agreement, wipe my tears, and look out the car window. It is the truth. I am about shared joy. I had not thought about myself in that way, but it moves in my heart right. I feel totally seen by Pat and I let it in. It is rare when someone sees another person for who she really is. It's an incredible gift

when it happens—someone recognizes your fear and extends a hand; a co-worker celebrates a talent and offers praise; a friend sees your beauty and reflects it back to you; a loved one looks inside your heart and shares what he sees.

Pat asks me if I remember when I first felt seen. Yes! When I was the corporate communications manager for NGM Insurance Company, I went to a week-long conference in Florida. As part of the sessions, I took a Myers-Briggs personality inventory. I can still remember sitting on the floor reading the synopsis of my personality as the tears dripped down my nose and onto the rug.

ENFJ (Extroverted, Intuitive, Feeling, Judging)—For ENFJs the dominant quality in their lives is an active and intense caring about people and a strong desire to bring harmony into their relationships. ENFJs are openly expressive and empathic people who bring an aura of warmth to all that they do. Intuition orients their feeling to the new and to the possible, thus they often enjoy working to manifest a humanitarian vision, or helping others develop their potential. ENFJs naturally and conscientiously move into action to care for others, to organize the world around them, and to get things done.

Having grown up believing I was gross, foul, and disgusting, I was shocked by this description that immediately felt true. I had been seen.

Pat and I arrive at the trailhead to find lots of other cars in the parking lot—a harbinger of what is to come. We head up the Blueberry Ledge Trail toward

the summit of Whiteface, a four thousand footer that happens to be between us and our goal of East Sleeper.

We immediately start seeing wildflowers and I am snapping photos right and left. I am in awe of each flower's unique beauty.

The conversation that began in the car continues on the trail.

"Why is it that we fight the very thing that we want most in life?" I ask this question with surprise and disbelief in my voice. "Why would we do that?"

This question comes on the heels of making the connection that the thing I want most in life is to be seen, and it is one of the things I never had growing up. As a kid, I perfected the art of being invisible, which kept me out of the direct line of anger and venom spewing around me at home. I was often afraid to come home, never knowing what mood my mother would be in. I was really good at not being seen, and not being seen meant safety. It was my way of coping as a child and I continue to live that way, even though the reason no longer exists. I refuse to see myself and I rarely let myself out to be seen.

As I'm taking close-ups of the wildflowers, reminiscent of last week's hike up West Sleeper, it occurs to me that I've just started to see the flowers, really for the first time in my life. But they are showing up to be seen. They are not hiding. They are right next to the hiking trail, smiling their beautiful petals at us. Huh. . . . To be seen, I have to want to be seen. I have to own my beauty and then share it with the world.

Like the wildflowers. Like sharing the story of finding my birth mother. I realize there is so much more of me that I keep secret.

We get to the ledges on Whiteface and up we go. Whiteface was our first four thousand footer and I was scared to death on the ledges two years ago. There are many spots where it is hard to find good footing and handholds, especially for short people. But today I know what I am in for. I can feel the fear come back but I hold my ground

and, with Pat's help, get myself up and over without trauma.

We arrive on the top at 1:15 and have lunch while a bunch of teenage boys yell and run around the summit. Peace eludes us.

We head off toward the Kate Sleeper Trail. When we see the snow, we high five with glee. We lugged our snowshoes all the way up the mountain so we might as well use them. On they go, and we walk balanced on the monorail of snow that runs down the middle of

the trail. Then we hit dry ground. We take our snowshoes off and walk until we run into the snow monorail again. Sighing, I put my snowshoes back on. I don't know how many times we take them off and put them back on, but I reach the you-have-to-be-kidding stage of exasperation. The trail is a mass of rocks, running water, branches, downed trees and rotten snow that doesn't support our weight with lots of post-holes made by people who wished they had snowshoes.

About midway to East Sleeper I voice my concern that it is late and really slow going and perhaps we should . . . I can't even bring myself to say the words. This is our fourth attempt and we don't want to turn around. But it is already 3 p.m. and we have another maybe six-tenths of a mile to go on very rough terrain before we reach the summit. Pat sees me. She registers my concerns. She says she is sure we will be able to get back to the ledges in daylight and suggests we keep going. We arrive on the summit of East Sleeper at 3:48, take a picture to prove we were there, and immediately head back to Whiteface.

This time we put our snowshoes on and just walk across whatever happens to be under our feet—snow, branches, mud, river, rocks, dry trail. We meet a few guys who are eyeing our snowshoes with envy, but we are on a mission to get back and don't let in how smart we are. With big relief we arrive back on Whiteface and head down the ledges without stopping to rest. I am nervous about going down, but it turns out it is much easier than going up. I just sit down and slide on my butt.

By this time my feet are killing me. I have small feet with narrow heels and have not been able to find boots that are right for me. I change into my sneaker-like Merrell's and immediately feel relief.

Our conversation rekindles once we are over the snow-filled ridge and past the ledges.

"Why can I see you so clearly?" Pat asks me.

The answer comes immediately. "It's the mountains."

Pat and I put ourselves out in the midst of nature, through all four seasons, and challenge our bodies to get up and down these peaks. Something happens to me in the process of climbing. It's like I sweat away a protective layer that envelops me, so that by the time I am on the top I am left with me, totally exposed. Just the truth. It just happens. The physical exertion and the natural splendor and the incredible expanses on the summits push me into my heart where I can only be fully me. So if I am scared, Pat sees it. If I am overjoyed, Pat sees it. If I am tired, Pat sees it. I am whatever I am. Back in my normal life at sea level, I am not so vulnerable. The protective layer returns and it is not so easy to see my emotions, or the raw

feelings and truths that make me who I am. I don't let them out on the streets like I do in the mountains, except at home with my husband. Another place I let out enough of me to be seen is in my writing. But writing is one step removed. I am not looking into your eyes as you read this.

But if I want to be seen everywhere in my life, then somehow I need to find ways to allow the me inside, the soft vulnerable truth of Nancy, to come out and be visible so people can know me. So people can see me. So I can be loved.

We arrive back at the parking lot at 8:15, surrounded by dusk. As the sun is setting we look back with gratitude over the fields to the mountains that just held us.

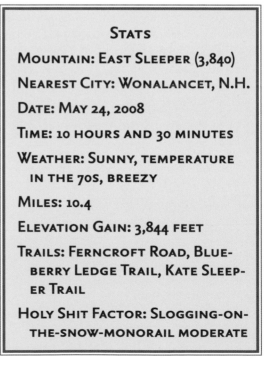

STATS

MOUNTAIN: EAST SLEEPER (3,840)

NEAREST CITY: WONALANCET, N.H.

DATE: MAY 24, 2008

TIME: 10 HOURS AND 30 MINUTES

WEATHER: SUNNY, TEMPERATURE IN THE 70S, BREEZY

MILES: 10.4

ELEVATION GAIN: 3,844 FEET

TRAILS: FERNCROFT ROAD, BLUE-BERRY LEDGE TRAIL, KATE SLEEP-ER TRAIL

HOLY SHIT FACTOR: SLOGGING-ON-THE-SNOW-MONORAIL MODERATE

33. A CANISTER OF CONNECTION ON REDINGTON

June 14, 2008, Kingfield, Maine

The world is so empty if one thinks only of mountains, rivers, and cities; but to know someone here and there who thinks and feels with us, and though distant, is close to us in spirit, this makes the earth for us an inhabited garden.

Johann Wolfgang von Goethe

I love it when we can share our summit moment with others who are just as excited about getting there as we are. But I doubt we will have company atop Redington, the only mountain on the New England Four Thousand Footer list that does not have a maintained trail. But there is supposed to be a canister on top that will hopefully hold the names of those who have summited before us, which is what I am looking forward to the most.

We arrive at the trailhead at 8:47 and head up the Appalachian Trail in the sun. In two hours we are on the top of South Crocker, surprised at the energy we have left. The path made by others on the same bushwhacking journey from the summit of South Crocker to the top of Redington is relatively easy to follow, most of the way. There are a number of overgrown areas where I can see the narrow path in front of my feet, but branches obscure the way and my body takes a beating. About halfway

to Redington, we enter a cleared area. As we follow the orange surveyor's tape that someone thankfully put up, I think about the canister on top. Renewed enthusiasm helps me push and fight my way through the now closed-in woods toward the summit.

When we get to the top of Redington at 12:20, the first thing we see is the tower that has blown down, leaving wires and debris everywhere. Ugly! Pat and I find a place for lunch in the sun, but can't wait to look for the canister. So we start searching.

"There it is!" I shout, pointing to a nearby tree trunk.

I am really glad Pat is tall because there is no way I can reach it. She stands on her tiptoes, unscrews the top of the canister, reaches in and pulls out a plastic bag with a pencil, pencil sharpener, and a notebook and single sheets of paper overflowing with names and descriptions of their hiking experiences. It's not other hikers in the flesh, but it is the next best thing. The canister holds the moment at the top for everyone and in opening it up and adding our own words, we join in the joy with everyone who has gone before us.

I understand there are a lot of people who want to leave the mountains exactly as they are, with no sign of humans left behind. But I love the canisters, just as I love the cairns and summit signs. For me, they represent the shared joy of hiking. It allows me to connect with others who have walked the same path. We are united with others in a shared effort.

Life can be isolating, because we are, in the end, alone. I am the only one who can live my life. But knowing there are others who are making the same journeys, up the same mountains, bushwhacking, getting scratched and

bruised by branches, then writing their stories and putting them in a canister to share, that is what life is made of. The connections we make with others matter most to me. Every connection, every person, every moment matters.

We sit down and eat lunch, then write our entry into the little notebook that I have in my pack, which I donate to the canister. Our entry recaps our mountain climbing history, but the numbers are irrelevant. What we are really saying is, *This is where we are on our journey. Where are you?* Through those words, we offer connection to the next group that summits and we leave a piece of ourselves on the top of Redington.

A canister of connection—how cool is that? So if you aren't hiking with a group of friends, and you don't get a standing ovation from fellow hikers when you reach the peak, maybe there is a canister that holds the dreams and accomplishments of other hikers that touches you. Or maybe there is a cairn standing tall built from all the rocks hikers have added—and you can make your own contribution. Or maybe you pass others on the trail who join you for a short portion of your hike. Fellow travelers all. We're all on the journey. There is nothing that separates us but the walls we put around ourselves. The cairns and the canisters and the standing ovations take down our walls and offer connection.

Pat and I get lost in the spruce bushwhacking down Redington, following the tape trail of someone else who also must have been lost. But we finally figure it out after getting scratched and scraped and slapped around a bit, and find our way back to the summit of South Crocker by 2:20. Then off to North Crocker. Ahhhhh, we are on a trail. All it takes is four hours of bushwhacking to remind you that having a trail is a pretty wonderful thing. We arrive on the summit of North Crocker at 4 p.m., my feet killing me from my new boots, and both of us feeling the effects of hiking. From there it is a relatively gentle five miles down to our car.

As I write this report I realize I did not read the entries other people had written and placed in the canister. That missed opportunity makes me sad. Why didn't

I? I guess I just didn't take the time or make the effort. I was intent on leaving a piece of myself, but not in the reciprocal act of letting in the joy or the dreams or the accomplishments of others. We had three mountains to climb and our ritual is to have lunch and go. But I wish I had taken the time to connect with others through their entries. As it was we offered a piece of ourselves, but we didn't get the joy of connecting with those who had come before.

That makes me think about everyday life—how easy it is to go through my day and not connect with others. It takes courage and a belief in myself to make a true connection. Often I am on a mission to get done whatever has to get done and I miss the moment when

I could connect with someone. It requires conscious effort to lift my eyes and meet the eyes of another. It might be looking eye-to-eye with a person on a sidewalk, or in a meeting, or on spin bikes. Anywhere. It might be showing my love to those I care for when they walk into a room. It might be taking the time to ask a friend how she is and then waiting patiently and listening for the real answer, my heart open. Connection comes in all kinds of ways, in seconds and over hours. And I know it when it happens because I feel the excitement of that connection. And I get to see the unique beauty in another human being. And it's available to me all the time! Little moments of connection are always waiting to happen.

I don't want to be the person who isn't available, or is only half available. I want to always be present and courageous enough to put myself, just me, out there, so I can take advantage of every precious connection moment there is. That would be really living, present in the moment, consciously. Can I do that? I know it would make every encounter more personal, more meaningful. And I crave meaning in my life.

Like hiking to the summit of Redington where there is no trail, connection takes risk and is hard work. Like getting scraped and bruised while bushwhacking, connection between humans can be messy, sometimes painful, and you may get lost before you find the way. And like the canister on top of Redington, the connection opportunity is always there.

Heart open, eye-to-eye, wanting to know you, here I am.

STATS

MOUNTAINS: SOUTH CROCKER (4,050), REDINGTON (4,010) AND CROCKER (4,228)

NEAREST CITY: KINGFIELD, MAINE

DATE: JUNE 14, 2008

TIME: 10 HOURS AND 30 MINUTES

WEATHER: SUNNY IN THE MORNING, CLOUDS IN THE AFTERNOON, TEMPERATURE IN THE 70S

MILES: 11

ELEVATION GAIN: 2,008 FEET

TRAILS: APPALACHIAN TRAIL, BUSHWHACK TO REDINGTON

HOLY SHIT FACTOR: OUR VERY FIRST CANISTER!

34. MILES TO GO BEFORE WE SLEEP—SUGARLOAF, SPAULDING, AND ABRAHAM

June 21, 2008, Kingfield, Maine

The woods are lovely, dark and deep, but I have promises to keep,
And miles to go before I sleep, and miles to go before I sleep.

Robert Frost

Hiking is a metaphor for my life. Every hike holds an opportunity to see myself more clearly. As I look back over the past two years, I realize I am different—in how I hike and how I live. I am changing.

Our plans call for two mountains, Mounts Sugarloaf and Spaulding. But Sue, manager of the Stratton Motel, tells us it is possible to add Mt. Abraham to our hike. She also tells us about recent rainfalls, and says the Carrabassett River is running high and the water crossing on the Appalachian Trail up to Sugarloaf might be tough.

We regroup. We decide to add Abraham to the plan, which means we'll need one less trip to Maine to finish the New England four thousand footers. We are climbing Sugarloaf, Spaulding and Abraham, three four thousand footers, in a little over fifteen miles. We decide to climb up the ski trails of Sugarloaf to avoid crossing the Carrabassett.

The next morning, after breakfast at the Stratton Diner, we are at the condos alongside Sugarloaf ski trails by 8:30 and up we go.

The second we hit the ski trail we are immediately inundated by black flies. I drop my backpack and slather myself with bug dope, batting away the flies and swearing loudly. Pat was smart enough to do this ahead of time. I'm sure I look pretty funny, and I can't help but laugh at myself.

Within minutes of setting foot on the trail, we are both breathing heavily climbing the steep slopes that afford skiers a thrill when they are going the opposite direction on snow. The view of the surrounding Bigelow Range becomes more and more dramatic as we gain altitude. We can see the tower on the summit of Sugarloaf and we keep climbing straight up. We arrive on top of Sugarloaf, the second highest mountain in Maine, at 10:30 and take a few pictures before continuing

along the Sugarloaf Spur Trail to the Appalachian Trail.

The hike from Sugarloaf to Spaulding is a bit over two miles. About halfway there we are offered a view of Spaulding looming in front of us. It looks massive. I gasp, which is my usual reaction.

"It looks like we haven't even started to climb," I whine. But then I remember what I have learned over the past two years of hiking—it always looks farther away, steeper and more daunting than it is. Always. And then I notice a difference in me. I used to let the massive mountain ahead of me eat away at my belief in myself, and would spend the next hiking hours dreading the climb even while I was doing it. But this time, I don't let what I am looking at zap my positive energy. I feel the calm inside of knowing it looks worse than it is and that I can make it—easily. And I do.

That is the first difference I notice on this hike. But more are to come. Pat and I are less talkative today. Often we talk about issues in our lives that we're processing, but today we are quiet. I find myself right here, noticing the plants, the beauty of the trail, the flowers lining the way, the moose droppings, the woods, and my body as it works. My mind wanders once in a while, but then it comes back to what is around me, like a meditation. I have let go of all perceived problems and stories and am just here, hiking, in the moment. I hear lots of talk and read articles about living in the moment, and it all sounds good. But I realize there are no words that can describe the power or feeling

of the actual experience of being in the moment.

We reach the top of Spaulding at 12:21 and have lunch. We talk with a couple who are doing almost the same hike we are, Tricia and Pete. It is good to know there are others on our journey today. We don't stay long on Spaulding—we have miles to go before we sleep.

From Spaulding it is almost four miles to Mt. Abraham. Even though I know the distance, I don't let it into my worry zone. I know it and I just keep walking. I feel energetic, strong, peaceful, complete. In the past, on a long hike, I would be psyching myself up for the long haul and cheering myself on internally. Today I am tranquil inside and don't seem to need anything. We arrive at timberline and meet Pete and Tricia again. They've just summited

Abraham and are heading down, saying they are nervous about rain. I give them a joyful high five for bagging three four thousand footers in one day before we head our separate ways. Although it looks like it is going to pour at any moment, by the time we get to the top of Abraham, the sun is out and the views are spectacular. With our hiking boots standing on the summit of Abraham, we have now climbed 102 mountains in a little over two years, sixty-three of the sixty-seven New England four thousand footers and seventy-seven of the hundred highest mountains in New England. Woo hoo!

From where we are standing we can trace our upcoming seven-mile journey back down Abraham, along the ridge, up over Spaulding's summit and down, more ridge, then up to the Sug-

arloaf towers, which marks where we will head down the ski slopes to our car. It looks very, very, very far away. But somehow, although I definitely register the distance, it doesn't get to me. It doesn't fester into doubt. It doesn't degrade into worry and angst about whether we will make it. We talk about the fact that we probably won't get back in time for dinner at the diner, which closes at 8:30. And, even though this is the summer solstice, we are glad we have our headlamps, because we just might need them. That's it. We head back, smiling, still full of energy and strength and calm and quiet.

Maybe this is my new way of being and I am seeing it clearly today, hiking.

In my daily life, I used to spend my time processing issues involving my past, worrying about all kinds of minor and major stuff, and stressing about whatever is coming up next. Much of my life has been filled with all that worry, angst, stress, and drama, day after day. It gave me something to do, something to focus on. I guess all that rigmarole gave me purpose. That is what I needed then. But now I am living differently. Over the past two years, it seems that gradually, almost imperceptibly, I have been letting go, bit by bit. I hold on to less. I am living my life more like I am hiking today in the mountains.

But I am left with a persistent, unrelenting question. If I don't have my past to define me and my worry and stress

to guide me and my stories and drama to provide purpose in my life, what is left? This question makes me feel so empty. I am raw and vulnerable in my emptiness. It feels heart wrenching to want something so badly and not know what it is or how to find it. I don't know how to re-fill myself or with what.

Yet I don't feel the emptiness as keenly when I am hiking. I am filled with the moment. I want to feel every day the way I feel when I hike on Saturdays. I want to feel as triumphant in life as I do on the summit of every mountain. I want to feel as empowered every day as I do when I see a massive mountain rising before me and I know I can reach the top. I want to feel as joyful in my daily life as I do when I am giv-

ing a fellow hiker a summit high five or a standing ovation. I want to feel as graced in my daily life as I do when I am walking along a trail surrounded by blue sky, warm sun, soft breezes, birch trees, and bright green ferns. I want to feel awe at home the way I do when I see alpine wildflowers. I want to feel as strong every day as I do when I make it up and down three mountains in twelve hours. And I want to feel that beautiful exhaustion of finishing a fifteen-mile hike after my daily workouts. I want to feel as fulfilled by what I am doing every day as I do when I check off another mountain on the hiking list. I want to live as intensely as I hike. But even that is not enough . . . .

Over the next seven miles of trail,

Pat and I retrace our steps down Abraham, over Spaulding, and back up Sugarloaf. Heading over the ridge, we pass some Appalachian Trail through-hikers who started at Katahdin in early June. Wow—and I think I have far to go! I give them a way-to-go-woo-hoo before continuing on. Not until we summit Sugarloaf and start down the ski trails do I feel the effects of the hike. Midway down the slopes, as we debate which trail to take to make sure we don't bypass our car, I realize that I am finally physically spent. With relief, we see the condos and Pat's peak-bagger-mobile. It's 9:05 p.m.—twelve hours after we started.

I take a very deep breath as I slip off my pack, another as I take the weight off my feet and sit down on the front seat of the car, and then a satisfied sigh as I take the first sip of my cold Snapple. I can feel my body still working internally, but I am done! There is no better feeling.

This hike magnifies the blessing of living in the moment and accentuates my desperate yearning for more meaning. Don't get me wrong. I have led a very meaningful life. I have a wonderful husband and two lovely daughters. I've had many rewarding professional and personal experiences. I am blessed to be hiking with Pat. I am incredibly lucky. It's just that I want more. I don't want to look at my past and say I'm done. I want to shine my light even brighter today and brighter still tomorrow and the next day—and I am not sure how to do that. This is not a new revelation for me, but the more I let go, the bigger and deeper the ache for purpose.

What do I really want? I want to change the world. I'm not saying I can. I'm just saying I want to. I am hungry to contribute to a greater good, to make a real difference. I want to know my life matters today and tomorrow. I want to express myself and use my gifts in a way that inspires others. I want to know in my heart that the world is a better place for my having been here.

I have not found the answers I am searching for, but I know I am on the trail.

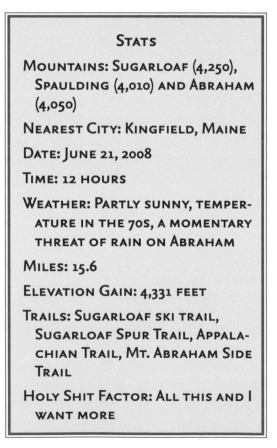

STATS

MOUNTAINS: SUGARLOAF (4,250), SPAULDING (4,010) AND ABRAHAM (4,050)

NEAREST CITY: KINGFIELD, MAINE

DATE: JUNE 21, 2008

TIME: 12 HOURS

WEATHER: PARTLY SUNNY, TEMPERATURE IN THE 70S, A MOMENTARY THREAT OF RAIN ON ABRAHAM

MILES: 15.6

ELEVATION GAIN: 4,331 FEET

TRAILS: SUGARLOAF SKI TRAIL, SUGARLOAF SPUR TRAIL, APPALACHIAN TRAIL, MT. ABRAHAM SIDE TRAIL

HOLY SHIT FACTOR: ALL THIS AND I WANT MORE

35. THE GIFT OF BALDPATE

July 5, 2008, Grafton, Maine

> *Climb the mountains and get their good tidings. Nature's peace will flow into you as sunshine flows into trees. The winds will blow their own freshness into you, and the storms their energy, while cares will drop off like autumn leaves.*

> John Muir

I'm writing this the week before my daughter Kelly's wedding. The luxurious hour Pat and I spent lying in the sun on the summit of Baldpate sits in my memory banks waiting for moments just like this. I am nervous. It feels as if one hundred elementary school children are playing an exuberant game of dodge ball in my chest. My legs are in perpetual motion and my feet have not stopped tapping, even though I have been sitting at my computer for the past few hours. My head is jam-packed with appointments and things I have to remember to do for the wedding and reception. And I am filled with worry about all the wedding details. Will everyone be able to find Alyson's Orchard? Will people get there on time? Will the weather hold out so we can have the wedding outside? Will the groom's parents like the wedding site? Will Kelly be able to relax and enjoy her wedding? To ground myself during this incredibly stressful time, I am going to helicopter back up 3,812 feet to the summit of Baldpate. I'll take you with me.

We leave Keene at our typical hardly awake hour of 5 a.m. and drive to Grafton, Maine. By 9:30 we are at the trailhead, which is right across the road from the trailhead for Old Speck where last summer we collected pocketfuls of mica and acted like little kids finding buried treasure.

We head up the mountain, taking our usual pictures of flowers and mushrooms and scenes that fill us with awe. By noon we are on the summit of West Baldpate, where we have lunch on a granite slab in an open area sprinkled with mica and surrounded by reindeer moss, sheep laurel, and alpine azalea. We have a beautiful view of where we are headed, the summit of the East Baldpate, which is the higher of the

two summits and the one that counts toward the hundred highest. It is a beautiful day.

Hiking in the White Mountains, like walking through the closet in *The Lion, the Witch, and the Wardrobe*, brings those who journey there into a magi-

cal realm that has the power to heal humans—a place where birds eat out of our hands, the natural world is exposed in all of its magnificence, the spectacular views are earned only through the demanding effort required to reach the summits, and the peace is profound. As Pat and I eat our lunch we are joined by a couple of gray jays squawking for their share of our treats. I put trail mix in my palm and watch as a gray jay tentatively lands on my fingers, takes an almond in its beak, and flies away, singing a thank you back to me.

After lunch, we gather our packs and head off to East Baldpate. It looks far away. But another property of the enchanted White Mountains is that distances are deceiving. A summit can appear miles away, but we always make it and it is always easier than it looks. At 1:10 p.m., in what feels like no time, we are on the summit. We take our packs off, find a relatively flat slab of rock, and lay our bodies down on the hot, hard surface to rest. A light breeze wafts over us as the sun warms us. It is perfect. It takes me a while to let myself sink into the granite. I giggle as I begin to relax, a response to letting myself feel the sheer joy of lying in the sun on top of a mountain with the world and its pressures at my feet and my best friend by my side. As time stretches and I am able to let in the warmth of the sun on my face and my legs, the feeling of the hard rock welcoming my body, I sink into it and let it take me. I close my eyes and I just am.

I just am. How often in my life does that happen? Almost never. Another gift of the mountains. When I "just am" I am nowhere and I am here. Nothing matters but the breeze and the sun and the hot rock I am lying on and my friend. Time doesn't exist. The wedding and all its stress evaporates, my To Do list disappears, my worries fade away. This is a rare moment on a mountaintop for Pat and me. Most often it is windy on the summits or too cold to linger, or we have miles and miles to go and can't spare the extra time. But today the temperature is warm and the hike is short,

affording us plenty of time to enjoy. I have never experienced the incredible "I am-ness" of just lying down on the summit in the sun quite like I do today. This will go down as one of my favorite moments in life. I can't think of a place that I would rather be than above the fray, on a sunny warm mountaintop. Pat and I linger here for an hour. It is a gift we give ourselves. I know the hours ahead, getting ready for Kelly's wedding, will be overflowing with excitement and stress, so I am soaking in the gentleness of the breezes to help carry me over until I am back in the magical realm of the mountains, peakbagging our next summit.

As we find ourselves ready to head down, Pat takes a pee break and notices a sign a few hundred yards away. We thought we were on the summit, but it looks like we have not made it yet. We leave our packs to rest in the sun a bit longer and walk the short, view-surrounded jaunt to the summit sign for pictures. The world stretches out from us in every direction. I take a deep breath, absorbing the beauty, knowing the world is humming down below, filled with life and love and tragedy and stress, and choosing to stay here, above it all for this moment. And the next moment.

Pat and I are so happy. The hike is beautiful. Nothing feels hard to me as we hike down Baldpate, slowly heading back into the real world. Coming down the way we came, gravity pulls us along, our legs braking the force of re-entry so that we can return to the world at a leisurely pace. We need a gentle transition today after an hour of lying in the sun. The mountains have a way of helping me find myself, preparing me for the hustle and bustle below. And when I am fully centered, not worrying about what happened in the past or what might happen in the future, not taking on the lives of others, but reacting to the world as Nancy, life always seems much easier. There is less stress, less drama, fewer worries. That is the gift of a mountain experience.

On the way down, Pat and I hike up a spur trail to Table Rock for the advertised extraordinary views. I am glad we take the detour. It brings us out above the world for one last reminder of the peace above the fray. The hike down from Table Rock is steep, straight down a staircase of rock. Wowsers! We get back to the car and our cold Diet Pepsi and Snapple at 6:30 p.m.

Having left the stress and worry on top of Baldpate, I am ready to immerse myself in wedding preparations.

I am off to pick up my mother-of-the-bride dress, then go to a much-needed spin class with Pat to use up this frenetic energy. And I know that all I have to do is stay in my heart and be present. If I start to worry and stress and re-engage in all the drama and stories that sometimes fill my life, I will helicopter back up to the summit of Baldpate, take off my pack of worries, and lie on a hot granite slab, soaking up the sun and the peace of the White Mountains to bring me back to me.

STATS

Mountain: East Baldpate (3,812)

Nearest City: East Andover, Maine

Date: July 5, 2008

Time: 9 hours

Weather: Sunny, passing clouds, light breeze, 70s

Miles: 10.9

Elevation Gain: 2,730 feet

Trails: Appalachian Trail

Holy Shit Factor: Peaceful in the moment

36. A WEDDING HIKE UP MONADNOCK

July 10, 2008, Jaffrey Center, New Hampshire

*I'm gonna love myself more than anyone else
Believe in me, even if someone can't see
A stronger woman in me.*

Jewel, **Stronger Woman**

I climbed Mt. Monadnock some six times in fifty years. Each summit sojourn gave me the same mysterious gift—a glimpse of endless possibilities. I loved the feeling of enormity that enveloped me on top.

But I am getting ahead of myself.

On Saturday my daughter will become Mrs. Kelly Ritter. Today, two days before the wedding, she is hiking Monadnock.

It is her idea, not mine.

On Thursday morning at 8:45 we gather. Pre-wedding jitters are ramping up big time, so I am hoping the heart-pumping aerobic climb will override the nuptial nerves and act as a calming agent.

I walk up to the park attendant to pay the parking fee. She looks at my five-dollar bill and tells me it is $4 per person, not per car. Whoops! We had e-mailed everyone the night before and told them the fee was $4 per car. No one has money. Pat, who lives across the street from the trailhead and is joining the pre-nuptial hike, goes up to the ranger and chats for a bit. She comes back, smiling, and tells me everything is taken care of. What a beautiful gesture. I start to tell her I'll write her a check to pay her back, but part-way through that litany I stop and look her in the eyes, and say, "Thank you."

We start up the Old Toll Road. I am sure Pat and I will be leading, having climbed over a hundred mountains in the past two years, but Kelly's sister Jess, the maid of honor (MOH), and her fiancé, Sean, who's just finished sapper training in the Army, are at the head of the pack. Along the way, we stop and take pictures of the flowers, the views, and the bride and groom. Everyone is climbing without much problem, although I hear side talk about not being able to walk tomorrow morning. We take a few rest stops, breathing with the bride. She wonders why hiking feels hard, since she has been kickboxing. I am so proud that she has started an exercise program. So while she is beating herself up because she thinks

she is not fit enough, I'm just loving Kelly. Before we know it we are above treeline. The wind picks up, an omen of the summit climate, and we keep climbing.

We arrive on the top to find the speedier hikers in our group nestled in a granite nook that's shielded from the whipping wind. We huddle in beside them and eat lunch. The MOH surprises everyone with wedding wands for the bridesmaids and a veil for the bride. All decked out with the matrimonial materials, we are ready to record the moment for posterity.

I don't know what the wind-chill is on top, but I've never seen so many goose bumps on so many arms and legs in my life! But the wedding party is bold. Off come the sweatshirts for the photos and we laugh at ourselves as the cam-era clicks away, Kelly's veil blowing in the wind.

I look at Kelly and Jess, sisters celebrating together on top of the mountain, arm in arm, and realize Don and I have reached the summit of raising children. We made it! Raising two girls, like climbing the mountain, had its ups and downs, places where the journey was easy and steep sections where we wondered if we were ever going to make it. Watching Kelly laugh with her friends on the summit, I wonder how is it possible she is all grown up and getting married. As Kelly shifts from daughter to wife, I am reminded of other life moments on this very peak that marked Kelly's journey from childhood to woman.

When Kelly was six years old and I was much heavier, I took her for her first hike up Monadnock. I was afraid she would have trouble getting to the summit because she was so young. I asked a ranger in the parking lot if he thought she could make it. He looked at her, then looked me over and said, "Lady, you're the one that's going to have the problem."

Kelly ran up the mountain, stopping once in a while to wait for me. As soon as I would reach her, panting and sweating and swearing under my breath, she'd head up the trail. At one point, when I finally caught up with her, sounding like I was ready to keel over, she looked at me with total disgust and said, "Mom, I can hear you breathing!"

Reaching the top was a triumphant moment for both of us. She and I bonded with each other that day on Monadnock, and the experience has remained with us. Standing on top, I experienced joy that I had never felt before—unexplainable, emotional, and powerful. We hiked back down and went out for ice cream to celebrate our achievement. I felt strong, happy, and close to Kelly. I was slightly aware that a door had opened inside of me, a door to so much more.

Four years later, Kelly had entered the my-friends-are-way-cooler-than-you stage. Don and I were in the that's-fine-with-us-because-you're-kind-of-snotty stage. We went back to the mountain with the Stones, family friends who have graced our lives since we were first married. Dave climbed with Don and I

while Kelly and Dave's daughter, Jenn, ran up the mountain together. On top, we felt the achievement in the endeavor, proud of ourselves and our children, taking in the gift of friendship. And again, I felt overwhelmed with something so intense inside of me on that mountaintop.

One summer day during Kelly's college years, we headed up the mountain a third time. On the trail Kelly confided in me that she had a hangover and felt terrible. I was angry. I didn't like that she had a hangover and I didn't want it to ruin our hike. Soon after the admission, Kelly started whining about how difficult the climb was.

"Oh, this is so hard! I don't know if I can make it," she complained.

"Holy moly, Kelly," I barked. "You are going to have to buck up if you want to make it to the top."

Kelly stopped on the trial and looked at me, hands on her hips. "Look, Mom, misery loves company. Just commiserate with me and things will go a lot better between us."

I thought about what she said. "Wowsers, this is hard," I responded, dragging my body up the next steep step. "I don't know if I am going to make it up either, Kell."

"Much better," Kelly said.

Mt. Monadnock has been a quiet, stoic witness to Kelly's journey through life. And the mountain has given us both gifts.

Each time I climbed Monadnock, I felt elated and filled with an excitement that was more than just reaching the top, I saw my true self: a strong passionate woman with huge potential. Of course, the words weren't there, just an incredible feeling that I couldn't name. For me, that glimpse has grown into a passion for climbing mountains and finding meaning in the process.

I don't know what Kelly's glimpses of triumph on Monadnock will turn into. Maybe when she is fifty she will be writing hike reports about her adventures in the mountains. I don't know. But I do know that if she listens inside, she will be led to the answers. I hope she sees the strong, passionate, exuberant, happy, beautiful woman she is. She is a shining light in our lives.

After celebrating matrimony on Monadnock with pictures and cheers, we start the hike down. I think about the upcoming wedding and feel no loss, only joy. We love Justin, and are thrilled to welcome him into the family, especially now that he has climbed Mt. Monadnock, a Sporborg rite of passage.

Kelly and Justin, I love you. I look forward to the family tradition of marking more milestones on Monadnock. My wish for you is that Monadnock's gifts will reveal themselves to you in exciting, life-changing ways, just as they have for me.

STATS

MOUNTAIN: MT. MONADNOCK (3,165)

NEAREST CITY: JAFFREY CENTER, N.H.

DATE: JULY 10, 2008

TIME: 4 HOURS AND 30 MINUTES

WEATHER: SUNNY, PASSING CLOUDS, LIGHT BREEZE, 70S, WINDY AND COLD ON TOP

MILES: 5 MILES

ELEVATION GAIN: 1,653 FEET

TRAILS: TOLL HOUSE ROAD, WHITE ARROW TRAIL

HOLY SHIT FACTOR: WICKED WINDY FOR A WEDDING

37. WALKING IN GRACE ON JAY PEAK AND BIG JAY

July 26, 2008, North Troy, Vermont

Like any other gift, the gift of grace can be yours only if you'll reach out and take it. Maybe being able to reach out and take it is a gift too.

Frederick Buechner

"You guys are walking in grace," the Reverend Alice Roberts says to Pat and me.

It strikes a chord and gives me goose bumps. I know something very special is happening to us. It feels like we are living more life than either of us ever thought possible a few years ago. We talk often about how lucky we feel being on this journey. Each time we talk about it, it is new, affirming, and thrilling.

How did we get here? How can we stay? Who do we thank?

We arrive at the Jay Peak trailhead at 9:30 and head up the mountain on the Long Trail. I am thrilled we are hiking a trail and not the Jay Peak ski slope, remembering the incredibly steep ski slopes at Sugarloaf in Maine. There is a marathon going on and people are running up Jay Peak today. I think I'll walk.

We reach the top at 11:30 and eat an early lunch before we start our bushwhack over to Big Jay. The views are hazy. Pat and I are in good spirits, talk-ing about the fact that we feel like we are riding a wave or, as Alice says, walking in grace. The simplest way to say it is our lives feel blessed. Really, that's it in a nutshell. Blessed.

From the top of Jay Peak, we head down and easily find the Long Trail off the ski slope. Now we focus on finding the left turn to the hiker-worn path that will lead us to Big Jay. We take a left on the first path we come to, but it ends abruptly. Continuing down the Long Trail, we see a snow fence. Pat checks out the path beyond the snow fence and is sure it is the path we are looking for. So under the fence we go and from there the trail is easy to follow. We run into a few more snow fences. Pat thinks their purpose is to prevent snowboarders from following the trail in winter.

The mud on the trail is boot-sucking hungry, and it is impossible to stay clean and dry. We are creative and work hard at avoiding the deepest mud holes, which requires lots of tree hugging, spruce grabbing, rock hopping, and log

jumping, all resulting in mud-splashing laughter. We encounter more mud and more snow fences, obstacles that could make one question the route. Most of the fences have been cut with wire cutters and the wooden slats pushed back so a person can get through. A few have not been cut but are loose enough that one of us can pull the fence up while the other gets on hands and knees and crawls under. It is clear to me someone does not want us there. But who? Why? Turning around does not even enter my mind and we continue. More fences and lots of ferocious mud and black water. By now I know that the longer I think about what route to take around the mud, the more I sink in where I am standing. So I just keep my feet moving

and, for the most part, I get out semi-dry. Once in a while one of us takes a wrong step, and the sucking sound of boot pulling out of mud cracks up both of us.

The hike is not particularly steep, but given the mud, fences, and blow-downs to work around or climb over, it is slow going. It takes about an hour to get to the summit of Big Jay. Immediately I see a glass jar attached to a tree trunk where the canister used to be. We take out the papers and read the two entries, including one from a guy last week wondering about the "asinine fences." We add our entry, take a picture at the wooded summit, and start back.

I wonder about the person who took the canister and with it the written

history of those reaching the summit—such a beautiful sharing gone. It is a shame. But I love the resilience of hikers. Nothing stops us. The canister is gone—well, here's a jar. Let's use this as a way to connect. Thank you to the person who put the jar in the canister's place, who reached out to the rest of us. Pat and I decide to get pads, pens, and jars and make sure we always have one set in our packs in case we encounter another bushwhack without a canister on the remaining hundred highest.

We decide to count the fences going back. I think there are ten. Pat thinks there are twelve. The mud, blowdowns, and fences don't slow us down. We know what to expect. Of course, we can't make it back without a little

mishap. I walk across a log, lose my balance, and in very slow motion, fall backward, backpack first, into a deep, wet, black mud hole. I am surprised how gently I land. Water immediately seeps in, everywhere. I am sprawled out in the mud and both Pat and I are laughing. Of course, Pat can't give me a hand without getting in herself. By the time I am out of the hole, we are both covered with mud and laughing hysterically.

More mud, more fences, more laughter, fence number ten, eleven, twelve, thirteen, fourteen. As we connect back with the Long Trail, I notice the back of a sign very high up in a tree. We both look at it. It says that Big Jay is closed for revegetation due to illegal cutting and erosion. Whoops. Missed that going in.

But the sign would not have stopped us. We are climbing the hundred highest and Big Jay is on the list, so we are on a mission. And all someone has to do is tell me I can't do something and I am pretty bound and determined to do it. Nothing much stops Pat and me. We are two determined women. When we are in our hearts, our decisions come from inside. Maybe that is why the fences didn't worry us, didn't make us pause and talk about turning around. We listened inside and knew Big Jay was waiting.

On the way back in the car, Pat and I continue our conversation about walking through this life on a path of grace.

"What do you think grace really is?" I ask.

"I think grace is a state of being, like the filter through which I can see and love," says Pat.

I pause, thinking. "So you think grace is an inside job."

Pat nods and I look out the window, letting that in.

"It's pretty awesome to think that is in me," I say in tears. Pat nods again.

Silence.

"I was doing my usual thing," I say, "looking for the answers outside of myself, putting someone or something else in charge. I always forget the answers are inside, and that it is only what is inside that matters."

Walking in grace, we're not in charge—our hearts are. Stuff just happens. And it turns out that the stuff that happens fits together and feels so right. Living inside out. And even when facing hard times, grace cushions the experience.

I've never felt this way before. But I am sure I am in it—grace, that is. And I am sure Pat is in it too—grace Pat style. I have given my heart control, my inner voice is calling the shots, and I'm along for the ride. And surprisingly, it's not hard, this ride I'm on. It's easy.

My life is running perfectly. When will the smooth ride end? When I start to doubt it or question it, or try to make sense of it or worry about it or change it. Then I fall off the grace wagon. And I get back on.

On a roll, in our hearts, riding the wave, walking in grace.

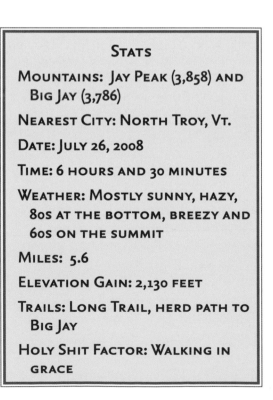

Stats

Mountains: Jay Peak (3,858) and Big Jay (3,786)

Nearest City: North Troy, Vt.

Date: July 26, 2008

Time: 6 hours and 30 minutes

Weather: Mostly sunny, hazy, 80s at the bottom, breezy and 60s on the summit

Miles: 5.6

Elevation Gain: 2,130 feet

Trails: Long Trail, herd path to Big Jay

Holy Shit Factor: Walking in grace

38. DOORKNOB JUNCTION—DORSET PEAK

August 30, 2008, South End, Vermont

> *The only journey is the one within.*
> Rainer Maria Rilke

We are at an intersection in the middle of the woods, halfway up the mountain, looking at a tree with doorknobs screwed onto both sides of its trunk. Yes, doorknobs attached to a tree. Now I know why they call it Doorknob Junction. Did the person who attached the doorknobs to the tree want to make us laugh? Or did he happen to have extra doorknobs in his backpack and want to lighten his load? Or was he saying something much deeper? Whimsy or soul-searching?

Doorknobs are everywhere in our lives, even in the places I least expect them, like out in the middle of the Vermont woods in the col between North and South Dorset. Each doorknob is an invitation to enter and see what is

behind the door and where the path beyond may lead. Once we choose, we walk through the doorway into a new realm unavailable to us just moments before. I love the mystery of not knowing what's behind a door, the thrill of adventure and new possibilities when I open a door to find out what it holds for me. The choice feels more serious when the doorknob I'm contemplating will change my life. I worry about whether I am making the right decision.

Actually, I don't think we can open the wrong door or make an erroneous decision or take a bad turn, whether in the woods hiking or in life. Every choice we make is the perfect choice for us in that moment. The door we open may lead us down a path filled with new experiences and excitement,

calamity, or confusion. But through every door we learn something new about ourselves—something that informs us about our next choice, and the next door we open. We can't go back, ever, not even by backing out the same way we came in. We can't un-know what we learn by opening a door, so even if we retreat, we have changed. We are changed by the choices we make and the experiences they bring.

Pat and I decide to go straight at Doorknob Junction and almost immediately find ourselves going downhill. That doesn't feel right since we are trying to get to the summit of Dorset Peak, so we turn around and head back to the junction to make a different choice. Next we turn right and head steeply up, a hopeful sign. When we arrive at the height of land, we find the remains of an old fire tower and a gas grill, but no summit canister. We figure this must be the lower of the two Dorset peaks. We head back down, now clear on what door to open next. We take the only path we have not yet taken. A sign on the doorknob tree points left to North Peak. Now we know North Peak is the higher peak, the one that counts. Up we go and in no time we spy the canister on Dorset summit, our eighty-third of the New England hundred highest. Each choice perfect. Each decision gives us information that narrows our choices, until we make the turn that brings us to the summit. But I am glad for the turns we took in our search. Of the 123 mountains we have successfully climbed, this is our first gas grill on a

summit! Plus, the knowledge gained in our search will enable us to write a trip report that will be helpful to those who follow behind us, because we are now clear on the way and can guide others. That's a gift of the journey. Once we know the way, we can offer guidance to those who come after.

The doorknobs on Dorset remind me of the many professional doors I have opened in my life and the resulting experiences that have helped me discover who I am, what drives me, what makes me feel whole. There were times I applied for jobs and did not get them, the doors remaining locked, a sure sign I was not supposed to enter. Other times I did not even see a door, but someone appeared holding one open for me, inviting me in, offering me a new opportu-

8/30/08
48948
64467
834 NEHH! Whoo hoo!
We are off to the
Grand Canyon to do a
rim-to-rim-to rim!
Love the canister as a way
to connect with all who come
after us! We are blessed!
Nancy + Pat
Whistler PZp/pa

nity. Other times I followed my instincts and wound up at an unknown doorway, ajar, beckoning me in, and I didn't think twice! Sometimes I chose among door number one, door number two and door number three. I worried and wrote pro-and-con lists and asked people for advice before turning a knob and walking through. Each choice perfect.

I worked in corporate America for twelve years as a communications manager for an insurance company, focusing mainly on helping employees and agents feel good about their contributions to the organization. There, I grew up professionally, finding my enthusiasm and exuberance for creative projects. I managed to work my way up the ladder to become an officer of the company. I even had my own parking space! I was sure money and prestige would make me happy, but once there, I found it was not what my heart wanted. During the same time I volunteered

for the Monadnock United Way for ten years and loved every minute of it (aha, a clue to what engages my heart), feeling I was doing something that mattered. From there, with great trepidation, I went out on my own and started Center Stage, a nonprofit organization. I created and directed community festivals in downtown Keene, including the Pumpkin Festival. I knew I was right where I was supposed to be and found my passion for thinking big on Keene's wide Main Street. I felt such joy and fulfillment announcing the 23,727 lit jack-o'-lanterns at the 2000 Pumpkin Festival, surrounded by family and volunteers and a celebrating community. I left after nine years, knowing in my heart I had done what I needed to do. I had discovered me in a very deep way. From there I consulted with a large healthcare network, driving from one clinic to the next, coordinating an internal communications program that reminded employees of the tremendous gift they give in caring for others. That grew into becoming a development director for a hospital and then for an arts and fitness organization. Those experiences helped me clarify my passion for meaning and the truth.

Now I am working for a dear friend, Ruth Sterling, helping her advertising agency communicate its strengths and gifts. Sterling Design & Communications' purpose is to serve the world by sharing its staff's talents. Not only are the people at Sterling brilliant and full of life, the clients are heroes, people working in organizations who care about those they serve, the products they make, and the communities they live in. I have also been subbing for a fitness instructor, teaching exercise classes for a wellness organization, and have found that I love the camaraderie and thrill of becoming strong and fit together. I have rediscovered the life-cheerleader in me.

Each turn, each new path provided me with opportunities to get clearer and clearer on me, my message, my life. Some jobs have felt great, some felt absolutely terrible, all were important. Each door I opened brought me closer to understanding who I am. Each job was a gift.

I wish I could be content with the journey as it unfolds, but I like to know where I'm going. When will I arrive at Doorknob Junction again in my life? Where is my next doorknob? Where will it lead?

For years I have been aware of an insatiable craving to matter in some important way, to make a huge difference on the planet. I don't know how. I don't even know if I am capable of such a thing. I just know it calls to me. Every day I feel this empty place inside of me that yearns to connect with thousands of people's hearts in such a magnificent way that they are changed by the experience. I probably sound delusional, but the truth is, the ache is there. And each time Pat and I arrive back at Door-knob Junction to try yet another trail, the symbolism of trying a different doorway to see where it leads catches in my throat. I feel that familiar hunger for more and the raw fear that I will

never figure it out, that I will never find the right door, and that I will leave the world still craving more, still wanting to make a difference in a bigger, wiser, deeper, greater, more meaningful way.

Doorknob Junction reassures me that there are doorknobs everywhere, that invitations to grow abound, and that life is full of opportunities to discover my purpose. I know I am on the right path. My fears keep me alert and alive. My yearning keeps me turning door-knobs, opening doors, and venturing out anew. My heart keeps me going in the right direction. And the journey brings me joy.

As we hike back down the mountain through Doorknob Junction, I turn and take one last look at the doorknobs on either side of that tree trunk. I smile and take a deep breath, knowing I am ever closer to finding who I am.

STATS

MOUNTAIN: DORSET PEAK (3,770)

NEAREST CITY: SOUTH END, VT.

DATE: AUGUST 30, 2008

TIME: 4 HOURS AND 30 MINUTES

WEATHER: CLOUDY, HUMID, 60S

MILES: 6.3

ELEVATION GAIN: 2,400 FEET

TRAILS: WOODS ROADS AND ATV TRAILS

HOLY SHIT FACTOR: TURNING THE KNOB, OPENING THE DOOR

39. A MOMENT TO LAST A LIFETIME ON SADDLEBACK

October 4, 2008, Oquossoc, Maine

> *You must be the change you want to see in the world.*
>
> Mahatma Gandhi

We are above treeline and have been for over three hours. There are 20 mph winds, 40 mph gusts, thirty-degree temperatures and a chill factor in the teens. Though it is only the beginning of October, the shrubs are covered with rime ice. Occasionally we glimpse fluorescent fall foliage in between the clouds that surround us, but for the most part we can't see any of the tremendous views we had hoped for. Pat and I are walking into the wind. My jaw is frozen and I slur my words when I speak. It's tough to be heard over the wind, so we're not talking much. My eyes are not focusing; I have to keep blinking to see. The wind whips my backpack straps into my face and pushes my fleece hat over my eyes. And yet, I have an incredible feeling of well-being inside of me. It's not pea-sized. It fills me.

I don't really know how to describe it because I've never felt it before. Never! How is that possible? I've lived fifty-four years and I have never felt this inner sense of well-being that seems to have coated my nerve endings, doused all the nasty voices in my head, kicked out all my fears, shoulds and can'ts, replaced my inner skeptic with a cheerleader and released a bounty of endorphins. The feeling is more even-keeled than excitement, greater than calm, more full than complete. It has erased all the hopes for a sunny warm day and left only contentment for what is. It has completely wiped out all my hiking insecurities and left only strength and self-assuredness. It's as if the inside of me has been emptied and all that remains is a surging life force that has no end, no limits, no separations, no concerns, nothing but potential and possibility and promise.

I want to live here forever. I want to hold on to this moment and never let it go. I want to feel this peace always. I want to super-glue myself to this place of wholeness and well-being . . . and I know I can't.

On the mountain I was in the experience. Now, sitting on my purple couch, I'm trying to figure it out so I can write about it. But the experience wasn't nouns and verbs and sentences. It required no thinking, only feeling. And now I am thinking, so I don't get it. Maybe it is not figure-out-able. But here's what I have so far.

All the inner voices that are normally yapping constantly were quiet. It's as if they up and quit their jobs prior to the hike and left me peaceful within. My critic, who continually barks at me, reminding me that I can't hike, I'm not strong enough, not brave enough, not good enough—she was nowhere to be found on Saddleback. My inner child, who is afraid of the cold weather and furious winds, either grew up or was taking a nap. And the parts of me that hold my anxiety and worry about being strong enough to get up and down mountains over four thousand feet high and along trails fourteen miles long carrying a pack, they had an attitude adjustment.

Perhaps the past two-and-a-half years of experience have had an effect on all my inner voices. Saddleback and the Horn are numbers sixty-four and sixty-five of the sixty-seven four thousand footers in New England—we have just two mountains left to complete the list. Our hikes have pushed me far beyond my comfort zone many times. Each experience pushed my leading edge out a bit more, and then a bit more, expanding my comfort zone one hike at a time. I am more comfortable in the elements than I was in 2006. The wind and the cold on Saddleback challenged me, but they didn't enter into me, they didn't change me, they didn't open up my raw

fear or past experiences. I stayed in me.

Along with growing in my comfort zone, I have also grown in the believing-in-myself department. Our hikes have brought me from the I-am-scared-to-death-that-I-can't-do-this place to I-hope-I-can-make-it to I-know-I-can-do-it. In the beginning, I questioned whether I was going to make it to the summit every time I stood at a trailhead. It took me a year and a half to think of myself as a hiker. Now I know I can do this.

So, this feeling of well-being is not a reaction to something outside of me—the cold, the steep, the wind, the mileage, the non views, although it is certainly as active, as equally alive as those things. The feeling comes from inside. The extreme conditions showed me how "in" I was to feel so peaceful with the weather raging around me. I wonder if my inner experience showed on my outside. I wonder if Pat could tell an amazing thing happened to me. I picture it as a light glowing from my heart out, intense and bright. If I looked like how I felt, I was shining.

If this experience happened to me, which it did, then it can happen to anyone.

So what really happened? Was it peace? Was it wholeness? Was it some kind of rite of passage? If I can figure out how I got to that amazing place, maybe I can get there again. Or I could write about how to make it happen and sell a million books. I could patent the formula if I could figure it out. Make big bucks if I could bottle it.

But it is even bigger than individual

experience, isn't it? Whatever is inside of us manifests outside of us. Peace within brings peace into the world. So if everyone could experience a "Saddleback moment" simultaneously, what would the world look like? Would we be fighting in Iraq? Would we be experiencing an economic crisis? Would the presidential election results be the same? Would corporations treat workers as they do today?

Something very special happened to me, in me, on Saddleback. I love knowing that life can feel like that. I love living life without my past traumas, my critic, my skeptic, or my fears. I love that I can let go of thinking and let myself just feel. Most of all, I love picturing the world as if we were all on top of Saddleback walking in wholeness and well-being. It starts with me.

STATS

MOUNTAINS: SADDLEBACK (4,120) AND HORN (4,023)

NEAREST CITY: OQUOSSOC, MAINE

DATE: OCTOBER 4, 2008

TIME: 10 HOURS

WEATHER: CLOUDY, TEMPERATURES IN THE LOW 30S, WIND 20 TO 30 MPH WITH GUSTS UP TO 40 MPH

MILES: 14.6

ELEVATION GAIN: 3,728 FEET

TRAIL: APPALACHIAN TRAIL

HOLY SHIT FACTOR: FILLED WITH WELL-BEING

40. BAGGING OUR SIXTY-SEVENTH WITH MICA AND PUMPKINS

October 25, 2008, Kingfield, Maine

> *If we all did the things we are capable of doing,*
> *we would literally astound ourselves.*
>
> Thomas Edison

It seems like a coincidence. Pat and I will bag our last two four thousand footers on the day of the Pumpkin Festival. The Pumpkin Festival in Keene, is one of the hardest, most meaningful, fulfilling, and beautiful things I have ever done in my life. Creating Pumpkin Festival was not unlike climbing mountains.

Pat and I are about to bag our last two peaks, accomplishing the goal we set for ourselves two and a half years ago. Climbing the sixty-seven four thousand footers in New England has also been one of the hardest, most joyous, rewarding, and healing experiences of my life.

Once I realize we will bag our last two peaks on Pumpkin Festival day, I know we need to mark the moment with pumpkins. I love the language of pumpkins at the festival—the faces, marriage proposals, special dates, hometowns, and political candidate endorsements, all carved in pumpkins. Each pumpkin speaks the heart of the carver. Pat and I carve "67 4,000 footers" into four pumpkins and Don brings them to the festival, signing them into the Guinness World Record log-in book. We are a part of the effort. We also carve a "6" in a tiny pumpkin and a "7" in another tiny pumpkin, glue mica pieces we have collected from all of our hikes onto their skins and pack them into Pat's backpack. We pin a sign on the back of each of our packs that says, "#67 today!" and off we go.

I have come so far! Signs on our backpacks announcing we are summiting our last peak? On our first hike up Whiteface we met a very nice group of people who asked us how many four thousand footers we had climbed. Pat announced proudly that Whiteface was our first. I was mortified and embarrassed that we were revealing to real hikers that we were know-nothing newbies! A year or so later, climbing Isolation, I realized that having people share their joy of bagging their forty-eighth four thousand footer brought joy to us also. By the time we hiked Mt. Jefferson, our New Hampshire forty-eighth, I was telling everyone. By the sixty-seventh, we are putting signs on our packs. I've learned through hiking how much joy there is in sharing the journey.

The Fire Warden's Trail heads up, then levels off, heads back up, levels off, then heads up steeply. I keep waiting for the really steep part, but it never arrives. Before we know it we are on the col between Avery Peak and West Peak.

I have come so far! For almost two years of hiking I carried more anxiety than gear. I worried that the mountain would be too steep and I would not be able to make it. Every hike I worried. I was afraid of the cold, the wind, the ice, the thunder, and the rain. I was petrified of the steep ledges with few hand or footholds, where the drop looked like it went down forever. I realized I knew nothing about hiking and my own inexperience kept me vulnerable and humble. Gradually my fears started to subside, my anxiety lessening as my time on the mountains increased. Finally, on Saddleback I experienced a feeling of wholeness and well-being and knew, beyond a doubt, that of course I could do this.

There are two young men on the col between the two Bigelow peaks when we arrive, and they spy the signs on our backpacks.

"All right!" one of the men says, clapping. "Sixty-seven—way to go!"

"That's great!" says his friend.

Pat and I beam as we share with these two fellows. It is great to have someone to celebrate with us. They take our picture on Avery Peak before Pat and I head down to begin the final ascent of our sixty-seventh mountain. It takes no time at all and before we know it, we reach the West Peak summit sign, together, smiling. We get out our pumpkins, light our tea lights, then set the camera timer and take a few pictures so we will always remember the momentous moment. We are all smiles, despite the wind and our cold feet.

I have come so far! Since May 6, 2006, Pat and I have reached the summits of a 133 mountains on eighty-three hikes walking over 750 miles with more than 225,000 feet of elevation gain. Me. Nancy Sporborg. A non-athletic fifty-four-year-old woman. Only three and a half years ago I met Pat and started walking a four-mile route between our work places, once a week. Only a few years before that I weighed eighty pounds more than I do now, and did not exercise. I am amazed at myself.

I have come so far! How did I do it? How did I climb these mountains? How did I even climb the first mountain? For that matter, how did I create the Pumpkin Festival?

I don't really know. Looking back on my life, each choice I made seems to make so much sense and fit perfectly, like puzzle pieces coming together. Yet going forward, I am never sure if I am

doing the right next thing. But here is what I do know. None of the things that have happened in my life came from me thinking through anything, weighing

any alternatives, listing pros and cons, or making thoughtful, thorough decisions. They all came through my heart. Feeling one moment at a time. And I took advantage of the moment when it arrived, the idea when it came, the opportunity when it knocked. I met Pat, we started walking, then walking hills,

then hiking. It has come to us and we have been open. I guess that is it. We have been open.

I see myself standing on the edge of possibility, heart to the sky, face to the sun, arms outstretched inviting the world in, a lit jack-o'-lantern by my feet and my pockets filled with mica, wondering what adventure will come next. Amazingly, they keep coming. This is riding the grace wave.

So what's next? That's the question everyone is asking. As far as hiking—there is always another mountain to climb. As far as my next life adventure—I don't know, but I am ready.

STATS

MOUNTAINS: THE BIGELOW RANGE—AVERY PEAK (4,088), WEST PEAK (4,145), SOUTH HORN (3,805)

NEAREST CITY: KINGFIELD, MAINE

DATE: OCTOBER 25, 2008

TIME: 9 HOURS AND 20 MINUTES

WEATHER: CLOUDY, TEMPERATURE IN THE LOW 30S, WIND 15 MPH, 8 INCHES OF SNOW NEAR THE SUMMITS

MILES: 12.3

ELEVATION GAIN: 3,583 FEET

TRAILS: FIRE WARDEN'S TRAIL, BIGELOW RANGE TRAIL, HORNS POND TRAIL

HOLY SHIT FACTOR: AMAZED THAT I'VE COME SO FAR

41. INSANITY ON VOSE SPUR

November 28, 2008, Bartlett, New Hampshire

> *Insanity: doing the same thing over and over again and expecting different results.*
>
> Albert Einstein

Insanity. That is our only excuse. Last weekend, with relatively little compass know-how and no real bushwhacking experience, Pat and I tried to climb Mendon Peak in Vermont. We got as far as the third cairn on the logging road, but once in the woods, blanketed in eight inches of new snow, it took us all of thirty seconds to figure out we were in deep trouble. We turned around and climbed Killington instead.

One week later and our plan is to

climb Vose Spur. We still have no compass expertise, although I know Pat has been reading a book and looking on the Internet for information. I, however, have done nothing. Pat's GPS is still in its original box. What are we thinking? We're not.

We climb up the Signal Ridge Trail to the Carrigain Notch Trail. We see the boulder that everyone talks about and know the bushwhack turn is coming up on the left. We feel about ten seconds of euphoria when we see the worn path. Thinking this is going to be much easier than last weekend's climb, I smile to myself. We lose the herd path no more than ten feet in. I look at Pat who is fingering a broken branch, a sign to her that others have passed this way. I am thinking we are in big trouble and start saying words to myself that are not acceptable in polite society. Pat takes a few more steps and pauses. Not a good sign. She has her compass around her neck and so may look, to any unsuspecting hiker, as if she knows what she is doing. But there are a few problems with what at first glance looks pretty darn impressive. The strap on the compass is too short; to actually see the compass, she has to take it off and hold it arm's length from her eyes. Pat stands wedged between two trees that are dripping raindrops all over her and her paper map. She holds the map level and twists the compass this way and that, talking to herself, a look of consternation on her face. Oh boy, here we go again. I quickly walk up to her wet perch to be of assistance and look at the compass and the map, as it I have some clue how to interpret what I am seeing. But then I realize I'm not fooling anyone. I have no idea what I am looking at. But, I think, maybe my presence will give Pat a brain boost and she will say, *Okay—this way.* Pat moves off in a direction and I follow. But I can tell she has no idea what she is doing either, so I get out our surveyor's tape and start tying neon orange tags to tree branches. Pat turns around and says to me, "Are you going to tie one here?" pointing to a branch next to her, clearly not happy. Yup, another clue this is going to be a very long afternoon. I start tying tape just about everywhere. Pat is worried we are going to run out of tape but doesn't say anything.

It is slow going because I'm tying tape every ten yards and Pat is fiddling with the compass. We both keep scanning the woods hoping we will stumble onto the path. When the rain picks up we put on rain gear and continue up the slope, trying to find the path of least resistance, having now given up all hope of finding a herd path.

Have I mentioned I hate bushwhacking?

Every tree branch is holding five times its weight in water, just waiting for me to walk by so it can drop its load on me. Oh, and how are you supposed to see where you are going and avoid being whacked in the face and eyes by every branch you pass? This clearly requires all kinds of new skills that I have not yet developed. I look up to get a bearing on where Pat is. I wipe my face off with my wet Gore-Tex sleeve, try to

dab at my runny nose, and spit a few pine needles out of my mouth. Pat fingers another broken branch like it is a clue to finding the Holy Grail. I don't know why I don't laugh out loud, but I don't (although I am laughing as I write this!). I look down at the ground and continue making my way up the slope, shaking my head and silently praying for the herd path.

We are soaked. My stringy hair is glued to my face—which is why my trail name is Slick. Pat's trail name is Curly and she looks a heck of a lot better than I do! I fight my way through the woods, verbally assaulting each tree as I pass, stopping often to tie tape onto a wet branch as it dumps its load of water down my back or onto my face or into my boots. Pat keeps looking up, as if she is going to see the mountaintop or the talus field that's our intermediate destination. Instead we see only gray clouds, mist, and rain all around us.

Pat turns around and looks at me. It's forty-five minutes and maybe two hundred yards into our bushwhack. "This is miserable," she says. "I say we turn around." She doesn't have to say it twice. We immediately do a 180 and begin following our surveyor's tape out. It takes me forever to untie the tape because I hurt my thumb in weight class and I tied the buggers too tight to boot.

I start breaking the branches instead of untying the tape. Get me out of here! We arrive back on the Carrigain Notch Trail, bummed and feeling stupid.

We both have energy left in our bodies—although our brains are pretty fried. So we decide to climb Carrigain, a neighboring mountain. Up we go, and in no time we are breathing heavily, sweating profusely, using our muscles, and letting our brains rest. We get to the ridge around 3 p.m. and turn around.

It's dark before we reach the river crossing that we bushwhacked around at the start of the hike. We meet a couple who tell us they lost the trail and think we are supposed to cross the river here. So we all cross—totally unsuccessfully. I end up just walking in the water, no longer caring since I am soaked anyway. We get across the river and . . . no trail. Again I start saying impolite words under my breath. We turn around and manage to get ourselves back across the water and finally locate the trail. Continuing down, we find the real river crossing and walk on across. We arrive back at the car soaking wet and very happy.

I decide I have to change my clothes. I am bare-bottomed, trying to get my underwear on, when a group of hikers comes into the parking lot, shining their headlamps my way. I'm laughing so hard I can't get dressed and I get all turned around in my underwear. I can hear Pat laughing from the other side of the car.

As Pat later wrote to me in an e-mail, "We salvaged yesterday in a really positive way. We are great when we can do that—wet and disappointed, we found a way to suck out the best that the mountains had to give us. And we found the best in ourselves."

We have twelve mountains left on the hundred highest list and we are committed to bagging them. But we'll never get them this way, that's for sure! So, according to Einstein, we better try something different. Like . . . maybe learning how to bushwhack?

STATS

MOUNTAINS: VOSE SPUR AND CARRIGAIN

NEAREST CITY: BARTLETT, N.H.

DATE: NOVEMBER 8, 2008

TIME: 9 HOURS

WEATHER: TEMPERATURE IN THE 50S, CLOUDY, GRAY, DRIZZLE, RAIN, CLOUDS, MIST

MILES: 13.5

ELEVATION GAIN: 3,406 FEET

TRAILS: CARRIGAIN NOTCH TRAIL, BUSHWHACK, CARRIGAIN TRAIL, SIGNAL RIDGE TRAIL

HOLY SHIT FACTOR: BUSHWACKING HELL

42. TWO DRIVEN WOMEN LOOKING FOR THEIR NEXT GOAL—MT. EQUINOX

November 29, 2008, Manchester, Vermont

> *When we are motivated by goals that have deep meaning, by dreams that need completion, by pure love that needs expressing, then we truly live life.*
>
> Greg Anderson

Oh no! Pat and I have temporarily run out of hiking goals! Does it matter? Do we really need them? Isn't there enough goal setting in the professional world without having to set goals in our personal lives?

On November 29, we climb Mt. Equinox, even though we've already climbed Equinox and checked it off the mountain list. We decide on this mountain located in Manchester, Vermont, one of the hundred highest in New England, because it is near a great breakfast place, has 2,800 feet of elevation gain in two miles, and is only an hour-and-a-half drive away.

We arrive at the trailhead and reminisce about our first hike up Equinox as we set out. This time, both Pat and I know what to expect—a steep and unrelenting climb from bottom to top. We are ready for it. It seems easier this time, shorter and less cold. We make it up and down the mountain in four hours and drive home.

When I walk into my house, I am hit with a moment of sadness when I realize I don't have a mountain to check off a list. I feel a heaviness that I have not felt before. I realize that completing our original goal of climbing the sixty-seven four thousand footers in New England is a beautiful blessing and an incredible loss. When we were bagging the sixty-seven peaks, each hike was unfamiliar. We never knew what was in store for us. That in itself is a gift. There is great mystery and anticipation entering into the unknown. What will it be like? Can we do it? Will it be really hard? The excitement of new adventure and the thrill of discovering what we are made of makes me feel incredibly, profoundly alive. By completing the list, we no longer have the dream or the excitement of the unknown to propel us forward. I feel empty, lost, and without purpose.

The essence of it is I live for meaning.

I found meaning in the big, challenging goal of hiking the sixty-seven four thousand footers in New England. And I want more.

Since hiking Equinox, I am tossing and turning in life, walking around half-hearted and disoriented, struggling to identify my next dream. What new big challenge can I find to fill me now? What will feed me for the next few years? What will keep me pushing, learning, growing, writing, and healing?

I realize as I write this that goals are not just goals. They are necessities, requirements for healthy living and essential to my happiness. They are dreams and hope and inspiration all mixed together into an essential daily vitamin for my soul. Having goals says that there is always an opportunity for more life—more challenge, more beauty, more fear, more learning, more joy, more healing, more love. I need them. I can't live my life fully without goals.

STATS

MOUNTAIN: MT. EQUINOX (3,848)

NEAREST CITY: MANCHESTER, VT.

DATE: NOVEMBER 29, 2008

TIME: 4 HOURS

WEATHER: MOSTLY CLOUDY, 40S

MILES: 5.8

ELEVATION GAIN: 2,880 FEET

TRAILS: BURR & BURTON TRAIL

HOLY SHIT FACTOR: EMPTY WITH-OUT A GOAL

We all have the power to give away love, to love other people. And if we do so, we change the kind of person we are, and we change the kind of world we live in.

Rabbi Harold Kushner

The winter hiking season of 2009 is short and incredibly intense. Then the worst fate: injury. Our challenge becomes to heal ourselves physically. As we mend, we discover, much to our surprise, that we are still on the grace wave, and have something important to do with our down time. Once back on the trails, we feel compelled to share our journey. We invite friends and family to join us hiking and receive the gift of seeing the mountains through their eyes, even while the beginning of the end is in the wind.

43. FLEXING MY COURAGE MUSCLE ON THE OSCEOLAS

January 2, 2009, Lincoln, New Hampshire

Every mile is two in winter.
George Herbert

Wearing snowshoes, Pat and I climb up an almost vertical slope on the Osceolas in the White Mountains. My hands grasp at any tree limb or rock I can find to help me pull myself up while I struggle to point my toes enough to get the front claws on my snowshoes to sink through the unconsolidated snow into the ice below so that I can gain eight inches up on the steep slope in front of me. My legs are screaming. I am thankful my snowshoes have Televators, metal bars that lift my heels a few inches off the snowshoes, easing the strain on my calves.

I feel a lightning bolt erupt in my chest and zap down into my gut as I look up to see that the trail continues up at this steep incline for as far as I can see. I start swearing. I glance down at my snowshoes and gather myself, taking a deep breath. I look up again and collapse into questioning my motives. *What am I thinking? Why am I doing this? Is this supposed to be fun?*

Another pause, another breath. I look down and take in the scene below me and a string of profanities rushes out under my breath. I am precariously perched on the side of a mountain with the trail slithering out behind me as if it is hanging limp from my snowshoes. It is a long way straight down. I glance at Pat, who is looking at me. She reassures me, tells me she is right there. In her reassurance I hear her confidence in me, which reminds me that I have climbed to the summit of many mountains, overcoming my fear of the cold and snow and ice. She knows I can do this. My friend is my mirror.

One thing I have learned in the mountains, though, is that having someone there with you, while comforting, doesn't mean he or she can do the work for you. In the end, it is me, and only me, who has to take the next step to get myself up the mountain. Pat can't do it for me. I have to do it under my own steam. In the end we do it alone.

I look up again, take a deep breath, and try to figure out my problem. I have the strength I need in my legs although I am certainly feeling the effort. But it is not my legs that are giving me pause. I seem to have lost strength in my courage muscle. It has weakened over the spring, summer, and fall hiking seasons from not being used. I have forgotten the difficulties of winter hiking . . . the cold, the hazardous footing, the frozen power bars, the frozen water, my cold wet body needing a change of clothes, and the fear that darts into my stomach when I realize how steep and icy the slope is and how easily I could slide uncontrollably down the trail if I misstep. I had forgotten the extra-added-ed oomph winter hiking requires.

I keep climbing. One foot in front of the other, one step at a time. As we trudge up, Pat reminds me, as she often does, "This is the good stuff!" I know she is right.

The steep section goes on forever! When we finally reach the ridge lead-

same thing. It is straight up and looks very far away.

Now that we are going down I become cold, but I don't want to change into dry clothes because I know I will be climbing soon and will start to sweat all over again. I'm hungry so Pat takes out one of my power bars. We almost break our teeth taking that first frozen bite and then we wash it down with water that's more ice than water, which produces an immediate piercing cold headache. I look up at where we are going, take another breath, flex my courage muscle to prime it, and take a step.

We arrive at the "chimney," literally a straight up section of trail. I remember this spot when we climbed it during our first summer hiking season. I was scared then and it was July! Now it is covered with ice and snow. We strap on crampons and start up. I just keep moving up and am okay until I hit a section of rock where there is no place for the crampon points to grab. That sends a jolt of lightning fear into my belly and I freeze for a moment. My courage muscle flexes. I lift my left foot and put it way up on the next rock ledge, lean my weight on it as best I can and take the next step up . . . and then the next. Once on top of the chimney, the trail is a series of short ups and downs to the summit of Mt. Osceola. We arrive at 12:20 p.m. and stay only long enough for a picture and boot tightening before heading back.

It is a long slog back to the summit of East Osceola. We are hungry and I am cold, but don't want to stop to change. I just want to keep moving. I am worried

ing to the summit of East Osceola, Pat and I high five, knowing, or at least hoping, that it will get easier from here. After a miniscule flat section, the terrain turns steep again and up we go. We reach the summit of East Osceola at 11 a.m. and almost immediately begin the steep descent toward Osceola Peak. After five minutes of hiking along an enclosed tree-lined trail, the sky suddenly becomes big and we see a view of Mt. Osceola. "Oh, my God!" I say. Pat is quiet—but I bet she is thinking the

about going down that steep section we hit on the way up East Osceola and I want to get that behind me. It turns out it is not as bad as I feared, thanks to crampons.

We arrive at the bottom of the steep section and I take a deep breath and let the relief flood through me. We are going to make it. Another deep breath—in and out. The last mile and a half feels like forever and my legs are tired. But my courage muscle got a great workout and is stronger for the experience.

As I walk the last mile I think about the questions I asked myself on the steep trail up East Osceola, struggling with my fear. The answers come.

What am I thinking? I am not. I am following my heart and my heart knows I can do this. My heart wants to do this. My hearts wants to show me what I am capable of, so that I will know what I am made of, so I will know who I am. So that one day I will stop questioning myself and rest in the knowledge that I am a strong, capable woman. These hikes don't make me stronger; they show me my strength. I am doing this because it is what I am supposed to be doing. I am hiking in the winter because every step up that steep slope in my crampons reminds me that I am alive.

Why am I doing this? Because I love a challenge. I love it and I need it. When Pat and I finished the New England sixty-seven four thousand footers in October, we were left bereft of goals and I felt completely lost. I couldn't find my enthusiasm. Luckily, winter kicked in and climbing New Hampshire's forty-eight four thousand footers in winter is the most daunting goal I have ever had the courage to commit to.

Having a challenge in front of me, in the form of goals or my Life List, keeps me alive and awake and focused and motivated and excited to be here on this planet, thrilled to have a chance to experience more and more and even more of life. My goals are my mirror, revealing who I am, reminding me what I can do, showing me I have all the courage I need.

Is this supposed to be fun? Years ago when I first started going to exercise classes, Pam, our instructor, used to say, "Now we're going to have some fun!" and then she would have us do some horrendous exercise that pushed us to our physical limits. Pam would be smiling at us, loving every moment of it, as we all struggled to get our bodies to respond and not give out before she reached the magic number of ten. And when it was over, Pam would look at us, eyes twinkling, and say, "That was great! Look how strong and fit you are!" And I would let that in. Pam taught me the "other" definition of fun: a challenge that will show you your beautiful self. It is fun to meet the challenge head on and realize I am a healthy, strong woman who can do anything she puts her mind to. There is joy in feeling the thrill of facing my fears and taking the next step up. Big joy.

To celebrate my fifty-fifth birthday I have dinner with two dear friends, Marty and Kate. I tell them about our Osceolas hike and share my fear of the cold and ice and snow and steep sections. They listen, they worry aloud, and they ask me why I am hiking in winter if it is so hard. They suggest I might want to dial it back a bit. They love me.

Then we talk about my new job as a fitness instructor, which starts in two weeks. Yikes! I confide in them that I am afraid I can't do it, that I won't be any good at it, that the people in the class will hate it. Tears fall. My friends are shocked and they immediately become my mirrors. They remind me of my journey losing eighty pounds, becoming fit, and changing my life. They remind me of my enthusiasm for cheering for others and my ability to motivate people. And they remind me that what I really want to do is inspire others on their own journeys to discover themselves. They remind me, just like winter hiking reminds me, of who I am.

Stats

Mountains: East Osceola (4,156) and Osceola (4,340)

Nearest City: Lincoln, N.H.

Date: January 2, 2009

Time: 7 hours

Weather: Cloudy, light snow, temperature in the 20s

Miles: 7.6

Elevation Gain: 3,100 feet

Trails: Greeley Pond Trail, Mt. Osceola Trail

Holy Shit Factor: Tough courage-muscle workout

44. I'M NOT READY TO GIVE UP ON THE TRIPYRAMIDS

January 10, 2009, Waterville Valley, New Hampshire

Never, never, never give up!
Winston Churchill

We head up the Pine Bend Brook Trail, which is very gentle to start. Having a relatively flat beginning to a hike gives us a chance to warm up by easing our bodies into the snowshoe shuffle. It also gives me a chance to warm up the old courage muscle as I adjust to the cold. I have a lot of anxiety about being cold that comes from a horrifying experience of running through the woods, freezing cold, as a child, and I carry that experience into the mountains with me in the winter. Each cold hike helps lessen the emotional charge.

A young man starts out about ten minutes ahead of us on the packed trail. After the first couple of miles, we hit a bend and find him coming toward us.

"There's too much snow up there. I had to turn around," he says.

We round the bend and immediately see what he's talking about. We are in a ravine. There is a wall of snow in front of us; the slope is very, very steep and there is no trail at all.

Pat is in front and she bravely pushes ahead, trying to gain enough purchase to move up the side of the mountain. Every time she puts her weight on top of the snow it collapses underneath her and she slides back down to where she started. I give it my best shot and end up lying face first in the snow below her. It is truly impossible to climb with snowshoes. There just isn't anything for the claws on the bottom of our snowshoes to grab onto other than loose powder.

The pivotal moment:

"This is crazy," I say.

"I'm not ready to give up yet," Pat replies.

I think about what she says. It's still morning. The sun is shining. If we turn around, what are we going to do with the day? We might as well give it a try. And, as I check in with myself, I am fine at this moment.

"Let's just get up there," Pat says, pointing to the top of the ravine wall.

It doesn't look that far. Pat's fire lights a blaze under my courage muscle and I am game.

We decide to try crampons because clearly snowshoes will not work. So we take off our snowshoes, put them on our packs, pull out our crampons and put them on—not an easy thing to do in freezing cold and deep snow on an incline.

We give it another try. Despite how deep the snow is, the crampons allow us to grab on to the ice below and we inch our way up the ravine. We take turns leading and before we know it, we are on top of the ravine and yes, we keep going. I'm clear we can do this.

We arrive at a clearing. There is a blaze on a tree, but it is not evident which way the trail goes from here. We head off in different directions, trying to find the next yellow blaze. I have no luck. I wind up in an open area with beautiful views and very deep snow but no blazes. I call for Pat, who is far above me. She hasn't found any blazes either.

Pivotal moment number two:

We keep looking. I join Pat up on a ridge, which we decide looks the most like a trail even though there are no markings. So we keep going. After getting up that impossible ravine there is no way we are going to turn around just because we can't find a blaze. No way, no how. We eventually find the next blaze, then get lost two more times. Each time we fan out and keep searching until one of us locates the next trail marker. It takes extra time, but by now we are two determined women. Nothing is going to stop us from bagging these peaks.

While climbing an incredibly steep section up to the top of North Tripyramid, I hear someone behind me. I'm embarrassed because I am grunting and groaning, slipping and losing my footing almost every step, the incline is so steep and the snow so deep. Luckily, this section of the trail is lined with trees and the spruce grab, pulling myself up with the help of a spruce branch, comes in handy.

A man below me says, "Gee, I hope we are almost there."

I turn around, grateful to stop trying so hard for just a moment. I take a deep breath as I speak to him. "I hope so, too," I say, but I don't put much stock in what I am saying. At this point, I know the summit will come when it comes and I might as well just keep going because I am not turning around now.

The man tells me he is hiking with two other people and that they are pretty spread out on the trail. Pat and I continue up, breaking trail, and that is the last we see of him.

We finally reach the top of North Tripyramid at 2 p.m., and we still have another summit to bag before we head back.

"It's late. What do you think?" Pat asks.

"I don't really want to be going down that steep section in the dark," I say.

"Well, it'll be dark by 4:30. If we keep going we will have to go down in the dark," Pat says.

We look at each other.

Pivotal moment number three:

I turn and start walking toward Middle Tripyramid. I just can't see turning around now and bagging only one of the peaks after this much work. We have headlamps and each other and I know we will be fine.

We make it to Middle Tripyramid, snap some pictures, and head back almost immediately, eating our semi-frozen sandwiches as we hike. We're back on North Tripyramid by 3:30 and now all we have to do is get down this monster in one piece!

We are tired and the trail is steep, so we slide down on our butts. There is so much snow that the sliding is pretty slow and safe. And it's a heck of a lot easier than the horrendous slog up the mountain. I whoop and laugh because it is impossible for me not to make joyful noises sliding down.

We get to the car under headlamp power at 6:45, incredibly proud of ourselves.

When Pat was first attempting to climb the ravine and I said, "This is crazy," I heard what I said, believed myself, and did an emotional 180-degree turn. In my mind, I was already heading back out to the car. A voice in my head said, *if that guy can't do it, then we can't do it.* And when I saw Pat sliding back, unable to move up the wall of white powder in her snowshoes, the voice in my head said, *see, told ya!* But you know what? That voice was not me.

That voice is my critic, who never believes in me and always has something negative to say about everything. Most people have one. It's the voice that says, you're stupid or fat or you will never succeed, or you're weak or ugly or useless or incapable or an idiot or you're doing it wrong. That is the voice I'm talking about. The good news is that your critic is always wrong. I've proven my critic wrong on every hike, on every trip to the Grand Canyon, and with everything I have ever accomplished. My critic told me I couldn't do it. What does she know? Nothing.

Yet, every time I hear her voice, I struggle with her. Why do I even listen? I have all the evidence I need to prove she is wrong.

"I'm not ready to give up," Pat says.

Give up. That's what my critic wanted me to do. But I do not give up. That is not me. When have I ever given up in my life? And when have I ever done what my critic told me to do? Not when I was trying to run the first Pumpkin Festival and was told by the Fire Department that there was not a chance that I was going to put even one lit jack-o'-lantern in downtown Keene. My critic said it was impossible, that I had been told no by the officials, and that I should just forget it. But I didn't do that. I called the city manager and asked him for advice. He suggested I ask the city council to reverse the Fire Department's decision. So I did. I went to a council meeting and pled my case with the Fire Department guys sitting in the back row. And I won.

I didn't give up when I had eighty pounds to lose and was so ashamed of myself that I couldn't look in the mirror without crying. I didn't listen to my critic, who was going wild telling me how gross, foul, and disgusting I was; that I couldn't stay on a diet, that I had tried before and always failed. My critic was brutal and I didn't listen. And I lost the weight and have kept if off.

I didn't give up when I left my corporate job and started my own communications consulting business with no existing clients and a new mortgage. My critic was appalled I would do such a thing, putting my family in jeopardy. She told me life was going to be hard now because I had given up good benefits and a cushy job for a fight to make a dollar. And, oh by the way, what was I thinking? I had no customers and no talent! But I made Sporborg Communications a success.

Pat's words—*I'm not ready to give up*—kicked the critic out of my space, making room for me. I was back in the hike. When I took the first step up wearing crampons, I knew I could make it, I knew I had it in me, I knew I was back in me.

As I get ready to start teaching fitness classes for the first time in my life, this hike touches my heart. My critic is loud and keeps tapping me on my shoulder, saying *Hey! What do you think you are doing?* Just like she did when I was running the Pumpkin Festival, losing weight, leaving corporate America, and countless other times. But a new chapter in my life is about to start, and my critic can't stop it from happening. I can choose to listen to her and have her chip away at my confidence, or I can kick her out and look forward to my first class with joy and anticipation.

Pivotal moment number four:

That's it! I kick my critic out. She's out sulking in a snow bank. And me? I'm packing my gym bag, practicing aerobics, and selecting the music.

Getting fit has enabled me to reach mountaintops. If I can inspire others to discover their ability to reach their own mountaintops, there can be no greater joy! I know I can do this.

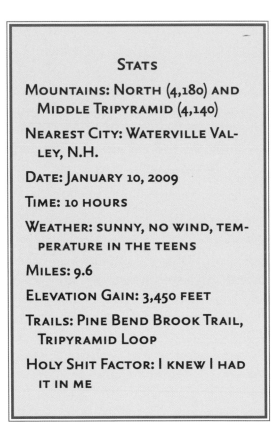

STATS

MOUNTAINS: NORTH (4,180) AND MIDDLE TRIPYRAMID (4,140)

NEAREST CITY: WATERVILLE VALLEY, N.H.

DATE: JANUARY 10, 2009

TIME: 10 HOURS

WEATHER: SUNNY, NO WIND, TEMPERATURE IN THE TEENS

MILES: 9.6

ELEVATION GAIN: 3,450 FEET

TRAILS: PINE BEND BROOK TRAIL, TRIPYRAMID LOOP

HOLY SHIT FACTOR: I KNEW I HAD IT IN ME

45. COMING HOME ON LAFAYETTE AND LINCOLN

May 9, 2009, Franconia, New Hampshire

I long, as does every human being, to be at home wherever I find myself.

Maya Angelou

Pat and I have not hiked since January 10. We had hoped to peak-bag through the winter, checking off the summits on the list of forty-eight New Hampshire four thousand footers, but that was not to be. Pat in-

jured her Achilles tendon and I pulled a calf muscle and that was that.

Of course, as the grace wave continues to take us on a ride of a lifetime, there is a greater good hidden in our injuries. We put our down time to good use, pulling together a presentation on hiking the sixty-seven four thousand footers in New England, and a Challenge Program geared to helping others discover their own inner strength and courage by reaching a mountain summit. The program is up and running and we are giving free hiking presentations every chance we get. It feels like we have come full circle. We hike the mountains and find our hearts. We share our joy with the world through our presentation and the Challenge Program. The feedback has been overwhelming. The hard part for me is to stop, breathe, and soften enough to actually let the praise, and the love, into my heart and feel it.

Eventually, Pat and I heal enough to begin talking about when we might get back on the trail. May 9 is the date. Nothing is going to stop us.

I remember coming home for Thanksgiving after starting my freshman year at Marietta College in Ohio. My heart beat with excitement as we drove up Hurricane Road in Keene. I remember being surprised and comforted that the house looked the same—same moss on the brick patio, same broken window on the porch. The dogs remembered me. The kitchen greeted me with its familiar smell; everything was in its place, the cluttered lazy Susan filled with notes, the salt and pepper shakers sitting in the middle of the kitchen table, the six chairs askew around the table.

I remember running up to my bedroom and walking into my own special space—my yellowed bedspread, pink flowered curtains, light from four windows filling the small room. I was home and it felt so good to be surrounded by the familiar and the comfortable. I had been away for so long I was afraid it would all be different, that it would be somehow changed, and I would no longer fit in. I was relieved to find that it was just as I had left it. It was good to be home.

Pat picks me up at 5 a.m. and we pull out of the driveway, leaving Dejah at home. Before she and my daughter, Jess, moved to Texas last year, Dejah climbed twenty-five four thousand footers with Pat and me. Now Jess and Dejah are living with us again while Jess's fiancé, Sean, serves in Iraq. So Pat and I have our trail dog back! Maybe she can get her forty-eight patch. Yes, dogs can get patches too for climbing the forty-eight four thousand footers in New Hampshire. Dejah has twenty-three mountains to go and we have about a year before Sean comes back to the United States and Jess and Dejah leave us again. That becomes our new goal: get Dejah her patch. It feels great to have a purpose that keeps us hiking! But Dejah gained some weight in Texas and I am getting her back into hiking shape.

Pat and I have been half kidding each other, wondering if we can still climb a four thousand footer after taking off three-and-a-half months, due to injury. But I know we can. It will be good to stand on the summit, though, so that

even the tiny little part of me that doubts can be reassured that we still have the right stuff.

We head up the Old Bridle Path and I take a deep breath. What a thrill to be back in the woods again: back in the black flies; the bright green of spring; the dark soil, dead leaves, and boulders beneath my feet; the warm smell of nature. Ah, I am surrounded by the comfort of the trail, back in the beauty of nature. It feels like I have never left, except for the excitement I feel inside at being back. Not only are the woods the same, but Pat and I are the same. We start taking pictures almost immediately of the trillium, the rushing water in the brook, wooden steps in the ledges, and the ladder built for giants. I love these mountains. I love reaching the summit under my own power, walking along the most beautiful trails in the world, encountering the most powerful weather and the kindest people anywhere. We are home, Pat and I. Finally. It feels great.

After the first mile or so, we come upon a man and woman taking a rest. We say good morning as we pass them. They follow behind us, and the man tells us that the White Mountain National Forest contains the largest alpine area east of the Rockies and south of northern Quebec. He explains that the area on Lafayette and Lincoln is home to many rare, threatened, or endangered species. He shares the history of Guy Waterman, who loved the alpine zone and put small boulders and large rocks along the sides of the trail above timberline to keep hikers off the alpine vegetation.

By this time, Pat and I are intrigued and listening intently. Neil Andersen introduces himself and explains that he is a volunteer steward of the alpine zone and that now, by virtue of having passed his knowledge onto us, we

are ambassadors for the alpine zone, responsible for caring for the fragile areas on the mountains and for passing on the knowledge. I am touched by the gentle nature of our interaction with Neil. Rather than hiring rangers to guard the precious alpine zone, the White Mountain National Forest and

responsibility, for caring for our fragile hiking environment.

We leave Neil and continue up the Old Bridle Path. Mayflowers line the sides of the trail—Trailing Arbutus, my favorite flower. Every year since I was a young girl I have walked to a small patch of flowers in the woods and cut some for my neighbor, my mother, and, if there was enough, for a little vase to put in my bedroom. For such a small, unassuming flower that's more leaves than petals, it has a big, bold, sweet scent that is truly exquisite. This year I was busy and never made it to the patch. But the world takes care of me. Here is my yearly mayflower moment on the Old Bridle Path. I bend down to take some close-up pictures and to smell the flowers. I am on-top-of-the-world giddy and we are not even close to the summit yet.

Then we hit the monorail. I knew it was coming. We had read hike reports that said that snow still graced the trails above three thousand feet. The monorail is like walking on a soft balance beam. But the Chinese gymnasts have nothing on us. Pat and I negotiate the snow with grace. We reach the Greenleaf Hut at 10:48 and have a snack before continuing on.

We arrive on the summit of Lafayette at 12:08, all smiles. It is cold and windy. I put on my hat and we find a place out of the wind for lunch. There are lots of people and dogs on top. Even if we don't speak, we smile, bonded together by a love and appreciation for all that surrounds us.

the AMC have chosen a kinder, gentler way. In the belief that knowledge breeds ownership and pride, volunteers are spreading the word, and the

I check in with Pat, who has not entirely healed and is still having issues with her ankle and groin. She chooses to continue on, so we head off to Lincoln and Little Haystack. It's cloudy and the sky is dark, but nothing can take away from the beauty of that ridge. I remember the first time we climbed Lincoln and Lafayette. It was our second hike. I had never seen anything like that ridge and was in awe of anything so magnificent.

We bag Lincoln at 1:45 and quicken our steps as the skies darken. We don't want to be caught in thunder and lightning above treeline. Before we know it we are back in the woods. The Falling Waters Trail has lots more snow than the Old Bridle Path and we are walking the dirty white balance beam for what feels like forever. There's lots of water running over the falls and the water crossings are tricky, but we manage to stay relatively dry. We arrive back at the parking lot at 5:15, take off our boots, and get in the car. Pat opens her Diet Pepsi, I pop my Snapple, and it starts to rain.

Here is what I know. I know that I am extremely lucky to have places in my life where I am at home, where I can let go of all that I am carrying and just be me, fully and completely. Places where everything is familiar and comfortable, where I can be loved and love myself more easily. Places that I hold in my heart and miss when I am not there. At home, with my husband Don, is that place for me.

And now I know that the mountains, with Pat, have become my home as well. From the trailheads to the summits, the mountains remind me of how incredibly lucky I am to be alive. Hiking brings me into the moment. I am blessed by every turn in the trail and by the perspective I gain when I look out into the vast expanses of blues and greens. The mountains bring out more of me. And each time more of me arrives, it is here to stay and I come back more whole, more completely me. I am coming home to me.

STATS

MOUNTAINS: LAFAYETTE (5,260) AND LINCOLN (5,089)

NEAREST CITY: FRANCONIA, N.H.

DATE: MAY 9, 2009

TIME: 9 HOURS

WEATHER: TEMPERATURE IN THE 60S, CLOUDY, WINDY AND COLD ON TOP, PRETTY DARK AND THREATENING WITH SUNNY BREAKS COMING DOWN THE RIDGE, WARMER AS WE DESCEND

MILES: 8.9

ELEVATION GAIN: 3,832 FEET

TRAILS: OLD BRIDLE PATH, GREENLEAF TRAIL, FRANCONIA RIDGE TRAIL, FALLING WATERS TRAIL

HOLY SHIT FACTOR: BACK-HOME-IN-THE-MOUNTAINS HIGH

46. EXPERIENCING LINCOLN & LAFAYETTE FOR THE FIRST TIME . . . AGAIN

August 15, 2009, Franconia, New Hampshire

I don't care how poor a man is; if he has family, he's rich.
Colonel Potter, **"Identity Crisis," M*A*S*H**

Today is different. Today I am giving myself a special gift— Sam.

Sam is my nephew and Pat and I are bringing him up his first mountains. I do not know Sam well, but the fact that he is in my life at all is a blessing.

Since finding my natural mother, Marge, I have been playing catch- up, getting to know my birth family—Marge, my sisters, Martha and Anne, and Anne's sons, Ben and Sam. Through years of getting together occasionally, we are now familiar and comfortable with one another, a family linked by the heart as well as by blood.

Sam is the first person in my birth family to ask if he can climb a four thousand footer with me. I know he is a runner and is training in hopes of making his college cross country team. I say, sure!

We meet at the Falling Waters trailhead, all of us arriving early. Sam is wearing running shoes, with a spare pair in his pack in case these get wet at the water crossing. He's wearing a book pack that has no belt for his waist or chest. I ask him how much water he has and his answer sounds appropriate. I make a note to myself to keep an eye on him, make sure his pack is not hurting him, that his running sneakers are holding up, that he has enough to drink. We all apply bug dope before heading up. I forget about sunscreen. The dogs, Pinta, Pat's housemate's dog, and Dejah, are both clearly excited about getting out of the car and bagging a peak.

Together we head up the trail. Sam says, "Oh, wow," when he sees the waterfalls and I think to myself, *If you think this is cool, wait until you see the Franconia Ridge!* We find ourselves in a line of hikers jockeying for position on the trail. That takes a while to shake out, but eventually we find our place and pant up the mountain chatting with fellow hikers.

I am not sure how Sam feels about climbing with two "old ladies" he does not know well. A handsome nineteen-year-old with a beautiful smile and bright eyes, he is about to start his sophomore year at SUNY Buffalo. He looks strong, happy, and sure-footed, and engages in conversation with us all the way up. He is patient with our pace.

I wonder if he wants to run up ahead, but he doesn't; he stays with us. Somewhere in the conversation about Sam's training runs, I realize he runs two miles in the length of time it takes Pat and me to run one. That keeps me humble. I find myself wondering if this hike will be a challenge for him at all. I know I am sweating and sucking wind, but I can't tell if he is. He's in the lead much of the time, glancing back to make sure we are behind him. As the trees get shorter and there is more and more room above our heads, our excitement builds. And then we are there—on the summit of Little Haystack. The Franconia Ridge stretches out in front of us. Sam has his camera out and is taking pictures. The sun lights up the trail all the way to Lincoln, in the distance. It takes my breath away. For me, there is nothing as beautiful as the Franconia Ridge on a sunny day.

We take more photographs and snack on trail mix, then start the ridge walk. I am just in love. Really, I don't know how to show it or contain it up here. I am surrounded by the most incredible beauty I have ever seen. The trail ribbons all the way to Mt. Lincoln, through stunning blues and greens. The clouds dance around the mountain summits. I am acutely aware that this is a blessing. I don't know what to say, or how to breathe, or what to do with myself. I am lost in the magnificence that surrounds me. I am sure I look composed, although I keep saying, "God, I just love it up here!" But inside I am emotional and unsteady, as if the

beauty is too much to absorb. This hike feeds me. It is the expanse that I love—that you can see the trail along the ridge all the way to the next peak, in front of you and behind you. I remember loving that expanse on our Presidential traverse, standing on top of Monroe and seeing the trail wind its way to Eisenhower. Such incredible grandeur. I feel a need to stop and honor it somehow, to breathe it in. Each step changes the perspective as we get closer and closer to the next summit, until we reach it and I get to turn around and see the trail wind down and back from where we came. I am so lucky to be here.

Sam takes lots of pictures while I ooh and ah, and I am hoping that he is ooh-ing and ahing too, on the inside. Not many people get to experience what Sam and Pat and I are experiencing at this moment. (Although I bet there are two hundred people on the ridge today.) I wonder what the world would be like if everyone could be here. I wonder if the beauty would melt away our anger and differences and leave us all feeling connected and grateful. That's how I feel. It is impossible for me to be angry or to hate when I am surrounded by this much beauty.

On the summit of Lincoln, we sit in the sun on a warm flat rock to enjoy our lunch. Pat is struggling, having difficulty breathing and experiencing tired legs due to exercise-induced asthma.

I wish she felt better, but that worry doesn't add to my experience or hers, so I try to let it go. Taking off my boots and socks, I wiggle my toes—one of the most exhilarating moments in hiking. I lean back and let the sun hit my face. In the distance I see Owl's Head and the Bonds, and more mountains behind them, and still more behind them. I am aware that I don't have the words to express what I am seeing or feeling in my heart. All I can do is hold the moment, let the experience soak into my core. This is the grace wave.

After a half hour or so, I reluctantly put my socks and boots back on and we take summit photos of the dogs. Then we head off to Lafayette and I am once

again in the moment, loving the ridge and its ability to drop me right into my heart. I shake my head as I walk, as wordless emotion floods my eyes with tears. It is a bit hazy today, so the mountains fade into the distance more quickly. But I can still see that they go on forever. There are clouds on the top of Lafayette, but I am sure they are going to clear by the time we get to the summit. They do. The top is crowded with chatting people and all I can do is breathe, barely containing my grateful heart. The experience is intense for me. It catches in my breath when I look out. It is so beautiful it hurts. And I get to see it with Sam.

A kind fellow hiker takes our picture on the summit of Mt. Lafayette. I glance at Sam. What a gift to be able to give him his first four thousand–footer experience on Lincoln and Lafayette! But there's more. This hike gives Sam an opportunity to see if hiking is in his heart, as it is in Pat's and mine. This hike opens the door to a world of mountain summits that are waiting for him to explore. It invites new possibilities. And it gives a new life perspective, from five thousand feet up, looking down.

We head down the Old Bridle Path, joining a visible line of people. Pat and I are not the fastest hikers, so lots of people pass us. Sam is very patient. At the Greenleaf Hut, we have snacks, take some photos, and then continue down. About a mile from the bottom, Sam asks to take a break, saying he is out of water. We give him more—we have plenty—and he shares his goldfish crackers with us. This is really the first time that Sam has mentioned being tired, and I am secretly glad that he is feeling something!

Revived by our break, we head down the rest of the way. Back at the trailhead, we take off our boots, sit on the curb, and breathe a sigh of relief. We take turns freezing our feet in the icy water at the bottom of the cooler that's been keeping our post-hike drinks cold. Sam's face is red from the sun and the back of his neck is covered with bug bites. They will help him hold the memory of the day a bit longer.

We hug Sam and say goodbye. Sam sits down behind the wheel of his car, lets his head fall back on the seat, closes his eyes, and lets out an audible groan. I laugh. He is tired! Woo hoo!

I want my birth family to know me, to see my heart. I let Sam see the whole, real me today. Me filled with the beauty of the mountains, me hiking strong and confident on the trail, me loving each moment on the ridge. It is as if I am saying, *This is what I love. This is who I am.* It is a gift to be seen.

And it is an honor to be with Sam on his first hike in the Whites. The experience changes me. Seeing Sam sweating, breathing deeply, smiling, saying "Oh wow" when he sees the waterfalls and gets his first glimpse of the mountain summits and the trail winding along the ridge in sunlight is like getting to experience Lincoln and Lafayette again for the first time. What a blessing.

Thank you, Sam. It was stupendous.

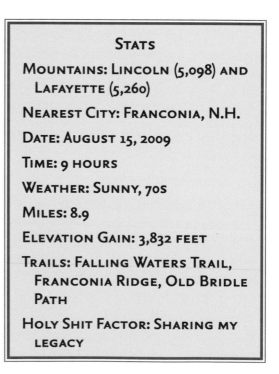

STATS

MOUNTAINS: LINCOLN (5,098) AND LAFAYETTE (5,260)

NEAREST CITY: FRANCONIA, N.H.

DATE: AUGUST 15, 2009

TIME: 9 HOURS

WEATHER: SUNNY, 70S

MILES: 8.9

ELEVATION GAIN: 3,832 FEET

TRAILS: FALLING WATERS TRAIL, FRANCONIA RIDGE, OLD BRIDLE PATH

HOLY SHIT FACTOR: SHARING MY LEGACY

47. DOING OUR BEST ON WAUMBEK

August 22, 2009, Jefferson, New Hampshire

Do the best that you can in the place where you are, and be kind.

Scott Nearing

Friday night, Pat and I make the decision to cancel our Challenge Team hike. It is an excruciating process. It feels like we have to dig really deep for this one. We've been working with a team of seven people for four months, getting them in shape physically and mentally to climb their first four thousand footer. Everyone is ready and very excited. Tomorrow is supposed to be the day. But the weather forecast calls for 80 percent chance of showers with a possibility of an inch of rain and thunderstorms. That means we will have to go with our plan B hike—Tom, Field and Willey—so that we are not above treeline in a thunder storm. It also means a really wet hike, with slick footing and no views. We are not comfortable taking the Challenge Team up a four thousand footer under those circumstances. So we cancel and reschedule the Challenge Hike.

I go to bed exhausted and toss and turn all night, wondering if we made the right decision.

Saturday morning, Pat and I head up to the White Mountains to pick up the cookies we ordered for the summit celebration that is no longer going to take place today. Hopefully we can freeze them. Our conversation on the drive up consists of replaying the agony of last night's decision, one neither of us wanted to make. As we drive, I pray that the skies open up and pour all day long. Bring on the thunder and lightning. Normally, I pray for sun, but today, if it rains and storms, I will feel better knowing we made the right decision. Rain spits at us all the way up to Twin Mountain; the sky's cloudy and gray. But it's not pouring.

At the Mountain Bean we pick up the cookies, which are decorated like four thousand foot mountains. We continue driving north to hike Waumbek. Dejah needs it for her forty-eight and it is a short hike, below treeline, so we know that even if it pours, we will be fine.

We arrive at the Waumbek trailhead and head up the mountain, replaying our decision and processing it. I keep asking Pat, rhetorically, "Where is the rain?" Every step I take that is not in the rain, the more anxious I get. We should have gone on the Challenge Team hike. *We could have hiked today*, I say to myself. It sprinkles on and off; we put on our raincoats then get hot and take them off. The rain is teasing us.

I feel tormented. Sweating and pant-

ing, I ask myself, *Why does this decision feel so hard?* What comes in reply is my childlike hope for the Challenge Team to have a perfect day on top of Mt. Eisenhower. Over the past four months I have come to know members of the team and really like and care for each of them. I want them to see the Presidential mountains in all their glory. I want them to reach the top of Eisenhower giddy with excitement and proud of themselves. I want them to be thrilled by the incredible 360-degree views of the Presidentials as they stand on the summit of Eisenhower. I want this four thousand footer hike to be one they will remember for the rest of their lives. One where the views will touch them in deep places. One where their own inner beauty comes shining through. I want it all—for them.

We are almost at the summit of Waumbek when we meet four hikers coming down. In talking with them we find out that at least one has climbed the sixty-seven four thousand footers in New England in every month of the year. Holy shit! We have a nice conversation and one of them mentions that the day turned out better than predicted. I smile and wish them happy trails as we part. Yup, the weather is definitely better than predicted, and I am pissed about it. Now that my critic seems to be winning the battle for my heart, I continue on down the "I'm no good" path, thinking I can barely call myself a hiker next to these people who have climbed over seven hundred mountains.

We reach the summit, take pictures, eat our lunches, and then head down. I am quiet. It's not raining, there is no thunder or lightning, and I now know we could have completed the Challenge Hike to Eisenhower. I am feeling guilty about it. We made the wrong decision.

My head is busy berating me and I am feeling lost in yuck of my own making.

Back in the car, we listen to a message on Pat's cell phone. It is a member of the Challenge Team saying the weather in Keene is beautiful and wondering how the weather is in the Whites. My head falls back on the seat; I close my eyes and utter an angry "blah." I feel terrible.

Then something happens. I pause for a moment and in that empty space my heart's rage for me kicks in. Finally!

We made the best decision we could with the information we had. That is all there is to it. We did the best we could. There is no need for blame or guilt. Why am I doing this to myself? If I had it to do over again, would I make the same decision? Yes. Was it the wrong decision, given the weather turned out to be better than expected? No. We made the best decision we could with the information we had. Period. We have nothing to feel bad about. It is what it is. This is life. You do the best you can and then you let it go and whatever happens, happens, and you learn, adjust and go on. There is no looking back. No shoulda, coulda, wouldas. No second-guessing. When I am doing the best I can, how can I ever be wrong?

I love that question. When I am doing the best I can, how can I ever be wrong? I love that it moves me away from simple right and wrong and into a deeper place where I can learn from each decision I make, with no guilt or blame. Each decision, perfect. I actually believe this. And that is where I want to live all the time. If we can look at our fellow human beings and give them the benefit of the doubt, knowing they are doing the best they can, it changes things, doesn't it? It forces us to hold our hearts open to everyone, because we are all in the same boat, doing the best we can with the information we have.

It took the drive up to Jefferson, New Hampshire, the hike up and down Waumbek, and the drive all the way back to Keene to get my head on straight about this. Finally, I am back home in my heart, knowing that all I can ever do is the best I can. By the time I arrive home I am at peace with our decision, and with myself.

Then it occurs to me. Instead of being angry that it didn't rain on Waumbek, why not be grateful?

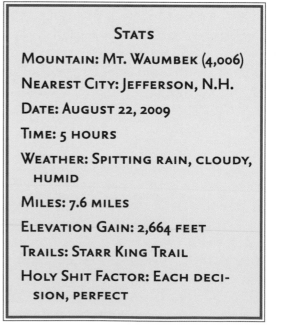

STATS

MOUNTAIN: MT. WAUMBEK (4,006)

NEAREST CITY: JEFFERSON, N.H.

DATE: AUGUST 22, 2009

TIME: 5 HOURS

WEATHER: SPITTING RAIN, CLOUDY, HUMID

MILES: 7.6 MILES

ELEVATION GAIN: 2,664 FEET

TRAILS: STARR KING TRAIL

HOLY SHIT FACTOR: EACH DECISION, PERFECT

48. THE CLEAREST DAY EVER ON EISENHOWER—THE CHALLENGE HIKE

September 6, 2009, Bretton Woods, New Hampshire

> *Keep me in your heart for a while.*
> Warren Zevon

As I climb, the trees get shorter and there is less ground cover, which gives the feeling of open space. There is more sky above me; more room to breathe up here. The air has a hint of chill in it and it is lighter; it feels more like sweet refreshment when I draw it into my lungs. The sun is so bright I am squinting, and it is warm on my face. Before I know it, I am above timberline on Mt. Pierce and there, off to my left, is Eisenhower. My breath snags on something way down deep and I stand there in awe. It is a perfect day. The wind is light and there is not one cloud in the sky. And the sky is so blue. Eisenhower's green- and gray-dotted dome dominates the view, with Mt. Washington and its towers clearly visible to the right. To the left of Eisenhower, I can see the castles on the Castle Ridge Trail and the caps on the Caps Ridge Trail heading up Mt. Jefferson. Oh, it feeds me, this vastness. I love tracing the trail as it winds its way to the top of Eisenhower. I can just barely see the cairns leading to the top, including the huge one on Eisenhower's summit. I love that I am lucky enough to see this. I love that my body got me here. I love that this is a part of my life. This is heaven to me. I want to breathe it in, let it become part of me so I never have to leave. How can it be this beautiful? It is the clearest day ever! I have not been in the Presidentials on such a glorious day. It seems almost unreal. I want to hold on to this moment, but it is gone and the next moment is here . . . and it is still this glorious day.

Adriana and Chuck, two members of our Challenge Team, catch up to me. I point excitedly. "There's Eisenhower!" They follow my finger and take in their very first view of our four thousand–footer goal for the day. I remember my first incredible view above treeline and how stunned I was. I couldn't stop saying, "Oh, my God, this is beautiful!" As I settle into the view, waiting for the rest of the Challenge Team to catch up, I feel the heavy weight of the rock in the

pit of my stomach. It's Rob. I felt it all the way up the mountain. It hasn't left me since I found out.

Two days ago I was talking with Rob. He told me he had not been feeling well, was having a hard time catching his breath, was bruising easily and feeling run down and lethargic. This is the

same guy Pat and I couldn't keep up with climbing Killington back in 2006. He just about ran up the mountain, and he had a cold. Rob tells me he is going to the doctor the next day. Shortly after his doctor visit I received an e-mail. "I have leukemia. I am heading to the hospital this afternoon for tests and to start chemo." I felt the rock being birthed within me, stirring to life in the pit of my stomach, and then sinking down into the depths of me.

How do I hold the glory of this crystal clear, perfect day and the devastating news of my friend's disease at the same time? How is it that I am here on

this mountain summit and he is lying in a hospital bed, his family by his side, all of them reeling from the life-changing nanosecond that it took for the physician to say "leukemia"? How do I come to peace with the fact that my friend is fighting for his life and I am standing on a mountaintop seeing views that go on for miles? I don't know how to do this.

For a few hours after I found out about Rob's diagnosis, I felt totally devastated. I imagined what he must be thinking and feeling, all of a sudden faced with a life-threatening disease. I thought about his wife and imagined how I would feel if Don had received the diagnosis, then jumped to trying to imagine life without Don. I thought about Rob's children, the oldest just a few days at college, and what this news must feel like to them.

It reduced me to tears.

Then I flashed back to a moment many years ago.

My mother was dying of Lou Gehrig's disease and had very little time left. My husband's Aunt Betty, the person in his family I loved the most, was dying of cancer. And our Siberian husky at thirteen years old was on her last legs. I remember driving home one day, sobbing, overwhelmed by all that was happening. And then I just stopped. This voice within me said, *You are not dying. But you're acting like you are. It is not happening to you. Live your life while you have it to live. You are not helping anyone by walking in their shoes.* That moment changed me. I stepped back into my own life and out of theirs. Of course I was sad, but I was no longer walking in their shoes; I was holding

them in my heart. There is a difference. When I held my mother and Betty in my heart, I just felt my feelings, not what I imagined theirs to be.

Standing at that stunning spot just above treeline, looking at Mt. Eisenhower, I close my eyes and I imagine reaching down deep inside me, grabbing that heavy rock from the pit of my stomach and throwing it aside. And then I scoop up Rob and his family and put them in my heart to hike Eisenhower with me.

The rest of the Challenge Team arrives and, after giving everyone time to absorb the view, we take the Webster Cliff Trail to bag Mt. Pierce, their first four thousand footer. The It's Not About the Hike Four Thousand Footer Challenge is a program Pat and I started this spring. The program mir-

rors the beginning of our hiking journey and offers others the opportunity to try hiking, with Pat and me as their guides, coaches, and cheerleaders. Seven people made the financial, physical, and emotional commitment to join our inaugural Challenge Team, and we couldn't have asked for a greater group. Over the past four months we have been getting in shape to climb a four thousand footer together—laughing, sweating, sucking wind, supporting each other, swatting mosquitoes, getting rained on, skipping rocks, and climbing stairs. The team is ready and today is our big day!

There it is! The Pierce summit cairn! One by one the team members arrive and we celebrate with high fives and woo hoos. As I look at the team, I think back to our first exercise session. We

walked four miles around town on flat sidewalks. We have come a long way in the past four months. I wonder what sitting on the summit of Mt. Pierce feels like to them? Then I stop myself. I can't know that either, just like I can't know what it is like to be faced with the diagnosis of leukemia. All I can know is my experience. As I look at each of them, laughing and joking, sharing trail mix and coming back from pee breaks, I realize I have become fond of each of them—Chuck with his jokes about Oreo cookies, the Red Sox and family dinners; Linda whose dry sense of hu-

mor always makes me laugh; Melanie with her pride and love for her children; Beth, who is drawn to the mountains; Adriana with her lively spirit; Fawn, full of inner beauty and belief in herself; Sarah, who has the capacity to deal with difficulties and continue on. I realize in this moment how proud I am of them, and that I will miss them when this hike is over. I close my eyes and imagine putting each of them in my heart.

As we walk along the ridge, Pierce gets smaller and farther away as Eisenhower looms closer and larger. I am aware of my heart vibrating with the glorious landscape around me as it holds tight to Rob and his family and, now, the Team. I turn around and come to a standstill. Off to the left there are mountains beyond mountains beyond mountains, one behind the other, fading with distance, until they are so light blue they fade into the sky. The trail winding all the way back to Pierce is clearly visible. It is hard to believe we have come all this way already. That is the magic of perspective in the Whites.

There's some grunting and groaning as we climb up the last, steep section to the top. I see the Eisenhower summit cairn and smile. One by one I cheer each member of the team to the top. Woo hoo! What a moment! As each person approaches, bringing his or her hands to mine in celebration, I think about them and their journey in the Challenge Program. Chuck signed up to get in shape to play with Olivia, his four-year-old daughter. Now he hikes with her. Linda is a role model for me. At sixty-nine years of age, she just lost Carl, her husband of forty-eight years. I can see the hiking has helped her through some of her grief . . . and there is still more. Fawn, a devoted mother, decided to do something just for herself. She glows with strength as she realizes she made it and gives me a high five. Melanie had a difficult summer, losing her dog, Whisper, and having to spend long hours at work. I have enjoyed getting to know her grown children through her. They are lucky kids. I can't help but beam as Adriana summits. Her passion for life

269

and for hiking shines in her enthusiastic expression. Beth has worked hard to get in shape to climb this mountain and all I have to do is look in her eyes to know that the summit has given her all she had hoped for. She is beaming. Sarah has been on a summit in the Whites before, but wanted to get back in shape to get up here again. Her hikes this summer have been a gift of respite to her, easing some of the stress of dealing with her son and his issues.

We break out sparkling lemonade and plastic champagne glasses and toast each other on our accomplishment. We hand out "I Did It" ribbons and, to my delight, people put them on. Then we sit back and enjoy our lunch under the biggest, clearest sky I have ever seen.

Eventually, reluctantly, we put our packs back on and begin the trek down, or, as Linda says, the "unfun part." I can see that people are tired and struggling. I could easily start to worry about them, ask them if they are all right, try to take care of them. But I know they are fine. I don't need to walk in their shoes; I need to stay in mine.

We come to my favorite spot on the Crawford Path. On the ridge there is a place where the trail opens up next to a cairn and the never-ending view of the fading mountains is spectacular. Each time Pat and I have climbed Eisenhower, I have taken photographs at this spot. I pause and share my love for this place with the team. I look up at Pat, at the back of the group, and we connect. She knows this spot is special to me; I can see it in her smile. I am flooded with memories of our hikes over the past three years, and I see just how special my journey has been and our friendship is. Consciously, with tremendous gratitude, I put Pat in my heart.

We arrive back at the idyllic spot where we had our first glimpse of Eisenhower and we all linger, taking in the view. I try to etch this scene into my brain so I have it as a screensaver in my mind and can see it whenever I want. Standing here, about to hike down into the trees, I don't feel the same anguish I felt climbing up. I am not walking in Rob's shoes, or anyone else's. I feel at peace, knowing I can't fix or change anything for anyone. All I can do is love them. Holding together in my heart the news of Rob's leukemia and this perfect Challenge Team hike brings me to a place of vulnerability and openness where I know I have no control. I am just living my life the best I can. This space brings peace into the world.

We head down the mountain. At the Mizpah Cut Off, two gray jays flutter by. We quickly pour trail mix into our palms and everyone on the team has a chance to feed the birds. One by one the jays alight on their hands, snatching nuts before flying off. I am so glad the Team has this amazing experience. I can see they are touched and awed by it.

Chuck reaches the trailhead first, with Fawn and me close behind. We cheer everyone back to the parking lot. Woo hoo!

I call Don and let him know we are all down off the mountain safe and sound. Hearing his voice, I feel a surge of gratitude for his love and support of my liking. As I put my phone away, I visualize putting Don in my heart with the rest of the gang.

At the Beaver Brook picnic area in Twin Mountain, we enjoy a picnic supper, complete with sandwich wraps tied up with four thousand–footer fortunes, whoopee pies, and four thousand–footer cookies.

I arrive home with a full heart. Rob and his family, Pat, the Challenge Team, and Don . . . all snug in there. I will keep them in my heart for a while.

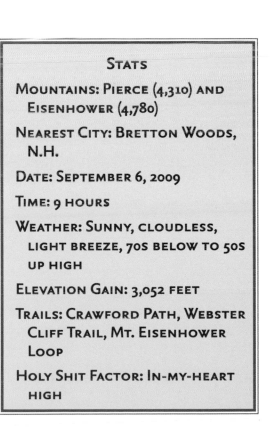

Stats

Mountains: Pierce (4,310) and Eisenhower (4,780)

Nearest City: Bretton Woods, N.H.

Date: September 6, 2009

Time: 9 hours

Weather: Sunny, cloudless, light breeze, 70s below to 50s up high

Elevation Gain: 3,052 feet

Trails: Crawford Path, Webster Cliff Trail, Mt. Eisenhower Loop

Holy Shit Factor: In-my-heart high

49. THE GIFT OF EILEEN—
WHITEFACE AND PASSACONAWAY

September 13, 2009, Wonalancet, New Hampshire

Each of us has a spark of life inside us, and our highest aspiration ought to be to set off that spark in one another.

Dr. Mark S. Albion

Eileen is like fireworks. You know those fireworks that go off in a series of bursts? I looked them up online. They are called multi-break shells. A burst of bright colorful stars comes out with a bang that ignites another burst of stars, birthing yet another colorful, shimmering burst of stars.

What I love about them is that you never know how many star bursts are in there and I ooh and ah a bit louder and with more surprise and delight with each one.

Eileen has climbed twenty-seven four thousand footers since she saw our presentation in March 2009. Each time she regales us with a story as we hike up Passaconaway and Whiteface, I feel I am seeing another colorful burst of Eileen shooting out into an evening sky, lighting up the world. I don't know how many colorful hiking bursts she has in her, but Pat and I are cheering her on.

The first time I meet Eileen she has tears in her eyes. Pat and I had just given our very first "It's Not About the Hike" presentation, sharing our hiking journey with thirty people at MoCo Arts Wellness Center on a Saturday morning in March. A pretty woman with curly, red hair comes up to me after most of the audience has left, tears ready to spill onto her cheeks, and tells me how she happens to be here. While collecting newspapers to take to the dump that morning, she paused to read the story about our presentation in the local weekly newspaper. She said she knew immediately she was supposed to go, but the event started in twenty-five minutes in Keene and she lives in Northfield, Massachusetts. She Googled directions, drove to Keene, and arrived seventeen minutes late. She said our presentation touched her in a very deep way. I remember feeling awed by whatever that greater power is that guides us to the next open doorway. The following day we received a four-page letter via e-mail from Eileen.

I feel so blessed to have serendipitously discovered you both and I think it was divine intervention or something that I allowed myself to be spontaneous and late! I was filled with a sense of joy, hope, gratitude and inspiration that is hard for me to really express on paper. Suffice it to say, I cried more on the way home. Not tears of sadness, but tears of gratitude. . . . After your presentation, instead of feeling just good, I was pumped! Exhilarated! Inspired as I have never been so inspired in my life!!!!!!!

The presentation itself was borne out of that same feeling Eileen had—the feeling we were supposed to do something. We had been talking about putting together a hiking program, but we were too busy hiking.

Sarah Ban Breathnach says, "Our deepest wishes are whispers of our authentic selves. We must learn to respect them. We must learn to listen."

We didn't listen. So the whispers got louder. We got injured. Both of us. At the same time. Pat injured her Achilles tendon, I pulled a calf muscle, and we couldn't hike. So we had plenty of down time to develop the presentation. I thought it would be easy to put together. We knew the title—"It's Not About the Hike." And we knew we wanted to talk about what our journey has meant to us personally. But it was far from easy. Actually, it was excruciating. I remember sitting with Pat at my dining room table trying to choke out how I felt about our hiking. It is deep stuff; in-my-heart stuff. I did not realize how deeply I had been touched by our hiking journey until I said it out loud. It was painful to share that deeply, to feel that deeply. It hurt to say the words. We cried. That was hard enough. Then

we had to find a way to put those feelings into a presentation to share with the world. And then we had to practice it until we could say the words without crying. We still get emotional sometimes, but how can we not? The journey is too close to our hearts not to feel it.

About three months after we gave that first presentation we heard from Eileen. On Saturday, June 13, at 11:04 p.m. Eileen e-mailed us that she had just bagged her first four thousand footer. She hiked Mt. Hale with AMC hiker Bob Humphrey, an inspiration himself, who continues to fan Eileen's hiking fire with his stories and his love of the mountains. She wrote in her e-mail:

As of today I have a new goal: It is all due to you and Pat fanning those embers in me that burst into flame when I met you both.

Walking in the light,
Eileen

Ever since that e-mail, I knew Pat and I were supposed to hike with Eileen.

On September 13, the three of us head up the Dicey's Mill Trail. What a reunion! It has been so exciting, sitting on the Internet sidelines, receiving e-mails about Eileen's hikes. But now we get to hear her stories first hand.

On the way up, Eileen shares her hiking journey. She started by signing up with the AMC, undertaking small hikes, then quickly graduating to four thousand footers. She hikes with the

AMC, with new-found friends, and solo. Nothing stops her. If she gets screened out of one trip, she finds another, or hikes by herself. She immerses herself in the hiking and is filled with joy. You can't help but feel it when you are with her. She has spent much of her life caring for others; now, she tells us, it is her turn. She says, "Maybe it is selfish, but I am doing this for me."

As we get close to the top of Passaconaway, Eileen tells us of a Bob Humphrey tradition. If a hiker has not been on a particular summit before, the group lets that person go ahead and reach the summit first. I love that. Both Pat and I step aside to let Eileen bag Passaconaway first.

Her passion is palpable as we hike the ridge between the mountains on the Rollins Trail. We reach our special lunch place, the place where Pat and I enjoyed lunch on our very first four thousand–footer hike. We sit on the same warm rock where we see Passaconaway to the left and Whiteface to the right, and an incredible view directly in front of us. We take off our boots and wiggle our toes, just as Pat and I did the first time. It is special to share this spot with Eileen.

We head to Whiteface summit, then continue on to the ledges. Rain begins to spit when we arrive and I am nervous about two spots that scared the begeebies out of me the first time I climbed Whiteface. But this time they are a cinch.

With each of Eileen's stories I am more impressed. She is on fire! There is

absolutely no stopping this woman. She will finish the forty-eight in no time and I am sure she will move on to the sixty-seven in New England, or start her second tour of the New Hampshire Whites. I can't wait to applaud her at the four thousand–footer awards ceremony. She is on her own grace wave and is full of happiness and excitement and enthusiasm for hiking. We arrive back at the car nine hours after hitting the trailhead, and reach home three hours later, feeling completely full of the experience.

Listening to Eileen talk about her hiking journey, like watching fireworks, is a special experience. It is even more special for me because I played a part, albeit small. Pat and I were sparks. Eileen was already packed with all the special hiking stuff, her fuse just waiting for a spark. Pat and I lit Eileen's fuse and that is all it took. Now we get to watch the spectacular show. As Eileen hikes and shares her experiences with others, maybe she will light someone else's fuse. The gift goes on and on.

I want to feel that I am making a difference in the world. I want to inspire others by being fully who I am. Giving the presentation allows Pat and me to share our journey and what we have learned with others. What a gift to be fire-starters, and to know we've made a difference in Eileen's life.

We have given our presentation nineteen times to approximately seven hundred people. Maybe some of those people were there because they heard the whisper inside themselves and knew they were supposed to be at the presentation. Maybe they too had a fuse, ready to be lit.

Sharing our journey and our joy with others by giving the presentation is riding the grace wave. When we are the spark of life that sets off another, it doesn't get any better than that.

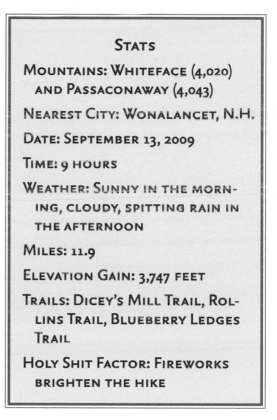

STATS

MOUNTAINS: WHITEFACE (4,020) AND PASSACONAWAY (4,043)

NEAREST CITY: WONALANCET, N.H.

DATE: SEPTEMBER 13, 2009

TIME: 9 HOURS

WEATHER: SUNNY IN THE MORNING, CLOUDY, SPITTING RAIN IN THE AFTERNOON

MILES: 11.9

ELEVATION GAIN: 3,747 FEET

TRAILS: DICEY'S MILL TRAIL, ROLLINS TRAIL, BLUEBERRY LEDGES TRAIL

HOLY SHIT FACTOR: FIREWORKS BRIGHTEN THE HIKE

50. IN A HURRY ON THE OSCEOLAS

October 3, 2009, Lincoln, New Hampshire

> *There is more to life than increasing its speed.*
> Mahatma Gandhi

Here is the short version in case you are in a hurry. I would rather savor than swallow whole. There you go . . .

Just in case you want to savor the message, here are the texture, feelings, and story behind the revelation.

I've done both—savoring and swallowing whole—in life and in the mountains.

I savored having my children sit in my lap, sucking their thumbs, while I read *The Little Mouse, the Red Ripe Strawberry and the Big Hungry Bear.*

I savored announcing the number of jack-o'-lanterns at the 1994 Pumpkin Festival to the cheering crowd. The auditor passed a sealed envelope to my daughter, Jess, who opened it. She passed it to her sister, Kelly, who took out the piece of paper and saw the number first, and then passed it to me, and I announced that we had more than doubled our goal with 10,540 pumpkins. The crowd roared. It was magic.

I savored the bowl of Italian Wedding soup I had in the cafeteria on top of Mt Washington in the middle of our Presidential traverse, after miles of hiking above treeline. I hummed "mmmm" in between every slurp of the steaming hot soup.

I savored the moment the minister said "I now pronounce you man and wife," and Kelly lifted her bridal bouquet to the sky in celebration of her new life with Justin.

My mother was always admonishing me not to swallow my supper whole. I'm not sure I learned that lesson then. I know there were many times as a young adult and a young mother that I swallowed life whole, gulping it down without taking time to notice the experience. I was in too much of a hurry to get all of life in. I can't give you specific examples because I don't remember them. When you swallow life whole, it seems our brains store those memories in a different place than the savored

memories. The savored ones are more easily retrieved. The times I swallowed whole feel lost forever.

Sometimes, though, swallowing life whole is the only way to go.

Pat and I beat book time climbing the Osceolas last Saturday. We have never come close to book time. (Book time is the AMC's approximation of the time a hike will take.) Book time for hiking the Osceolas on the Osceola Trail is five hours, forty minutes. It took us five hours and fifty minutes, but that included breaks, food stops, clothing adjustments, and taking pictures, easily fifteen minutes of extra stuff.

So we swallow our Osceola hike whole. We don't usually hike like that, but these are unusual circumstances. We are working on getting Dejah her patch for climbing the forty-eight mountains in New Hampshire over four thousand feet high. We would like to do it before the snow flies because once winter arrives, we can't really be sure we are going to reach the summit, ever. It's always a wait-and-see-what-the-weather-is-and-how-we-are-doing game.

We arrive at the Osceola trailhead at 8:30 on a rainy morning. But we are prepared for it, physically and mentally. I wear my zip-off pants, two light Techwick shirts, and my rain jacket. I feel strong and we motor up the mountain, while the rain falls on and off.

Now, when I say motor up the mountain, I mean it. Before long I am soaked inside and out. I am wet on the outside from the rain and the trees. Every time

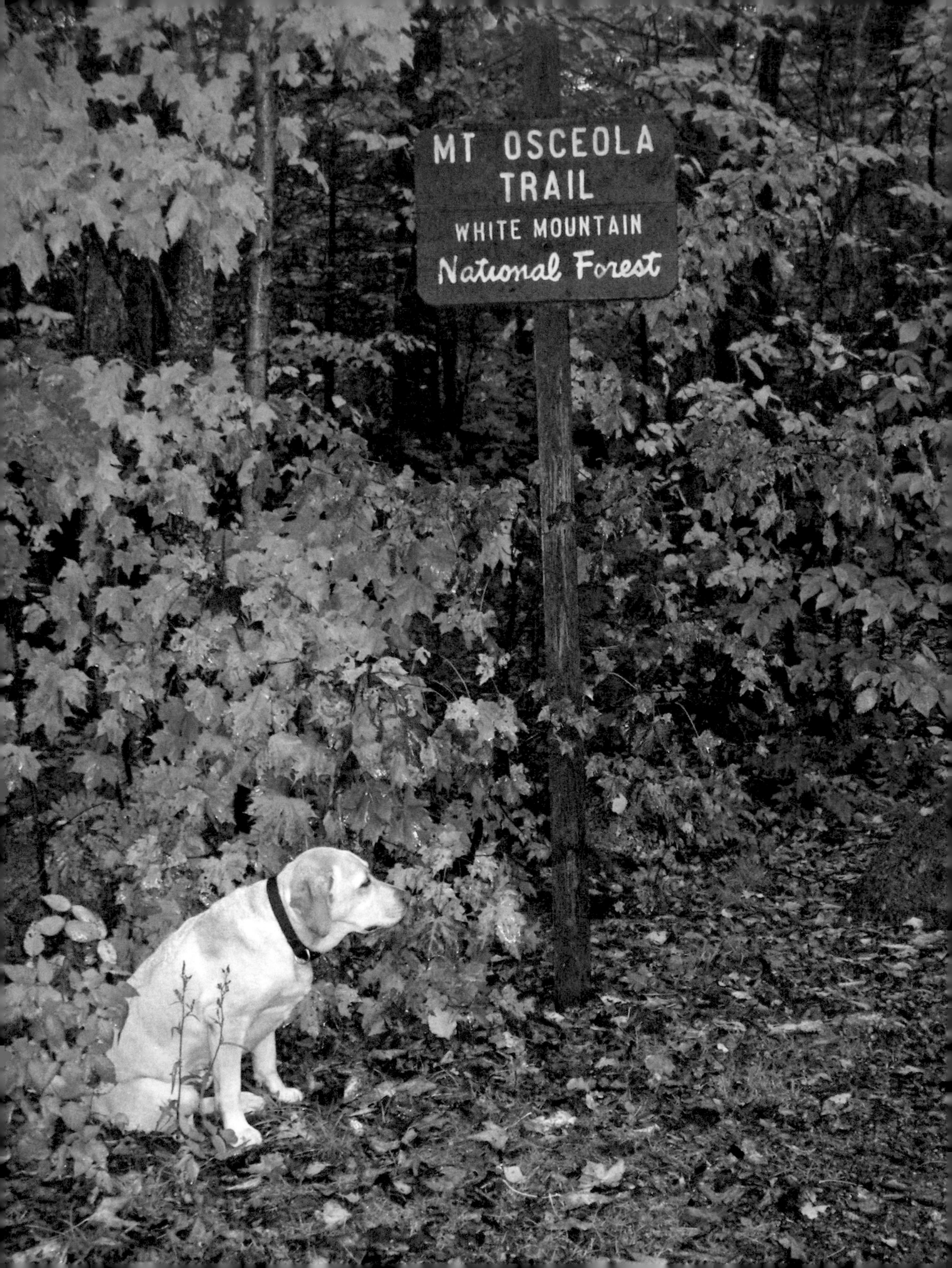
MT OSCEOLA
TRAIL
WHITE MOUNTAIN
National Forest

I use a tree trunk or branch to pull myself up the trail; it thanks me by dumping a load of water on me. The water runs through my hair, plastering it to my face, and continues around my neck and then down in between my shoulder blades, forming a running rivulet down the middle of my back. Oh, so comfortable. And my sweat has soaked through my clothes.

Once wet, there is really only one thing I can do to stay warm: keep moving at a good pace. We stop for a bathroom break, and I jump up and down on the trail as I wait for Pat. As we near the summit, I am getting cold so we stop so I can wade through my pack to find gloves and, later, hand-warmers. They are last year's hand warmers, and I learn, to my dismay, that hand warmers run out of oomph after a while. These got a bit warm for an hour, and then went cold.

By 10:30 a.m. we are on top of Mt. Osceola, which is enveloped in rain clouds and offers no view at all. I take a picture of Dejah on her thirty-ninth peak sitting on one of the pylons.

We head down the steep descent between the two mountains. I remember the chimney, a down and then straight up section of the trail, from our previous hike, but it isn't too bad. We are down and on our way up East Osceola, arriving at 11:18 on Dejah's fortieth peak. I take some pictures, turn around, and we're back on top of Osceola in no time. The temperatures have dropped and gusts of wind blow right through me. We are both soaked and cold.

I know I should stop and change into dry clothes, but I am so cold that I feel like the only thing I can do for myself is move as fast as I can and not stop. We get out of the wind and take out our sandwiches, but I eat mine as I hike down the mountain. I just can't stop. I finally give in to take a bathroom break, which, when you are that wet and that cold, is no fun at all.

The second I get back on the trail, I move down the mountain as quickly as I can, trying to build up some body heat. I'm okay, but I can't stop. Pat and Dejah are right behind me. I focus on putting my feet on solid rock, or between boulders, avoiding the slippery downward-facing roots, staying balanced, and moving as fast as I safely can.

We arrive back at the car at 2:20 p.m. and immediately change into dry, warm clothes, then sit in the car with the heater on full blast until we warm up. Ah . . .

There is nothing on this hike that I savor. Writing this hike report, I realize that this hike is like life. We convince ourselves that we have to do something, when we really don't. And then we do it as quickly as possible, in order to get it done, so we can hurry to the next thing, or the next mountain, so we can check that off and move to the next. Swallowing life whole.

The moments we savor turn into blessings in our lives, to be remembered again and again with joy. The moments we swallow whole disappear

into an abyss of missed opportunities.

In hindsight, I'd rather hike more slowly, in decent weather, enjoying the hike, instead of rushing down the mountain to stay warm. I'd rather get less done and have more moments with meaning, have a longer To Do list and more blessings in my life, less mission and more kindness, fewer patches and more moments to savor.

STATS

MOUNTAINS: OSCEOLA (4,340) AND EAST OSCEOLA (4,156)

NEAREST CITY: LINCOLN, N.H.

DATE: OCTOBER 3, 2009

TIME: 5 HOURS AND 50 MINUTES

WEATHER: CLOUDY, BREEZY, OCCASIONAL RAIN, 50S

MILES: 8.4

ELEVATION GAIN: 2,950 FEET

TRAILS: OSCEOLA TRAIL

HOLY SHIT FACTOR: SWALLOWING WHOLE

51. THE SPACE BETWEEN US— GALEHEAD AND GARFIELD

October 12, 2009, Twin Mountain, New Hampshire

Each friend represents a world in us, a world not born until they arrive, and it is only by this meeting that a new world is born.

Anaïs Nin

On Saturday I receive an e-mail from Pat, who has hurt her knee and will not be able to hike on Monday. Our plans to make a traverse of the Bonds collapses. I am disappointed. We have only three more hikes before Dejah can get her patch, and this is the big daddy of all hikes— four mountains, twenty-plus miles. We want to get it checked off before winter

arrives. All week I have been working myself up mentally and taking it easy physically, and have reached the point of being psyched for the challenge.

At first, my disappointment takes the form of anger at Pat. There are times I don't like myself much. This would be one of them. I sit and stew for a while.

The stewing goes something like this: *Damn. It's supposed to be a beautiful day Monday, with sunshine and foliage. My calendar is clear. I am going to*

spend Monday wishing I were hiking.

Then a light comes on inside of me and I realize something pretty big: I can stay at home on Monday and be mad at Pat, or I can meet Pat for lunch on Monday and we can feel sorry for ourselves together, or I can continue to live my life. I can hike.

Hike without Pat? We have hiked more than 160 mountains, over a thousand miles together. It has been about us, our journey. I don't know if I can do that. But it doesn't feel right staying at home on a beautiful day, moping that I'm not hiking.

As I stew, I become aware of a calm voice inside of me saying simply, *hike alone.* It is an empowered voice, not angry, not vengeful, just clear. It doesn't try to convince me to go or to quell my fear. It just says, *hike.*

I tell Don I am going. He says, "Go. Be careful."

I don't want to hike twenty miles alone, so the next thing to decide is where I will hike. I am goal-oriented; it's just that simple. I know I have to hike a mountain that counts for Dejah. So I choose Garfield, a ten-mile hike on Dejah's list. I e-mail Pat that I am going, but say little else. I don't want to rub salt in the wound. I know she already feels terrible.

I am up at 4:30 a.m., and leave my driveway by 5. Being alone in the car reminds me how different this day will be. I go to the Tilt'n Diner for breakfast, as Pat and I always do. I sit at the counter instead of a booth. Breakfast doesn't taste as good alone. I eat half of it and am on my way. I get to the trailhead parking lot, put on my boots and at 8 a.m. head up the mountain. But I soon realize that I am climbing the wrong mountain! I parked in the Galehead lot, 1.6 miles from the Garfield lot, by mis-

285

take. Pat would never have made that mistake. Oh, well, Dejah needs Galehead too, so I keep hiking up the Gale River Trail.

It's peaceful. I feel strong and am sweating and panting as I move up the mountain. There are a few river crossings and I miss having Pat to confer with about the best place to cross. Instead, I just start across, get halfway there, and realize there might have been a less-wet option. I see a few people coming down from the Galehead Hut and I greet them enthusiastically. *Thank God*, I say to myself, *people!* We chat, but that is all we do. Chat. When Pat and I hike, we really talk, share, and explore who we are. I let out what is in me and it falls on caring ears. But there are no caring ears around me today. Dejah is different, too. She is leading! She is usually right behind me, never in front. Maybe she thinks she needs to show me the way, as Pat is not with us.

I arrive at the Galehead Hut at 10:30 and immediately head to the summit of Galehead, a half mile up. On the way I meet a woman. Her name is Pat—can you believe that? She just bagged number forty-eight on top of Galehead. I woo hoo and clap for her, but it sounds hollow without Pat's cheers to complete the standing ovation. I summit Galehead at 10:50, take Dejah's picture, and head down.

I had decided on the way up that if I got back to the junction of the Garfield Ridge Trail before noon, I would try to bag Garfield, too. It means I will have to hike a very rough three miles with some short, steep ups and downs. And it means I will have to walk 1.6 miles along the River Loop Road once I get down the mountain in order to get back to my car in the Galehead lot. I arrive at the junction at 11:52 and head out along the Ridge Trail.

The ridge is rough, very icy, and treacherous in spots where I have to find a way around tilted icy granite slabs. Dejah just slides down.

I finally get to the Garfield waterfall, a straight-up section of trail leading to the summit that features water running down the same steep rock steps that you hike up. It rises eleven hundred feet in less than a mile. Wowsers. If Pat were here, we would exchange eye-rolls and a few curses to celebrate the challenge. I pant and rest every few steps. Inside I am calm. The empowered voice has taken over and I feel sure of myself, not afraid, just in the experience. I am not thinking a lot; I'm just concentrating on the next step. I arrive on the summit of Garfield at 2 p.m. and am gifted with a 360-degree view of red-carpeted valleys between blue mountains. I want to stay and soak it in, but it's windy and cold on the top. A fellow hiker kindly takes my picture with Dejah and I chat with some young men as we look over at snow-covered Mt. Washington.

I head down the mountain and stop at the junction of the Galehead Trail to eat my bagel. I share it with Dejah, who is very appreciative. Then I head down the very gentle 4.8-mile Garfield Trail which goes on and on and on. On the last mile, I chat with two men and an

eleven-year-old boy as we find our way around a flooded section of trail. I realize as I talk with them that they are my ticket to the car. Perhaps they will give me and Dejah a ride to the other parking lot. They are hiking faster than I am, but I keep up and we arrive in the parking lot at 4:35. They gladly give me a ride to my car.

I make the hike in 8.5 hours—13.5 miles, 3,848 feet of elevation gain. Quite a hike. I am tired. Dejah is sound asleep within seconds of getting in the car. The traffic is horrendous on Columbus Day evening, so all my attention is on the road. I'm home by 8:30.

I did it. Now I know I can hike solo. And I know that hiking with Pat is a much richer experience.

There's me. And there's Pat. And then there is the special place between us where we meet, and I think that is where friendship lives. When I am hiking with Pat and we are on the summit of a mountain, soaking in the views, that space swells with joy, whether we share the experience verbally or not. There is her joy experiencing the views and there's my joy, and in that space in between us, the joy comes together and it multiplies. It's magic. And it's synergy—the whole is greater than the sum of the individual parts. It feels huge. And we each have a choice to let in that bigger version of joy or to keep our joy at our own size. Boundaries.

When we meet someone who has just

summited their forty-eighth and we cheer, there is my woo hoo and Pat's woo hoo, but together we sound stronger and bigger than just the two of us. Our enthusiasm multiplies and our cheering is magnified.

When one of us is sad or wading through difficult times, a similar thing happens. When I am in a tough place, and I talk about it with Pat, the words sit between us and the power of the struggle seems to be cut in half. When she is in a hard space and shares it, the same thing happens. And when the struggle sits between us, we have another choice around our own boundaries. We can let it in and go to that place of struggle with a friend, and struggle together. Or we can make a healthier choice, one I am learning to make. We can let the struggle sit there between us, see it, and meet it with compassion. Being compassionate lessens the struggle for the other. I am learning that I can still be in a place of joy and be compassionate with Pat when she is in a place of struggle. It all happens in the magic of the space between us. The deeper that space, the more room for the healing and the joy to snowball. Love makes lots of room between people who care for one another.

When I hike alone, there is no Pat and, therefore, no space between us. So my joy is just my joy. Worthy and wonderful, but just mine. There is no one to share it with, and therefore no way to multiply it and let it grow. When I am nervous hiking alone, my fear sits in me. There is no one to say it aloud

to, no one to hold it and care that I am in it, and certainly no magic space that diminishes my fear through the sharing of it.

Although I think "the space between us" is there among all human beings,

the quality of the space varies depending on the relationship of the people. Pat and I have a deep friendship that has developed over miles and miles of trails and through many out-of-our-comfort-zone experiences that left us feeling vulnerable and dependent on one another. We are close. The space between us is blessed.

My hike alone was great. Hiking with Pat is more than just greater. It swells to fit the space between us. It is our

energy magnified to a power that can lessen sorrow and fear and help us heal through the act of sharing our experience. The combination of the two of us expands our joy until it overflows the trail. What we have is remarkable.

I know that, given the choice, I choose to hike with Pat rather than alone. I choose me and Pat and that remarkable expanse between us called friendship. Am I glad I went hiking alone? Absolutely. I would never have seen this so clearly. Sometimes we have to experience what we are missing to know how much we miss it.

STATS

MOUNTAINS: GALEHEAD (4,024) AND GARFIELD (4,500)

NEAREST CITY: TWIN MOUNTAIN, N.H.

DATE: OCTOBER 12, 2009

WEATHER: SUNNY IN THE MORNING, CLOUDY IN THE AFTERNOON, LOW 40S, HIGH 50S

TIME: 8 HOURS AND 50 MINUTES

MILES: 13.5

ELEVATION GAIN: 3,848 FEET

TRAILS: GALE RIVER TRAIL, GARFIELD RIDGE TRAIL, GARFIELD TRAIL

HOLY SHIT FACTOR: FRIENDSHIP IN THE SPACE BETWEEN US

November 8, 2009, Waterville Valley, New Hampshire

In order to really enjoy a dog, one doesn't merely try to train him to be semi-human. The point of it is to open oneself to the possibility of becoming partly a dog.

Edward Hoagland

This is a very special hike, and there's lots of evidence. The most obvious is that Dejah is wearing a bright orange vest with a white sign pinned to it that reads, "#48 today." I never dress up dogs, but today she has bragging rights and I'm just helping. In my backpack, I have a hand-made blue ribbon with a gold "48" in the button's center, for the special moment when she actually stands on her forty-eighth peak, having climbed all the four thousand–foot mountains in New Hampshire. I also have two marrow bones for Dejah to celebrate with Pinta, and two white chocolate truffles for Pat and I to commemorate the long-anticipated moment.

We are hiking up the Pine Bend Brook Trail. Pat and I climbed this trail in winter and it will be interesting to see what it is like in November, before snow . . . maybe.

We arrive at the trailhead at 8:15 a.m. and open the back door of the peakbagger mobile. The dogs explode out of the car, eager to begin the hike. The trail is generous in giving us time to warm up our legs. The woods go on and on to either side of us—birches and hardwoods, bereft of leaves, let us glimpse further into the inner world of wilderness. The trail is covered in foot-deep dried leaves that hide the rocks and mud beneath, so I don't know I've stepped in a mud hole until I sink in. I love the crunch of walking in the leaves as I shuffle through them. It reminds me of being a kid, piling the leaves up into a huge mound, and jumping in, screaming with glee, letting the leaves conceal me. I loved the feeling of being covered; pieces of the leaves would get into my shirt and my pants and in my hair and I would be so uncomfortably happy.

The Pine Bend Brook is on our right as we hike. "Huh," I say to Pat, "I remember the brook being on the other side when we did this in winter." She rolls her eyes and smiles at me. Uh oh. We're going to have to cross the brook. In winter, the water crossings were frozen and covered with snow. This time of year they can be challenging if the water is high and the temperatures are low. It is not long

before we reach the first of many water crossings and it is a breeze; boulders lie just where we need them, to help us stay dry. The dogs splash across, slurping up some cool refreshment along the way. Now the brook is on the left and everything feels right.

I watch Dejah galloping up some

stairs that trail workers built for us. I am always touched by the incredible work volunteers do to make it possible for hikers to reach these summits. The strength and energy it takes to build bridges over brooks and granite steps up mountains is hard to imagine. I am indebted to the trail workers. Pat and I clap and cheer for them whenever we are lucky enough to run into them on the trail.

Dejah turns around on the steps to look at me, checking to make sure her Grammy is with her. I look at her and smile, my love for her bubbling up in a spontaneous response of joy. "Hey,

Dej," I say in my high-pitched, soft, I-love-babies-and-animals voice. "How ya doin'?" She looks at me with her dark brown eyes and tilts her head, as if to say, *What are you saying, Grammy?* The second our eyes meet, her tail wags, which then wiggles the entire back half of her body. That's her love coming back to me.

I met Dejah when she was three weeks old, when I accompanied Jess to pick out her puppy from the Lab litter.

When Dejah first came to live with us, we established a morning hiking ritual that continues today. I tiptoe upstairs and crack open Jess's bedroom door at 4:45 a.m. Dejah has her nose to the door, and she erupts out of the bedroom, slamming her tail on the walls of the hall, snorting and twisting and turning with exuberance. She runs down the stairs, jumps over the last treads, and waits for Grammy to catch up. As soon as Dejah sees Pat's car coming up the driveway, she grabs one of her stuffed toys and stands nose to door, tail wagging furiously, anxious to greet Pat. She hops in the back of the car, joining Pinta, and immediately lies down and starts sucking on her stuffed zebra, quieting herself for the long drive ahead.

For a year and a half, until she and Jess moved to Texas, we enjoyed Dejah's company on the mountains, hiking through all four seasons. They returned, a year later, and we welcomed them with open arms. We have them for a year; they will leave in the spring.

Now it is November, and we are only two mountains shy of our goal: bagging the forty-eight four thousand footers in New Hampshire with Dejah.

As Pat and I continue up the Pine Bend Brook Trail, we are amazed that we did this hike in January. Not only did we complete it, but we broke trail in three feet of new snow for most of the hike. Incredible. We are impressed with ourselves as we climb up what feels like a never-ending steep ravine. It's fun to be amazed by ourselves when no one else is around to think we are bragging. I glance at Dejah, who is bounding up more man-made steps in this perpendicular section of the trail, looking svelte and fit, totally unaware of the feat she is about to accomplish. She is in the moment and doesn't need to feel good about what she has done or will do. She just feels good while she is doing it. What would it be like to live life that way?

The trail gets very steep, then rewards us with a more gradual climb, then levels off. We are on top of a knoll, the trail winding gently through the flat woods, when I glance to my right and see a massive monster mountain standing like a giant peering over my shoulder. I hope that is not North Tripyramid, though I know it is. But, I remind myself, it is always easier than it looks. It's like a one thousand-piece puzzle—incredibly daunting when you take it out of the box. When I stick with the one-piece-at-a-time mentality it becomes possible. Of course, Dejah doesn't look at the mountain, or care about what is to come. She is happy hiking with Grammy and Grammy's best friend. No worries, just contentment.

As we get closer to the summit, the hiking gets very steep, more like boulder climbing and we pull ourselves up with our arms as well as our legs. We start seeing snow and ice, although not enough to put cleats on our feet. I hear voices and realize there are people on the top. Someone to celebrate with! We crest the top at 11:30 a.m. and woo hoo and clap for Dejah's forty-seventh. She is busy sniffing everyone, which gives them a chance to read the sign she's wearing. A few hikers offer congratulations.

We head off to Middle Tripyramid, Dejah's forty-eighth, and as we walk I remember the gentleness of this ridge from our winter hike. It is kind and mellow, with an easy descent from North Tripyramid and then a gradual ascent to Middle Tripyramid, giving us a chance to walk in a more relaxed manner in the woods. I find myself thinking about the fact that we are about to reach another goal. But then what?

My theory is that I'm on a grace wave. It's pretty amazing how it works. Before Dejah came back, I was feeling that old familiar ache of dissatisfaction, which means I need something big to strive for. When Dejah bounded in the door needing twenty-five mountains in order to earn an embroidered piece of

fabric, I came alive again. That's the grace wave handing me a purpose. Big goals push me from the inside out, and I love that feeling. When I'm not striving for the next big thing, I feel empty and directionless. Once I put the blue ribbon around Dejah's neck and finish this hike report, I will be back in the "what's next" phase of life. And that place of not knowing is the hardest of all. I dread it. But no need to go there quite yet.

It takes us half an hour to walk the wooded ridge between the mountains. Dejah is in her usual spot, right behind me, her nose almost touching my calves. We reach the tree-covered summit of Middle Tripyramid at 12:10 p.m. for the big celebration. It is a bit anticlimactic because Dejah is not celebrating. Pat and I are smiling, woo hooing, and clapping. Dejah is busy visiting other hikers who are eating their lunches, hoping for a handout. I call her back. "Sit," I say and she sits and looks very hopeful. I give Dejah and Pinta marrow bones and they gnaw on them while Pat and I eat lunch. I present her with the blue ribbon, which she sniffs and then ignores. We take a few pictures, snapping our fingers, calling her name and whistling, trying to get her to look at my digital camera at the exact second it decides to click. One of the other hikers takes her picture too. She is a celebrity and I am pleased; she is clueless and happy.

We head back to North Tripyramid and then down the mountain. It's steep and the boulders are slippery, so we spend a fair amount of time scooching down the wet rock faces on our butts, which are soon cold and wet. Dejah keeps looking back at me, wondering why Grammy moves so slowly when all you have to do is jump down! But she waits patiently, her tail wagging as I get closer.

We arrive back at the trailhead at 4:45 p.m., just as darkness is settling in, after eight and a half hours of hiking. Dejah and Pinta jump in the car and settle into sleep. We don't hear anything from the back until we turn in to my driveway three hours later. Don greets us with a standing ovation, but Dejah runs right into the kitchen to see if there are any leftovers from supper on the floor. She is oblivious to the fact that she claimed a prize today; that she has done what only a hundred other dogs have done. I lower myself slowly onto our purple sofa with a sigh of relief. Dejah jumps up, lies down, puts her head in my lap and closes her eyes. I love this part—feeling the exhilaration of exhaustion as I relax with Dejah. An hour later, I head to bed. I bring Dejah up to Jess, who is watching TV in her bedroom. "Night, Dej," I say. She turns around and looks at me, wagging her tail, as if to say, *It was a great day! Thanks, Grammy.* I blow her a kiss. Maybe Dejah is my basic training for when my kids have kids and I am a real grandmother. Now I know what to do. I will take my grandchildren for walks to get them in shape, give them treats, hike the four thousand footers with them so they earn their patches, and cuddle up with them on the couch at night.

In the beginning I thought I was climbing these mountains for Dejah. Now I know I did it for me. I got the gift of Dejah for forty-eight mountains and had a few years of being a Grammy. There is something so incredibly special about being with her. She is free, unencumbered, and uninhibited. She does not worry about water crossings, steep or slippery trails, or the height of the mountain ahead. She does not care what people think, or about goals, accomplishments, or patches. She is full of never-ending curiosity, wild enthusiasm, boundless energy and irrepressible love. She lives and loves so everyone can see.

I hope some of her has rubbed off on me.

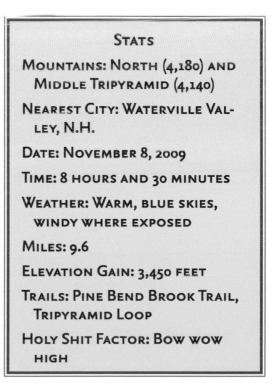

STATS

MOUNTAINS: NORTH (4,180) AND MIDDLE TRIPYRAMID (4,140)

NEAREST CITY: WATERVILLE VALLEY, N.H.

DATE: NOVEMBER 8, 2009

TIME: 8 HOURS AND 30 MINUTES

WEATHER: WARM, BLUE SKIES, WINDY WHERE EXPOSED

MILES: 9.6

ELEVATION GAIN: 3,450 FEET

TRAILS: PINE BEND BROOK TRAIL, TRIPYRAMID LOOP

HOLY SHIT FACTOR: BOW WOW HIGH

53. PUSHING OUR LIMITS ON LOWER WOLF JAW

December 12, 2009, St. Huberts, New York

Only those who will risk going too far can possibly find out how far one can go.

T.S. Eliot

Today will be a challenge. We are hiking our third mountain in the Adirondacks. It is a four-hour drive from Keene, New Hampshire, to St. Huberts, New York, and although it may be only 170 miles, culturally it feels like a continent away. The Adirondack map is harder to read, the trails have names but also numbers, the trail signage is completely different, and our hiking plan for the day is more difficult to pull together because the guide books are based on trails and not on mountains. Pat and I can't quite make sense of it all yet. In the Whites we are home; in the Adirondacks, we are still tourists. It is cold and windy today. We don't know how much snow we will find, but we are prepared with crampons and snowshoes. I have learned not to fast-forward into a hike and anticipate what we might find. That just makes me anxious. I prepare for the worst and then I take one step at a time, staying in the moment.

We are climbing Lower Wolf Jaw. This mountain and its partner, Upper Wolf Jaw, were named by Alexander Wyant, a well-known artist who painted the peaks and said the two peaks and the deep col between them looked like a great pair of wolf jaws.

We start out in the parking lot of the Ausable Club. Only members can drive inside the club grounds, so hikers have to walk half a mile from the parking lot to the trailhead. Coming back to our cars on this road is going to feel like forever. We reach a gate and behind it a snow-covered dirt road that leads to the various trailheads. We walk three-tenths of a mile to the trailhead and off we go. Whoops, not so fast.

Pat says, "This doesn't seem right." We check the map. The people who designed the Adirondack map could take a lesson from the White Mountains mappers. As a fifty-five-year-old, I can read the White Mountains map without glasses, but the Adirondack map is tough. Realizing we are going the wrong direction, we retrace our steps and head out on the trail that takes us on a bridge over the Ausable River to the West River Trail.

The path is still wearing all of its new snow; no one has come before us to break trail. I'm feeling strong. I break through a foot of new snow, as the trail winds up and down along the Ausable River for a mile. After hiking a good distance, and after consulting the hard-to-read map a few times, we arrive at a trail junction and realize that we could have taken the road all the way to this point. We make a mental note of this for our return trip. We head up the Wedge Brook Trail, which has been broken out.

Pat is having a hard day. One boot is too loose, her pack is not sitting right on her hips, and she can't seem to tighten the waist belt enough to get comfortable. She is struggling from the get-go. We've all had days like this. In addition, we think Pat has exercise-induced asthma, so on some hikes she has a hard time breathing and her legs get tired quickly because they are not getting the oxygen they need. It is hard enough hiking in winter; it must be close to impossible if you can't breathe. It looks like this is going to be a difficult hike for Pat. She falls behind me and I slow down, hoping she catches up. The problem is that it is cold today, with wind that makes it feel even colder. And

I am sweating, so I'm wet. Whenever I stop to wait for Pat, the cold immediately seeps into my body. I can't stop for long or it becomes too hard to build my body heat back up.

The trail is steep and hard-going. Pat is just within my sight when I turn around. The wind blows and I feel chilled because I have slowed down. I wait for Pat, who reaches me, winded and struggling, and I ask how she is doing. She tells me, between breaths, that her legs are really tired.

"Maybe we should turn around, Pat. That would be fine with me," I say. And I am clear that it would be fine with me.

I want to do what is right and look to Pat to let me know if she wants to turn around.

"It wouldn't be fine with me," she says. I hear resolve and fight in her voice.

I suggest we eat something, hoping that will boost her energy level. We chomp on bagels overflowing with peanut butter and jelly while we hike. I huff and puff my way up a very steep section. It is harder for Pat because she uses poles, so eating, holding poles, and maneuvering up a steep section while having trouble breathing is impossible. I wait and she catches up to me. She throws her bagel in the snow in frustration. I pick it up and eat it; it's snow covered and yummy.

As we climb, Pat lags farther and farther behind. I wait until she catches up and then hurry ahead. When the trail finally levels off, we meet hikers who are coming down the trail. One of them has a beard of icicles; I can't stop looking at it. They tell us there are some steep sections up ahead. *What do you mean?* I ask myself. *We haven't already hit the steep sections?* They also tell us they broke the trail to Upper Wolf Jaw, but that no one has been to Lower Wolf Jaw, our destination. In my mind I figure we will climb Upper Wolf Jaw instead, staying on the broken-out trail. Mr. Icicles turns and points his pole at Lower Wolf Jaw, a massive snow-covered mountain in the distance. Oh, my God! It looks like we have not even started to climb the mountain.

We start up another steep section before the trail levels off and we climb more gradually between the two mountains. I see Upper Wolf Jaw jutting into the blue sky, straight up to my left. I can't see Pat behind me, and I struggle to stay warm while I wait for her. Until the past six months or so, when she started developing breathing problems, our hiking pace matched. I don't like being separated, so I decide to go back to meet her. Going back and forth is a good way for me to stay warm and stay connected with Pat.

We reach the decision point. Do we climb Upper Wolf Jaw, which is .9 miles of packed-out trail, or do we climb Lower Wolf Jaw, which looks on the map to be .3 miles of unpacked trail?

"We can do point three miles of anything, can't we?" I ask Pat. She agrees. I know she is struggling and I'm clear I will be the one breaking the trail to the top. I take off, unfazed, breaking trail through two to three feet of new snow. The trail is straight up. No kidding. Straight up. There are places where I have to brush off the snow to find what is under it and where I can put my snowshoes to get enough traction to climb up. Often I take a step up and just slide back down, bringing an avalanche of snow with me. I take another step and slide back down. The trees on the side of the trail are draped in snow; sometimes the only way to pull myself up is to use their branches as handles, and when I do that, the tree dumps its load of snow on my head. We look like snowmen. I finally see blue sky ahead and tell Pat I feel hopeful. Translation: we are almost to the summit. But when I get there, I see that the trail turns and heads straight up again. A curse comes into my head but I keep it in check. I continue slogging straight up. Ah, blue sky. "I'm hopeful, Pat!" I get there and see that the trail again turns and heads straight up. "Shit," I say under my breath. I get to a place where the trail is literally perpendicular and I see no way of dragging myself up. I'm up to my hips in snow. We help each other over a chest-level rock, Pat shoving me from behind and then me pulling her up. We keep going. Blue sky again, then dashed hopes again.

"Maybe we should turn around," I

say. I don't mean it. We've come too far and are too close to retreat. I'm just venting my frustration. Pat, in spite of her difficulty breathing, doesn't want to turn around either and is staying close behind me. I am crawling, moving at a snail's pace because I have to take three steps to move one. We continue hauling ourselves up over three feet of snowfall toward the top.

I get to a place that looks like the height of land. "This must be it, Pat." I say. "There are supposed to be views," she says.

I look around me and see no views. "Shit." We continue on.

It's funny how our expectations affect our performance. I feel fine. But I expect to climb .3 miles. Once we reach what feels like a third of a mile, it gets harder to continue on. But physically, although I'm challenged, I feel strong and confident breaking trail.

I see blue sky again, but am nervous about getting our hopes up, so I say nothing. Behind me, Pat says, "We're almost there." I can barely hear her over the sound of my own breathing. I crest the last huge vertical section and stand on the top of Lower Wolf Jaw. There are views off to one side. Pat takes a few pictures. It is 3:50 p.m. We have never reached a summit this late in the day. We will be descending in the dark. My hope is that we get down the really steep section between the two mountains before the sky turns totally black. We spend maybe a minute on the summit and head down.

Going down the steep sections is eas-

ier because I can slide on my butt. We don't build up speed because there is too much snow, so we get down safely. Pat is far behind me again, struggling with balance. I am very cold, now that I am drenched with sweat and using less energy. We get down the worst of

the vertical section and Pat says she is going to stop to pee, change her shirt, and eat something. I take off my pack and mittens to get a fresh pair of hand warmers. Within thirty seconds I am absolutely freezing.

"I can't stay here," I say. I frantically yank my mittens back on, throw on my pack, and start moving. Pat comes to the same conclusion and we quickly head down. I am far ahead of her, so I go as fast as I can to build up body heat and then slow down and wait for her to catch up. A few times I turn around and head back to find her. She has fallen. It's hard to watch Pat struggle and not be able to help her. The best thing I can do is cheer her on and keep us moving.

"You can do this, Pat! You've got it! We're getting there!"

At dusk, we meet another hiker. When he tells us he is heading down to the Garden parking lot, we realize we are on the wrong trail. We turn around and head back up the mountain. I am cursing to myself because I don't want to upset Pat and I don't want that hiker to hear me. We don't have to go far before we come to the missed intersection. The sign there says St. Huberts. Huh? Isn't that a town near Keene Valley, New York? The trail name would be helpful! Pat recognizes the spot right away and I finally remember it. This time we take the right trail and head down. It is steep and my boots are too loose, so my toes are hitting the front of the boots. But I am freezing and the thought of stopping to remove my ice-covered gaiters to tighten my boots is too much. And, I know that I am really okay. I may be pushing an edge, but I do it knowing I am all right. I still have strength and a sense of well-being— although it is being tested today. So I keep moving fast to build body heat, then I wait, cheer Pat on, and then move again.

By now it is pitch black and we wear headlamps, but we have the trail we broke out to follow back, which makes trail-finding easy. We watch for the intersection with the river trail, knowing that we want to take the road this time.

I keep thinking it is around the next corner. No. Maybe the next. No.

We finally hit the West River Trail and I know the intersection for Lake Road is coming up. Well, maybe not. Holy shit, it feels like we've walked another mile.

Finally. There it is. We take the trail that we believe will lead us over a bridge to the road that will bring us back to the Ausable Club road and then to our car. We cross a bridge. Good sign. Then we hit what looks like it could be a road and walk for quite a way. I worry we went the wrong way when we come upon another bridge. We didn't expect another bridge.

"I think we should go over the bridge," I say to Pat. We debate it and finally decide to follow the way most of the other snowshoe prints have gone. Over the bridge, I automatically turn left and start walking and Pat says, "No, we need to go right." My instincts say go left, but Pat is really good with trail directions, so I turn around. As we hike, in my head I am thinking this is definitely the wrong way.

"Pat," I say. "At the end of the bridge there was a sign that said Wolf Jaw. It was facing the other way, as if hikers would be approaching the bridge and sign from the other direction. I think this is the wrong way." We keep walking. I am thinking that we should turn around when Pat says, through tears, "I am so disoriented."

When Pat says this, I feel the part of me that wants to collapse in fear, the part that is afraid of being lost in the

dark, of never finding our way out, of freezing to death in the snow. But I just don't go there. I keep those thoughts on the periphery. I take strength in being with Pat, and stay centered.

"I think we should go the other way." I say.

Pat gets out her compass and I kneel down and spread the map out on the snow. It is pitch black, and we are tired and cold. I can't find a North, South, East, or West indicator on the map.

What? Don't all maps have that? "Shit." Pat suggests we line up the map so Lake Champlain is vertical.

I am so cold, and the edges of fear are closing in around me. I turn the map around, and orient myself. "It looks like we should be going northwest," I say.

Pat looks at the compass and points back the way we came. We turn around. She continues to struggle with breathing and seems to have very little energy left. She slogs. I am clear we have to keep moving. "Try and keep up with me," I say. She does.

"We can do this, Pat. If this is wrong, we'll just turn around. We know we're close. We'll figure it out. We can do this." We walk for what feels like forever and see a sign for Nippletop Mountain Trailhead. We look at the map using the light of my headlamp. It is almost impossible to see without glasses. It looks to me like there is a trail off the road we hope we are on, going to another mountain. I take it as a good sign and we keep going.

Finally, we pass the trailhead we took in the morning and know we are on the right road. Relief floods my body and I relax just a bit. We keep walking for what feels like miles. We finally arrive at the gate, and have another half mile on the road to the car. It is the longest half mile I have ever walked. I don't let myself feel how cold I am, even on this last plod to the parking lot. I don't absorb how tired I am. I just keep walking. Pat and I are quiet, each in our own little hell, praying for the end.

There is the car. It is 8:10 p.m.; we have been hiking for almost eleven hours, the last four in the dark. We dump our backpacks, jump into the car, and turn on the heat full throttle. I sit there, rubbing hands together, every muscle in my body contracting, trying to stay warm. The heater is going full blast, but I feel nothing. We take bites of a bagel, but the jelly is too sweet and sticks in my throat. My hands are icicles, but we are safe. We will get warm. We sit in the car for twenty minutes before we

feel life coming back into our bodies. Relief slowly sinks into my muscles and I begin to relax.

The moment slowly comes into focus. We head out of the parking lot, starting the four-hour drive home. We blast the heat for quite a while before turning it down. All the way home we talk about the experience. Talking about it helps affirm what we feel inside. Was it really that hard? we ask each other. Yes. Was it really that steep? Yes. Was there really that much unpacked snow? You bet. Did we get lost, twice? Holy shit, yes. Does that map just suck? Yes.

Pat drops me off in Keene and has yet another half hour to her house in Jaffrey.

I dump my backpack in the hall, kiss my husband, and head upstairs. I stand under the hot spray of water in the shower, filled with relief and gratitude.

I love feeling that powerful, resilient person inside of me. It is good to know I have her when I need her. I guess it shouldn't surprise me. That strong resilience inside kept me safe in an unsafe household growing up. When I think about how strong I was as a child, I am amazed. And that same part of me kept me strong, pushing the rock uphill, creating and running Pumpkin Festival when obstacles mounted up into mountains. We all have that strength in us. The blessing of this hike is that I reconnect with that part of me.

Having had this experience, I know that next time these circumstances present themselves, I will put more

stock in turning around, which I believe requires even more inner strength
than continuing on. Being strong in a
crisis is one thing; being strong so the
crisis never happens is something else
entirely.

The hard part is knowing how far I
can push my own envelope before I really need to turn around; and how far Pat
can push hers before she is in danger. I
trusted Pat to tell me if she needed to
turn around. And for whatever reason, whether she knew she could do it,
wanted to push her limits, didn't want
to let me down, or was in denial about
the severity of her asthma, she chose to
forge on. Where is the point at which
danger overrules forging on? How do
I know when we reach that point? I
knew Pat was struggling, but could
not tell if she had reached a physical
limit and was suffering. I felt she was
pushing herself outside her comfort
zone safely. So much of my healing and
growth have come from putting myself
way outside of my comfort zone and
not turning around, but continuing on.
That is true of this hike as well. I re-
learned how strong I am and what I am
capable of because we kept going. If we
had turned around at the first sign of
Pat's discomfort, or even the second or
third, I would never have found that inner reserve of strength that carried us
to the car. I would not have found that
extra hunk of me that took charge and
kept us moving. I would not have had
the blessing of knowing more fully who
I am. We kept going and I got a gift.

STATS

**MOUNTAIN: LOWER WOLF JAW
(4,175)**

NEAREST CITY: ST. HUBERTS, NY

DATE: DECEMBER 12, 2009

TIME: 11 HOURS

**WEATHER: SUNNY, COLD, WINDY, IN
THE TEENS AT THE TRAILHEAD**

MILES: 9.6

ELEVATION GAIN: 2,825 FEET

**TRAILS: LAKE ROAD TRAIL, WEST
RIVER TRAIL, WEDGE BROOK
TRAIL, EAST RIVER TRAIL**

**HOLY SHIT FACTOR: ARE WE GOING
TO MAKE IT?**

54. A BIRTHDAY CELEBRATION ON NORTH KINSMAN

December 31, 2009, Franconia, New Hampshire

> *It is our light, not our darkness, that most frightens us.*
> Marianne Williamson

Pat and I spent the last day of 2009, Pat's birthday, on a hike so special that I am sure neither one of us will ever forget it. It wasn't the hike so much as it was the space we created on the trail. It felt sacred, like hallowed ground, so touching that talking about it in the car on the way home seemed like a violation of what we had created. I knew it would take a while before I could talk about it comfortably. A day or so later, I asked Pat to write down what she had said on the trail; I told her I would do the same.

This report is about what happened while we were doing what we always do, putting one foot in front of the other, climbing up and down mountains. Hiking has a meditative rhythm. Couple that with the physical exertion required to reach the summit while being in the midst of the beauty and splendor of nature and that takes me out of my head and into my heart. Once there, in the midst of a hike, something special almost always happens. It isn't planned. It never is. It just happens.

We have been keeping an eye on the weather, looking for the most favorable window for a hike during the Christmas holiday. Unfortunately, the forecasts have been calling for snow and cold all week. Thursday looks to be our best bet, so we are climbing the last day of 2009, a great way to end the year. It is also Pat's birthday, and there is no better way to celebrate than with a hike.

Climbing up toward North Kinsman feels more like a struggle than a celebration. Although Smith and Dickerman's guidebook says the Mt. Kinsman Trail is moderately steep, I am pushing my legs farther than they want to go today.

That's because of what we did three days ago. The gym where I teach a biweekly free weights class has been closed for the holidays, but both Pat and I wanted to keep training. So I led a class just for Pat and me. I mixed high intensity aerobics with free weights. By the time we were finished, we had done thirty lunges on the right, thirty on the left, thirty plié squats and thirty squats

using hefty weights. We did dumbbell press and flies, butt, back, and ab exercises. The next day I was a bit sore, but by Wednesday I was walking up the stairs funny, getting out of my car gingerly, and lowering myself onto the toilet seat with a groan. Apparently Pat was having similar issues.

Thursday morning Pat pulls into my driveway at 5 a.m. Dejah hops in the back of the car and greets Pinta. I get into the car with effort. Pat smiles a yeah-my-legs-still-hurt-too smile.

We head to the White Mountains. It feels good to be traveling on New Hampshire roads going to a familiar mountain. We have been climbing in the Adirondacks since late fall. But once we hit December 21, the Winter Solstice, the hikes count as "winter hikes" and we get back to work on climbing the New Hampshire forty eight four thousand footers in winter. The plan is to climb North and South Kinsman today.

We are surprised by the lack of snow at the trailhead and start off with our snowshoes strapped to our packs instead of our feet. That, however, doesn't last long. About a mile into the hike, we need snowshoes for traction. The climb starts out on a gentle incline, but long before we reach the summit, we are huffing and puffing and our legs are reminding us that they don't really want to work this hard today. About three-quarters of the way up the mountain, I wonder how I am going to get to the summit of North Kinsman, much less that of South Kinsman; my legs ache

with each step. We reach the top of the first peak and I ask, "How about just one mountain today?" Pat readily agrees.

As we snowshoe down, I am thinking about it being Pat's birthday.

"I want to celebrate you today, Pat," I say. "How about if you tell me all the ways that you love yourself, as a way to celebrate your birthday?" This is not something that I thought about ahead of time. It just came out of my mouth. I just said it.

There is complete silence as we walk down the trail. I hear our snowshoes shuffling through the snow, occasionally grazing a rock or some ice. I am aware of the silence, and slightly aware that what I have just suggested might not be easy, but I let it sit out there among the trees as our bodies move along the trail.

"I love," Pat says slowly, "that I am loyal."

"Yes, you are."

Long silence. We keep walking. I am in the moment, not thinking about anything, encouraging Pat in my heart.

"I love that . . . I love adventure," Pat says.

We keep walking, Pat in front, then Dejah, then me. Pinta is way ahead, hoping to catch a squirrel. Another long pause filled with snowshoe plods.

"I love that I laugh," Pat says.

I smile, thinking about the times we have laughed on the trails.

"I love my intelligence and common sense," she says. Long pause. "I love that I read."

We continue snowshoeing down the trail, letting gravity help us as the snow softens our footfalls. The world around me is black and white; there are tree trunks and snow as far as I can see. Pat wears a bright salmon top that shines on the monochrome trail. She seems to get brighter as she opens up.

We pass a heart that someone has drawn in the snow, and I stop to take a picture. This trail must bring out the love in those who walk its distance.

"You can join me, Nancy. Tell me what you love about yourself."

I let her invitation sink in and rumble around inside to see what comes out. Wow. This is not an easy thing to do. I flash back to a time years ago. I am sitting on my therapist's couch; she asks me to tell her things I like about myself. I am silent, tears running down my cheeks. I keep thinking, working, trying to find something that I like about myself. I say nothing.

We keep moving down the mountain in the snow-covered silence, in our own spaces, open to what might come into our hearts.

"I love that I find meaning in everything," I say, slowly. As I say this, the emotion behind the words fills me, tears come to my eyes and I struggle to get the words out. Not only am I saying what I love about myself, but I really mean it.

After another long silence: "I love that meaning matters so much to me." More tears.

Silence. Snowshoes scraping along the trail.

"I love my kindness, my tenderness," Pat says.

311

I push my parka hood off, disregarding the cold, and concentrate, wanting to make sure I don't miss anything Pat says.

"I love that I am capable and can do many things," Pat says.

"I love cheering for others and being cheered," I say.

"I love that I see the glass half full," I add.

Each time I say something I love about myself is an experience. It is not just words coming out my mouth. While I walk in the snow, a thought pops into my heart. I hear it, think about it, and feel the emotion building within me. I start to say it aloud and find a lump of something stuck in my throat. Maybe it is fear. I keep talking, tears streaming down my cheeks, emotion choking my voice and airway. As I say the words aloud to Pat, I hear them in a new way. When I put them out into the world, I hear them and know them to be true.

"I love that I get excited about stuff," I say.

"I love the mother in me," I add.

"I love that I have learned to trust people, and I love that I have the fortitude and resilience to keep going when I am outside of my comfort zone," I say.

Tramping through the woods, listening to my snowshoes shuffle through the snow, I am aware that something important is happening. I have never said these things about myself; never even considered them before. Never. And in saying the words, it feels like I am actually knowing, at a very deep level, that they are true. I own them. I own that I am a loving mother, a cheerleader, an optimist, a meaning-maker; that I am enthusiastic, resilient, and trusting. Yes, I know and love these things about me.

"I love that in spite of the depression that I suffered for most of my life, I never gave up and committed suicide," Pat says.

I honor the hugeness of this statement in silence. Then I say, "Pat, that is so big."

Time goes by, the trail moves under our snowshoes, the affirmations of who we are coming sporadically, blessing the space, our relationship, our selves.

"I love that I went through trauma in my childhood, raised by parents who could not see me, because that experience made me who I am today." The sentence drops like a loaded bomb out of my mouth, and rises like fairy dust into the woods.

"I know my mother missed something awesome when she chose not to know me," I add slowly, filled with the emotion of lost chances.

"Wow, Nancy," Pat says.

We keep going, each statement a revelation to the speaker, a deeper owning of who we are. I realize that we have created sacred space here, in the woods on the Mt. Kinsman Trail. The trust, acceptance, and vulnerability that surround us as we do this exercise-turned-celebration is nothing short of miraculous.

"I love my eyes," Pat says. Tears run down my cheeks when I hear her say this. They keep flowing as we walk. My mittens have become Kleenex. I won-der if my tears will freeze on my face; it is cold.

"I love that I know what I want, that I know who I am," I say.

"I love that giving up is not something I easily do," Pat says.

I think back to the heart we saw drawn in the snow. Simple. Beautiful. A message to everyone hiking by that there is love everywhere, always. We just have to open ourselves up to it. Pat and I find it here today. I am in awe of the hugeness of the space we create by doing this. We are different now. I own more of who I am and that is conta-gious. The next time someone tells me I am inspiring, I might be able to really let it in, maybe even rejoice in it. And when I do that, I give the other person the space to find where they are also in-spiring. Once we own it, we don't have to hide it or deny it. We can live it. And the world becomes more inspiring.

"I love that I can say what I love about me," I say, remembering the day in the therapist's office when this space was unavailable to me.

"And I love that there is always more," I say.

Yes. There is always more—more that I will love about myself, more life possibilities, more sacred spaces, more meaningful celebrations and more in-credible hikes. Always more.

STATS

MOUNTAIN: NORTH KINSMAN (4,293)

NEAREST CITY: FRANCONIA, N.H.

DATE: DECEMBER 31, 2009

TIME: 7 HOURS

WEATHER: CLOUDY AND COLD, LIGHT SNOW, TEMPERATURE IN THE 20S

MILES: 8.2

ELEVATION GAIN: 3,208 FEET

TRAIL: MT. KINSMAN TRAIL, KINS-MAN RIDGE TRAIL

HOLY SHIT FACTOR: CREATING SACRED SPACE

Saying farewell is also a bold and powerful beginning.
Aron Ralston,
Between a Rock and a Hard Place

Something's not right. I feel it inside, but I'm afraid to say the words. I begin to explore my feelings as I write hike reports. Reading the words, minutes after my fingers hit the keys, my eyes fill with tears. How can this be the end? I won't let that happen. But it already has.

55. WASHINGTON SOLO

June 19, 2010, Bretton Woods, New Hampshire

Be faithful to that which exists nowhere but in yourself.

André Gide

You know how they say old people are set in their ways? As I grow older myself, I realize that's not accurate. Older people are not set in their ways. They've had a lifetime of discovering who they are—what they like and what they don't like—and now they know. Once you know who you are, you are free to stick with what holds meaning and delight for you and let all the rest go. And since we have only this life, the sooner we figure out who we are and what we like—and start living from there—the better.

It really boils down to "time is of the essence." Why do anything for even one second that isn't truly who you are? Of course, it can take years to figure it out, years of trying things and testing this and that. It did for me. And it has taken me even more years to realize there is a pattern to it all. What I like to read reflects on where I like to hike, which also says something about the work I do, and how I like to do it.

The same is probably true for everyone. How you play is also how you work and raise your children, and how you live your life. I'm not advocating that you change anything. On the contrary, I'm suggesting knowing who you are and then living who you are with no deviations. But what does this have to do with hiking?

I know I am supposed to hike on Saturday. I know it from the inside out. That happens to me. A moment comes and I know something for sure that I didn't know before. And once I know that I am supposed to do something, there is no sense in trying to talk myself out of it. I have to follow my heart.

It's Saturday at 7:30 a.m. and I am driving on Route 302, heading to the Presidential Range in the White Mountains. My plan is to climb Mt. Eisenhower and then hike over to Monroe—I want to see those incredible views again.

The sun is out and the sky is blue; it is a gorgeous day for hiking, except Pat is not with me. Worried about her breathing problems, she decided to take a weekend off. I miss her already.

As I drive, I begin to question my plan. It is a perfect above-treeline day and we don't get many of those. Why not go for Washington instead of Eisenhower? Why would I climb the twelfth highest mountain in the state when I can climb the highest? This is part of who I am. There is really no middle ground with me—it's all or nothing. The biggest, the best, all out, or why go?

So, I change my mind and decide to climb Washington. As I pass Clinton Road, which goes to Eisenhower's Edmands Path trailhead, I see that the road is closed. I couldn't climb Eisenhower even if I wanted to! I arrive at the Ammonoosuc Ravine trailhead and begin my ascent of Washington at 8:07. I remember the trail begins at the Cog Railway, initially following the Ammonoosuc River. But soon the staircase begins. Really, a stone staircase, forged by trail workers, leads me up the mountain.

I love the waterfalls at the gorge, about halfway up. I was spellbound by them the first time I saw them. The sight of the water cascading down the mountain sparked awed silence back then, but today, I chat with other hikers as I walk along the falls. I dip my bandana into the cold water and put it around my head to keep cool. I love feeling the shock of cold water dripping through my hair, onto my neck, and down my back. And I love looking at the falling water. But it doesn't blow me away. I have been here before.

There are lots of people on the trail,

so even though I am alone, I am not alone. I miss Pat's presence, and there are plenty of kind people around to chat with as they pass me or I pass them. It is the perfect day to climb Washington, a rare event given the mountain is home to some of the world's worst weather. Halfway up, the air is still hot, tempered by a light breeze. It is a bit hazy, though, so you can't see forever. Still, I know I am lucky to be this high up wearing a sleeveless top, loving the temperature.

Dejah keeps me company and seems happy to be climbing. She runs ahead of me often—a sign that she still has lots of pep. I arrive at the Lakes of the Clouds Hut and continue on. Dejah takes a quick dip in the pond near the hut and then we head up the last mile and a quarter to the top.

I reach the summit of Washington at 11:15 and it is packed. The Mt. Washington Road Race is underway today: a thousand people will run up the auto road to the summit, 7.6 miles, gaining 4,727 feet in elevation. The peak is covered with runners wrapped in Mylar blankets. I walk to the summit sign and wait my turn for a picture. Someone kindly snaps a couple for me, and then I head quickly off the mountaintop, away from the crowds.

Dejah and I find a warm rock on the way down and sit to enjoy lunch together, looking out at the view of the northern Presidentials.

As I eat my Lost Pilgrim wrap (turkey, stuffing, and cranberry sauce), I notice how I am feeling. I wouldn't say I feel let down—it is too beautiful up here

to feel anything but awe. But it is not a new awe for me. I have been here before, seen this exact view. It feels familiar. It's a repeat. I realize, as I eat lunch, that familiarity takes some of the shine off the experience; having been there before makes the moment less unique, as if today is a day that will fade from my memory instead of standing out. I realize that I like the thrill of new, first-ever, once-in-a-lifetime moments.

I wish I could be satiated climbing the same mountain every hike. I have a friend who climbs Mt. Monadnock in Jaffrey, New Hampshire, a few times a week. I love that about her. I wish I could do that. Then I would be secure in knowing that my mountain is always right there waiting for me. I wouldn't have to wonder what the next hike would be or deal with the uncertainties of new territory. But that is not me; I

like new. I realize how well suited I was for the goal of climbing the sixty-seven four thousand footers in New England. Every hike brought a new mountain. I never knew what I would see or what challenges would greet us.

I get that every hike is new, even if I've been there before. But climbing the same mountain, even on an unfamiliar trail or in a different season, is not new enough for me. I like the surprise and thrill of every hike being a first-time adventure. My essence is about new experiences, and it is the totally unknown, uncharted moments that thrill me completely. When I reach treeline on a mountaintop I have never visited and am confronted with a never-seen-before view of the world—that is what I love. And if I am going to hike, why not go for a new experience every time?

After lunch, Dejah and I head down

the Jewell Trail. The first third of the trail, above timberline, is rocky. We get much warmer once we are below the trees where the breeze is blocked. Dejah pants and I give her the last few drops of water from my bottle. Luckily, we reach a stream three-quarters of the way down and she and I both cool off. Thus refreshed, we hike the last mile down to the Cog Railway, arriving at 3:15.

Dejah and I find a soft patch of grass near the parking lot. I take off my backpack and lie down on the soft sod. Ah. The moment of complete relaxation after a hike is the best! I lift my head to check on Dejah and she is right beside me, sound asleep. With Washington behind us, we rest in the sunlight for a while before heading to the car. People walk by us on the road to the parking lot and I notice they glance in our direction and smile—an exhausted hiker and her dog taking a well-deserved rest.

My first solo hike up Washington reinforces my conviction that climbing a mountain for the second time lacks the luster of the first experience. Sitting on top of Washington, six thousand feet up, I was surrounded by magnificence, yet I wanted it to really dazzle me, to feel more tingly, and more effervescent. The view was the same one that took my breath away the first time I saw it. I remember feeling I was on top of the world then. This time, I felt like I was on top of Mt. Washington.

I am not a repeater. I have realized this before, but perhaps not so clearly. I realize this is true about me across

into the world, something beyond what others expect or have envisioned. So what I thrive on in a work environment is the same as what I try to bring into the world, which is also exactly the same as what I yearn for in the mountains. Who knew life made so much sense?

I will never take the beauty of the White Mountains for granted. But I have seen them, I know them. The Whites are part of me. I want to be exposed to different beauty—an unfamiliar mountain, an unknown experience, a new thrill, a tingly moment. Bring on the glitter and the sequins in life. Why be a repeater when there is a world of new out there?

the board of my life. How I live is how I hike is how I work.

I won't read a book twice. I won't watch the same movie twice. I won't watch a TV rerun. I even hate it when a reality TV show comes back from a commercial break and repeats the last few moments as a refresher. It drives me crazy.

This same theme shows itself in my work life, too. I am not good at maintaining. I don't do status quo very well. I like not knowing what I am going to encounter in the next project. It's what I don't expect that excites me. My career has followed this pattern: I move into a new position, bring what I have to offer to the organization and then, when the projects or circumstances begin to repeat themselves, I move on to the next challenge. When I work on a new venture, I try to bring something surprising

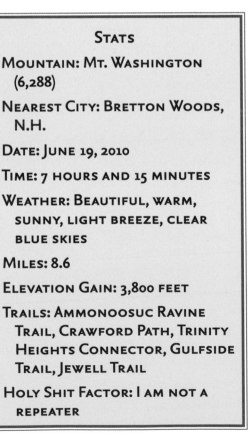

STATS

MOUNTAIN: MT. WASHINGTON (6,288)

NEAREST CITY: BRETTON WOODS, N.H.

DATE: JUNE 19, 2010

TIME: 7 HOURS AND 15 MINUTES

WEATHER: BEAUTIFUL, WARM, SUNNY, LIGHT BREEZE, CLEAR BLUE SKIES

MILES: 8.6

ELEVATION GAIN: 3,800 FEET

TRAILS: AMMONOOSUC RAVINE TRAIL, CRAWFORD PATH, TRINITY HEIGHTS CONNECTOR, GULFSIDE TRAIL, JEWELL TRAIL

HOLY SHIT FACTOR: I AM NOT A REPEATER

56. THEN YOU STAND— EISENHOWER AND FRANKLIN

July 3, 2010, Bretton Woods, New Hampshire

> *You get mad, you get strong*
> *Wipe your hands, shake it off*
> *Then you stand.*
>
> Rascal Flatts, **Stand**

We are on the grace wave on this hike.

No doubt about it.

We decide on Eisenhower, for the views and the fact that it is not a killer mountain. Pat has seen numerous phy-sicians about her shortness of breath and muscle weakness and the tests have all been inconclusive. Pat still feels she has no answers. It is frustrating for me so I can only imagine what it must be like for her to wonder what is happening to her body, to not know how to fix it, and to

worry that she may have to stop climbing mountains. I am sure she is anxious about our hike, but I don't bring it up. We are both hopeful that today will be different.

We arrive at Edmands Path trailhead at 8:30 a.m. As we are getting ready, a woman who read a feature article about our hikes in a New Hampshire newspa-per approaches. She tells us she checked out our website and read some of our hike reports. She is climbing the forty-eight four thousand footers in New Hampshire with her son, but today is hiking solo. She makes our day and we haven't even started hiking yet!

It comes as a surprise to me that people we don't know have read about

us and looked at our website and been touched by our experiences. It's weird to think that our message goes beyond the circle of people we know or have met giving pre sentations. Our sphere of influence is growing. I love that—we can touch people's lives without even knowing them. And then I realize that we all do that. Every day. What we do and how we do it affects those around us, and those around them. We all influence others and we don't even know we're doing it! We're forging connections. We may not notice it until someone brings it to our attention, like the woman we met at the trailhead. But when I really let in that we are all connected, I get goose bumps.

Dejah and Pinta bound up the trail. I stand back and let Pat take the lead. I want her to go at whatever speed feels right for her. I want Pat to have a suc-cessful day. Sometimes it is hard for me to go slower than my usual pace, so I wonder if it will be frustrating to stay behind. But today I feel comfortable bringing up the rear. Pat sets a good pace and seems to be doing fine.

Edmands Path is a sweet trail, and takes us up the mountain without any really steep grades, just a steady in-cline. Before we know it we are in a stiff breeze on the shoulder of Eisenhower, above treeline. Off to our left we see Franklin in the foreground, with Wash-ington, Clay, and Jefferson lined up be-hind. I hear Pat say "Oh, wow, I thought I might never get up here again." I am behind her, but I know she is smiling. I am too. This moment, when trees give way to shrubs, the sky gets bigger, and the woods fall away, is why we hike. It is magical up here. There is something al-most heart-breakingly beautiful about being up on the mountains, more in the sky than on the earth, that touches my very essence. And now that place of more sky than earth has become familiar to me; it feels like home. My response to reaching treeline is a heart sigh. *Ah, I'm back. This is where I am supposed to be.*

That's when I know I'm on the grace wave. But I already know that today. I knew it when we walked into the Mountain Bean this morning for sand-wiches and saw the owners, Chris and Elizabeth, smile. And I knew it when we met the woman in the parking lot who had read the article about us.

We reach the Eisenhower Loop junc-tion and head up to the top. We tag the huge cairn, which sits at the very zenith of an already crowded summit. We don't stay long, but head down the rock-lined trail, sky all around us, on a search for a nook or cranny out of the wind to have lunch. It takes a bit of exploring, but right in the crook between the mountains we find a sunny, sheltered spot. We park our gear and sit up on a ledge looking out at Franklin, Monroe, and Washington while we enjoy our Mountain Bean wraps. The dogs enjoy the extra turkey pieces that Chris put in the bag with our lunches. He clearly has a soft spot for dogs, and for us.

We finish lunch, don our packs, and are just heading off toward Franklin when we hear a "woo hoo!"

"Oh wow, it's Eileen!" Pat says.

I am stunned as we walk over to greet our friend. How is it possible that we would meet her here, now, today? Grace wave, big time.

I love Eileen. Ever since she came to our first presentation, she never misses an opportunity to tell us that we changed her life. She is persistent. And that is what it takes to get me to let in that I made a difference.

As we stand on the ridge talking, I am reflective. Both of these women have been through hell.

Late last fall, Eileen developed debilitating neck and arm pain that had her fighting just to get through each day. She stopped hiking and went on disability leave from work. Then the most devastating news: she lost her beloved brother in March. Pat and I went to the calling hours on Cape Cod. When we walked into the funeral home, packed with people, there was Eileen in the receiving line, eyes red from crying, her broken heart visible to everyone in the room. All we could do was hug her and tell her we loved her. I don't know how she has managed from moment to moment since then. But she has. She's just started hiking again, trying to get back in shape to do what she loves most.

Pat has been struggling with exercise-induced asthma for a year. While training for a marathon this spring, she came down with shingles and meningitis, which landed her in the hospital. Back on the hiking trail this summer she has been plagued by shortness of breath and severe muscle fatigue that has turned hiking into a test of will.

As we talk in the sunlight above treeline, I realize I am witnessing a triumphant, extraordinary moment: Pat and Eileen standing on top of the Presidential Range. It seems so ordinary, yet I know it is extraordinary. This is their moment. They made it. They can do this. They are back on the mountains they love, smiling. These two women are the epitome of strength and determination, perseverance and grace. They never, ever gave up.

"My plan was to just bag Eisenhower," says Eileen. "I felt like maybe I could do that. And I wanted to go alone, so I wouldn't hold anyone up if I couldn't make it. Once I got there, I felt great, so I continued over to Franklin." Pat is looking squarely at Eileen, nodding, knowing. She gets it; she's been there.

And I get it. I have been there too. There is a sisterhood born of the trials of being human.

There is solace here for Pat and Eileen, above treeline, closer to heaven than anywhere else. There is comfort for them in each other and in these mountains. Being here seems to have a way of taking away the cares of the world. I see it in their faces. They are not thinking about their recent struggles. For the moment, that angst has been swept away by the wind, the warmth of the sun on their faces, and the view from almost five thousand feet up.

Eileen is headed down the mountain and we are going up to Franklin, so reluctantly we part. For at least half an hour after we turn in different directions I feel disoriented and sad. We weren't ready to go down and Eileen was. I realize now, looking back, that I was grieving the moment when we turned and went our separate ways. I wanted to hold on to our sisterhood a bit longer.

We reach the summit of Franklin, take off our packs, sit on a hot rock, and rest. I love this part—we take off our boots and let the wind caress our toes. This is paradise. The dogs are more than glad to take a break, Pinta curling up while Dejah rests next to Pat, enjoying being patted. After a good half an hour, we reluctantly put on our packs and head back. Off to the left of

Eisenhower are mountains that start off green and dissolve into a medium, full-bodied blue; mountains beyond that are lighter blue; even more distant mountains blend into the sky. I want to find a way to make the scene part of me so that I always have it inside. It is too beautiful to let go. I don't want to leave. I hike down the mountain, keeping the battle within, within. Outside I look like a hiker going down the mountain. Inside I am struggling to tear myself away from the blue-green expansiveness of above treeline.

We hike back down the mountain on Edmands Path and as we progress, Pat slows up. I can tell her legs are feeling the hike. But the discomfort seems mild compared to other hikes, and I am hopeful that her symptoms will continue to lessen. We arrive back at the car at 4:30 p.m. eager for my cold Snapple and Pat's Diet Pepsi. Pinta hops in the car, anxious to get going. Dejah lies down in the parking lot, and falls asleep.

Today I watched as my two courageous friends fought their way back into their lives and their bodies. For me, the grace wave gift provided an opportunity to stand back and see Pat and Eileen in a triumphant light, instead of a struggling darkness. I have felt bad for Eileen, wishing that I could assuage her grief, wanting to take her physical pain away so that she could hike. And I have felt sorry for Pat, dealing with illness and medical issues and difficulty doing the thing she loves to do more than anything else. On the ridge between Eisenhower and Franklin, I realized they don't need me feeling sorry for them. It doesn't feel good to me or to them. This is their path and they are doing just fine. Today was a glorious celebration of the human spirit and all that we can accomplish in spite of what life throws at us.

I got to witness courage today. Real courage. That's what I saw: two women battling to find themselves amid the recent remnants of a life hard-lived.

Standing on top of the mountains, Pat and Eileen announced to the world: Do not count us out. We will not give up. We will be back. Again and again and again.

Grace wave.

STATS

MOUNTAINS: MT. EISENHOWER (4,760) AND MT. FRANKLIN (5,003)

NEAREST CITY: BRETTON WOODS, N.H.

DATE: JULY 3, 2010

TIME: 8 HOURS

WEATHER: BEAUTIFUL, WARM, SUNNY, LIGHT BREEZE, CLEAR BLUE SKIES

MILES: 9

ELEVATION GAIN: 3,678 FEET

TRAILS: EDMANDS PATH, MT. EISENHOWER LOOP, CRAWFORD PATH

HOLY SHIT FACTOR: I WITNESS REAL COURAGE

July 24, 2010, Manchester, Vermont

We must learn to reawaken and keep ourselves awake, not by mechanical aid, but by an infinite expectation of the dawn.

Henry David Thoreau

I had a rebirth halfway up Mt. Equinox. The experience reminds me that the potential for renewal is ever present.

I am literally pouring sweat. It runs down my back, drips down my legs, and streams down the side of my face. My clothes have absorbed all they are capable of holding. My top is clinging to me like spandex, which is not very becoming. I look like I have wet my pants, and feel like it too. My shorts fit like a soaked diaper, full and drooping. The backs of

329

my hands glisten in the sun and I can almost hear a "squish, squish" when I walk since all the sweat eventually ends up in my boots. Panting, I take one step after another up the steep incline that makes up Mt. Equinox. My outlook on this hike deteriorates the hotter and wetter I feel. I have never hiked in such humid weather. I can't really look up, because sweat drips into my eyes and stings, and my soaked bandana is of no use.

Dejah and Pinta are panting. "Isn't there a spring up here somewhere?" Pat asks, when we are halfway up the mountain. We remember a sign where the trail turns right. I realize we are almost there. "Upper Spring," the sign says. We take off our packs and head to

the spring, planning on giving the dogs an opportunity to drink. I hope we don't have to climb halfway down the mountain to get to it. But within a minute, we hear water running, and soon find a pipe coming out of the side of the mountain, with clear water flowing out of it onto the hillside. Pinta checks it out timidly. Dejah puts her mouth under the heavy flow and tries to bite the stream.

I know exactly what I have to do. I hesitate, but not for long. I move to the side of the pipe and lower my head under the water. Wow! It is freezing cold! I stay under until my head and hair are soaked and then I surface, a huge smile on my face. Woo hoo! I scream out of sheer joy. I laugh, wiping the cold water

from my face and feeling it run down my neck and back. I laugh again. How can I not? Relief. But it is more than relief. It is a total fix, a new outlook, a reawakening, a rebirth of sorts. My life feels back on track. The hike feels doable, and I am back in me. I feel so alive. I am tingling. Exhilarated! Emotionally, I don't even resemble the woman who dragged herself to the spring only moments ago. Physically, I am even wetter than before. But this feels like Christmas and my birthday and Easter all rolled into one. I am seeing the world through brand new eyes.

As we continue to hike, I think about how thankful I am that we went to the spring. I could so easily not have gone! I was on a mission to get to the top so I could stop trudging uphill. Had it not been for the dogs, I might not have taken the extra time and extra steps.

The dunk in the spring is a rebirth. Today has other moments of renewal. This morning we go to Up For Breakfast in Manchester, Vermont. I have blackberry peach granola buttermilk pancakes with warm real maple syrup. If that doesn't push me out of my current eating rut, I don't know what will. An hour later while walking from the road to the Burr & Burton trailhead, we pass dozens of wildflowers. Seeing flowers immediately takes me out of the keep-walking-we-have-to-get-climbing mode and makes me stop and take notice. Flowers are all about rebirth. They are born to bring beauty to this corner

of the planet. I look at the individual petals intently; notice the colors and the intricacy and shape. I am in awe, and that brings me into a world of wonder that feels new and refreshing each time.

As we finally reach the tower and then the wider trail that leads to the inn at the top of the mountain, I realize I need to dunk myself in a cold spring of life. This incredible rebirth I am feeling as a result of plunging my head in the freezing spring water is exactly what I need in my life. I am feeling stuck, goalless, same-old everything, and depressed. I need a new outlook. I need to see life through new eyes. I want to feel exhilarated, vital, and woo-hoo excited.

I find myself wondering what a re-birth in life would look like. Moving to an awesome place? Having grandchildren? Taking on a project that has the potential to change the world? Climbing a mountain in Colorado or Italy, or maybe Africa's Mt. Kilimanjaro? Walking the John Muir Trail in California? Winning the lottery? Applying to be a contestant on "The Amazing Race"? Taking a job guiding paddleboats down the rapids of the Grand Canyon? Moving to San Diego to live near Kelly, or following Jess wherever she lands?

Or maybe my rebirth is something I can't even imagine yet.

But here is what I know: I am ready. I want to dunk my head in the cold water of life and come up feeling that I love life so much I can't stand it. So I am putting it out there. I am ready for a change. I am sweating up a storm of discomfort with life in its current rendition and it is time for a transformation. What will that look like? And when I see it will I know it? Will I be brave enough to stick my head under the freezing cold water?

We have lunch on the top, scones from Up For Breakfast, amid wildflowers galore. Then we head back down the Burr & Burton Trail. Although the trail is only two miles one way, it rises over 2,775 feet in elevation; so it is steep. We make good time going down and before we know it, we are back at the "Upper Spring" sign. I know I have to dunk my head again. It is not even a question in my mind. Both Pat and I totally submerge our heads in the gush of water from the pipe, and we take videos this time so we have a reminder of the moment. I leave the spring and the mountain feeling full of everything wonderful.

I want every day to have an Equinox spring dunking. I want every day to contain an exhilarating moment when I feel energized and refreshed and full of life.

I am fifty-six years old. Over half of my life is over. If I'm going to have a rebirth, shed my paradigm and step into a new way of thinking and living, now would be a good time. But I have a few questions. Do I have to make the rebirth happen? I think so. Or at least I have to choose it. I have to move toward it, just as I chose to go to the spring. And I have to choose to put my head under

the water. No one is going to do that for me. Friends might encourage me, but I have to be in the right place and make the decision to dunk. Will I know the spring of life when I see it?

We have a new named moment. An "Equinox," a rebirth, when in one exciting moment we see the beauty and potential in life, and see ourselves at the center of that moment. So when the time comes, and I recognize it, and I dunk my head under the cold spring of life and come up giddy, we will know I have had my "Equinox."

I can't wait!

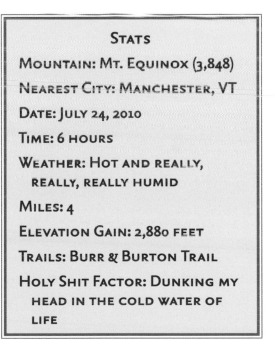

STATS

MOUNTAIN: MT. EQUINOX (3,848)

NEAREST CITY: MANCHESTER, VT

DATE: JULY 24, 2010

TIME: 6 HOURS

WEATHER: HOT AND REALLY, REALLY, REALLY HUMID

MILES: 4

ELEVATION GAIN: 2,880 FEET

TRAILS: BURR & BURTON TRAIL

HOLY SHIT FACTOR: DUNKING MY HEAD IN THE COLD WATER OF LIFE

58. ACKNOWLEDGING THE TRUTH ON BOOTT SPUR

August 1, 2010, Jackson, New Hampshire

> *Risk! Risk anything! Care no more for the opinions of others, for those voices. Do the hardest thing on earth for you. Act for yourself. Face the truth.*
>
> Katherine Mansfield

I stand on the Lion Head Trail, the summit cone of Washington over my shoulder, tears in my eyes. Pat stands opposite me, tears brimming in her eyes. This moment has been a long time in coming. I hate the words as they come out of my mouth, but they are true. I have said them before. But this time, my heart is right out there next to the words, and I let myself feel their weight.

"I want our hiking to be magic, but it's not anymore. I want to love it as much as I did in the beginning, but I don't." Silence wraps around us like the wind that blows over the Presidentials.

Those words have been building inside of me for some time. Ever since Pat and I got patches for climbing the New England Four Thousand Footers and Dejah got hers for the New Hampshire Four Thousand Footers, hiking in the White Mountains has lost its sheen. It feels regular instead of magic, normal instead of iridescent. And that wouldn't be so bad if I weren't a glitter kind of girl. I love the sparkles in life.

I have tried to soothe this discomfort by focusing on the mountain lists we are still working on. We have twelve left of the hundred highest mountains in New England. They are all trailless peaks, so we'll have to bushwhack, using a compass to find the way to the top. Here's the thing: forcing my way through dense forest, getting beat up by spruce limbs, crawling around, under, and through trees and branches, following no trail, does not call to me. I wish it did; but it doesn't. So my drive to climb the hundred highest is waning. In a similar vein, we have started climbing the forty-six Adirondacks in New York, but almost half of them require bushwhacking. Great goals, but not for me.

When we decided to climb the sixty-seven four thousand footers in New England, I knew in my heart that was what I was supposed to do. But I don't have that same feeling about our remaining mountain lists. At fifty-six, I have a pretty good idea of who I am, and I have to honor not just who I am but who I am not. I am not a bushwhacker and I am not a repeater.

How do I let go of hiking in the White Mountains? Just asking the question feels hard. Over the past five years hiking has brought me great joy, pushed me past my comfort zone, and challenged me physically and emotionally. It has come to define who I am—I am a peakbagger. And if we are not hiking, what binds me to Pat, my mountain-climbing sister? Is it just a matter of saying no, I don't want to hike in the White Mountains any more? Wow, that would be like draining my world of all its color without any clue where to find the crayons.

I keep thinking my next goal will materialize, as the marathon did. In December I had an epiphany that I was supposed to run a marathon. So we did. Pat and I ran 26.2 miles. The moment I crossed the finish line I knew running one marathon was enough. Now I am back in the mundane, doing what I have been doing, bored and dissatisfied. I feel like I am tossing and turning in bed, having a rough night's sleep. I can't find a comfortable position, the sheets stick to me, and there is no breeze. Even though I am uncomfortable, I don't want to stop doing the thing that has given me the most joy until I can find its replacement. But the next thing is not here yet, and the mountains no longer give me my sparkle fix.

Our goal today is Mt. Washington. We start out from the Pinkham Notch Visitor Center sharing the Tuckerman

Ravine Trail with lots of other people. It is not long before the Boott Spur Trail takes us off the main thoroughfare and onto the trail-less-traveled for a quiet but steep ascent. Once above treeline, the sun plays a game of hide and seek using the clouds as cover, splaying light in a huge paisley pattern on the green treetops far below us. As we climb Boott Spur, the shoulder of the great Washington, we are teased over and over by false summits, while the actual peak of Boott Spur remains elusive. Ah, there it is. Whoops, not quite. Maybe that is it. Nope, a bit more to go. When we finally arrive on the summit I look over at Washington and am awestruck. The trail from here to there is barely discernible, marked by huge cairns that gradually disappear into the jagged steel gray of the king's immense boulder-strewn surface. Mt. Washington's massive cone looks like an entire mountain and, although we know there are lots of people ascending it, we can't see them. I realize I don't want to climb anymore. I don't need to bag Washington. Been there, done that. I don't want to push myself, because I just don't feel like it. It is not important to me today. Boott Spur is a fifty-five hundred–foot mountain. We got our exercise. Pat agrees that we don't have to climb Washington. We are tired and the magic and euphoria usually attached to our hiking is absent.

We head down the mountain. The landscape seen from the ledge on the Lion Head Trail is pretty spectacular, but Pat and I are engaged in a moment of truth and I am not paying attention to the views.

"I want our hiking to be magic, but it's not anymore. I want to love it as much as I did in the beginning, but I don't." Just saying the words aloud brings all my fear and grief to the surface. Now we can't pretend it's not happening.

"How do you feel about it, Pat?" I ask.

"Hiking has become a nightmare for me," Pat says. "I never know what body is going to show up. It's not fun anymore. I keep trying to make it feel like it used to."

We continue moving along the ridge toward the top of Lion Head. Once there, the views looking back and down into the ravine remind us of how far down we need to go. We don't stay long; we know what lies ahead will be challenging, so we start the steep descent that will eventually bring us into Tuckerman's Ravine and the 2.3 miles back to Pinkham Notch.

For much of our hike down, we walk in silence. But it feels different than the silence that enveloped us during the first half of the hike. This silence feels heavy with the realization that life will be different now. I keep flashing on the question: What is next for me? For us? What if I never find something else that feels this good?

I remember asking that exact question when I left the Pumpkin Festival. I loved the magic and thrill of the event, and the meaning behind the festival. When I left, I was afraid that I would never do anything that big or awesome or fulfilling again. But I was wrong. Little did I know I had mountains to climb.

I have to let go of hiking in the White Mountains before I can find my new goal. And I know how to let go. I've done it enough in my life. I let go of my hope that my parents would love me. I let go of my prayer that my sister and I would be best friends again. I let go of the desire for Jess to keep her beautiful curly hair instead of straightening it. I let go of Rajah, my beloved golden retriever, as he slipped away from life. I let go of my daughters, year by year, as they grew out of my lap and into the world. And with each letting go I understood that I can't really hold on to anything.

The grief feels poignant nonetheless. I have experienced such immense joy hiking with Pat. The accomplishment, growth, physical and emotional strength, personal confidence, and awe I have experienced has been extraordinary. It is hard to let that go, to stop trying to recreate those feelings when they are no longer there.

So, I am feeling the loss of the wonder that hiking in the White Mountains once held for me. As I write that sentence, I realize I am focusing on loss. What if I focus on the excitement of whatever comes next? I could welcome

the delight that I know is hiding around the corner, waiting for me to loosen my grip on what was.

It is a long hike down. We get back to our car at 6:30 p.m. Dejah jumps in the back seat, stretches out from door to door, and is asleep in moments. Pinta snuggles up on her bed behind Pat's seat and rests. We sit in the car and down cold drinks and let our bodies sink into the car seats. I move my toes, separating them for the first time after hours of them being squished together in my boots. We know we have been to our edge today. As we rest in the car, we are quiet. It's a big space we are in. It feels good to have acknowledged the truth.

The beginning of an end began on Boott Spur.

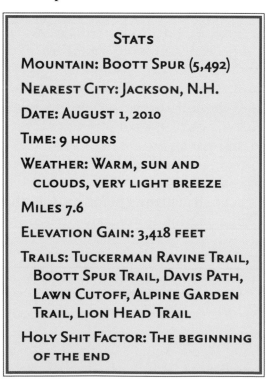

STATS

MOUNTAIN: BOOTT SPUR (5,492)

NEAREST CITY: JACKSON, N.H.

DATE: AUGUST 1, 2010

TIME: 9 HOURS

WEATHER: WARM, SUN AND CLOUDS, VERY LIGHT BREEZE

MILES 7.6

ELEVATION GAIN: 3,418 FEET

TRAILS: TUCKERMAN RAVINE TRAIL, BOOTT SPUR TRAIL, DAVIS PATH, LAWN CUTOFF, ALPINE GARDEN TRAIL, LION HEAD TRAIL

HOLY SHIT FACTOR: THE BEGINNING OF THE END

59. FOLLOWING LIFE'S ARROWS TO A WEDDING—NORTH MOAT MOUNTAIN

August 7, 2010, North Conway, New Hampshire

*She's a wild one
Runnin' free*
Faith Hill, **Wild One**

This hike has a pleasant surprise—arrows. Yup, arrows pointing us in the right direction. I love that. Sometimes I doubt my choices and wonder if I have veered off the path. An arrow is so reassuring. I wish life had arrows pointing us in the right direction. That would take care of a lot of the guesswork, doubt, and angst that goes along with making life decisions.

The other pleasant surprise about this hike is that the trail offers views almost the whole way up. We are not in the woods long before we break out on a ridge with a view and then, on a

pretty regular basis, find ourselves on open ridges with the horizon defined by mountains and, beyond them, more mountains. The incredible vistas are also signs we are on the right track, as is the eroded path that winds its way up the mountain, and the time-worn blazes we come across on the open ledges every once in a while. But the ultimate reassurance is the handmade arrow signs.

As I walk along the ridge, immersed in the rich colors of summer, from the intense blues and greens just over the cliffs below my feet to the wide expanse of muted blues and greens that eventu-

ally merge with the sky, I find myself thinking about the arrow signs and wondering why I love them so much. I know why right away. I am at a crossroads in life, rethinking work, adventures, and even where I want to live for the second half of my life. I am in a place of not-knowing, and that makes me think of Jess, my youngest daughter, who is getting married on Saturday. She is in a place of knowing. It seems she always has been.

From the very beginning, Jess had a mind of her own and exercised it every time we asked her to do anything. Her temper and her stamina for pushing back until she got her way combined for a merciless wallop that left Don and me wondering if we were meant to be parents. She was always testing us.

Jess met Sean when they worked at the Colony Mill, a local marketplace; they started dating when they were in high school. They had a fairly tumultuous relationship at first. Sometimes, when one of their fights would leave her crying, I would try to console her, while suggesting that perhaps Sean was not the right guy. But I was wrong, and she knew it.

They'd break up, then get back together, and we would go through the cycle again. I was sure the relationship would not survive. I was wrong again. It more than survived. Sean joined the Army and matured into a strong, handsome, responsible young man. He served for two years in Iraq, while Jess worked and waited. When he came home on leave, he asked Don and me if he could marry Jess. "I love Jess and I want to spend my life with her," he said. It was then, looking into his eyes as he told us how much he loved our daughter, that I realized what Jess knew all along. Sean loves Jess with all his being.

Pat and I stop on the ridge and check our watches to see if they agree with our stomachs, which are calling for sustenance. We find an out-of-the-wind nook with a view and have some lunch. I am thinking we must be on the top of the mountain.

As Pat and I eat, I am deep in thought. I realize that we can only live our own lives and only know our own way. Everyone has their own unique arrows to follow, which direct them along their own personal path. I can't know Jess's path. Only she knows. Maybe as parents we think we know the right path for our kids, and we guide them as best we can, until the moment comes when they take over. Our jobs are essentially done, often long before we are ready.

After lunch, I have some fun taking pictures of Dejah against the backdrop of the New Hampshire mountains. I love this dog. And if Jess had followed my advice, I would never have had the joy of Dejah. When Jess was in college she wanted to get a dog. I urged her not to, saying dogs take a lot of time, work, and money; that it was the wrong time in her life for a dog. She didn't listen. Jess clearly was following her own life arrows, ones I could not see. She bought a yellow Lab, named her Dejah, and proceeded to bring her everywhere she went, introducing her to college life. As a result, Dejah is an easy-going, sweet, well-behaved, intelligent dog, and an adored member of the family.

Pat and I collect our stuff, pack up, and head out. Not only are we not on the top, but, it turns out, we have quite a way to go. The next open view arrives and I am sure we are on the summit now, so I take off my pack and lie down in the sun. But we're not there yet. Back on the trail, up and over a few more humps, and we finally arrive on the top with clear views all around us. As I soak in the landscape, it dawns on me that this is the view I want of my life. I want to be able to see it all, to be able to see my destination so I know where I am going. Standing on top of Moat Mountain, I can see for miles and miles. I want to see my journey as if from the top of a mountain. Then I would be sure I am going in the right direction. But that is not how it works. We can't see the whole journey; we see just the next step. And once I take that, I see the next step. We don't get a whole view of life except when we look back.

We head down the mountain, into the woods, where the views are much more like those we have of life—just a step or two ahead of where we are. We arrive back at Diana's Baths—a series of granite terraces, cascading falls, waterspouts and rock basins along Lucy Brook. We had hoped to sink our tired bodies into the cool water, but it is packed with people so we keep walking, Pinta and Dejah looking longingly back at the water.

We get to the car, enjoy our cold drinks and begin the long drive home.

We're at the Bedford Village Inn. It's Saturday, August 14, a few minutes before 6 p.m., and Jess asks me to button the buttons that run down the back of her wedding gown. I'm touched to my core by this moment. She looks so beautiful that my heart swells—so full of love it hurts. I kneel down behind her, realizing I will hold this memory in my heart forever. I begin at the bottom and work my way up, each tiny button surrounded by lace and ivory splendor. As I struggle with each, I can see Jess smiling at me as a little girl, her eyes big, bright, and full of life. It's hard to believe that she is all grown up and about to be married.

The wedding is supposed to begin at 6. It is 6:05 and the photographer says, "It's time."

Jess responds: "This is how I roll. This is my show. They can wait."

I relax a little and laugh to myself, realizing that it has always been Jess's show. How can you not love that about her? She knows who she is and she stays true to her path, every step of the way.

At 6:15, Don walks me to my seat in the front row. I am surrounded by 175 friends and family members, all sitting in their white seats, blue skies above, bright green grass beneath, encompassed by flowers as the strains of Pachelbel's Canon fill the air with a breeze of music. Here comes Jess, on Don's arm. The girl I gave birth to twenty-five years ago, bathed in her beauty, smiling, radiant, walks toward her husband-to-be.

most cherished gifts today."

Jess and Sean turn to each other and recite their vows. They look in each other's eyes, and their faces reflect the love they have for one another. That is when I know for sure this is right.

Maybe I can't see their future lives laid out like the vista from the mountaintop, just as I can't see mine. But I can see in this moment that Sean and Jess truly love each other. They are on their own path, following their own arrows. May it take them to the summits of many mountains. May they know the joy of loving each other for many, many years, the joy Don and I, now married for thirty-three years, know. And may they have a strong-willed, beautiful, brown-eyed little girl, just like Jess, to remind them that we all have our own paths.

She reaches Sean, hugs her Dad, then comes over and hugs me. My breath catches in my throat, tears sting my eyes. I'm thrilled to be included in the giving away. Jess takes Sean's hands.

The officiant says, "Family is paramount to this union. Jessica and Sean are both mindful and appreciative of the strong and fine examples of marriage their parents continue to provide for them. These examples will be their

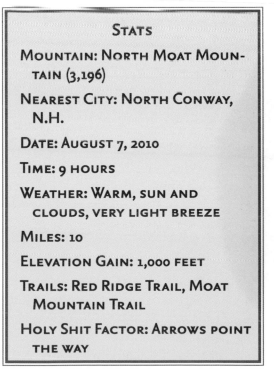

STATS

MOUNTAIN: NORTH MOAT MOUNTAIN (3,196)

NEAREST CITY: NORTH CONWAY, N.H.

DATE: AUGUST 7, 2010

TIME: 9 HOURS

WEATHER: WARM, SUN AND CLOUDS, VERY LIGHT BREEZE

MILES: 10

ELEVATION GAIN: 1,000 FEET

TRAILS: RED RIDGE TRAIL, MOAT MOUNTAIN TRAIL

HOLY SHIT FACTOR: ARROWS POINT THE WAY

60. LET GO AND MOVE ON

When one door closes another door opens; but we so often look so long and so regretfully upon the closed door, that we do not see the one which has opened for us.

Alexander Graham Bell

Let Go & Move On. These are the words I carve in the pumpkins that I bring to the Pumpkin Festival. It is the twentieth anniversary of the event and, as its creator, I have been asked to light the pumpkin towers and say a few words to the fifty thousand guests who are pumpkin-gazing on Main Street. This is it—my chance to go back to the event I birthed, to finally let it go and move on. That seems to be my universal task these days.

The weekend after the festival I visit Naushon Island with Pat and two dear friends, John and Mary. We walk all over this incredibly beautiful island. The trails are covered with crackly brown, yellow, and red leaves; the branches of beech and oak trees reach out to us as we walk by. We are surrounded by meadows and bordered by the blue waters of Buzzard's Bay.

John says to me, "You know, you have developed a following. And I know you are going through this transition right now, but don't leave us out. You have a gift of sharing. And even though you are in a difficult place, we want to be a part of your process."

What a gift, those words. For me, it is hard to trust that people want to know about the tough stuff. I imagine people willingly cheering us up and over mountains, but not wanting to be dragged through the dark, boot-sucking mud of personal turmoil. Maybe that says more about me than about others.

I love to share the good stuff. Our hiking over the past few years has definitely been the good stuff. Going to sleep at night after a hike, my body pulsing from the extreme effort, I was always filled with gratitude. I loved the way my body felt tingly tired after working so hard. I loved that I always had a hike to look forward to. Each day of the week brought a sense of elation that grew as we closed in on Saturday, when we would hit the trails again. I loved the hikes; I yearned for the mountaintop

views. Each hike blessed me with my friendship with Pat. The fact that we had a long list of mountains to climb that would keep us busy for years gave me a false sense of security that I could hold on to this euphoria forever. I remember being filled with so much excitement I could hardly stand myself, sitting in the car on the way home from many hikes, talking about all the mountains to come. I thought the hikes and the accompanying joy would never end.

But it has. This is the tough stuff. Telling the story of Pat and I conquering a mountain is easy. Saying publicly that our hiking adventures are over feels devastating. Because once I say it, you will all know that I am just human, just struggling along through life like everyone else. I wish I still wanted to get up at 4:30 a.m., drive three and a half hours, hike all day straight up and then straight back down, drive three and a half hours home, and flop into bed, my body buzzing. I want to want to do that. But I just don't. I'm done. Whatever is in me that determines my life path, of which I seem to have no control, has clearly laid down the law. This is it. It is time to move on. I can fight this realization, or I can go with the flow.

But how do I let go of the very thing that makes me feel good?

Wait a minute . . .

I'm basing how I feel about myself on what I do. But it's not about what I do, it's about who I am. Climbing up an ice slide on a four thousand footer, I discover my courage. But I don't lose my courage once the hike is over. It's still

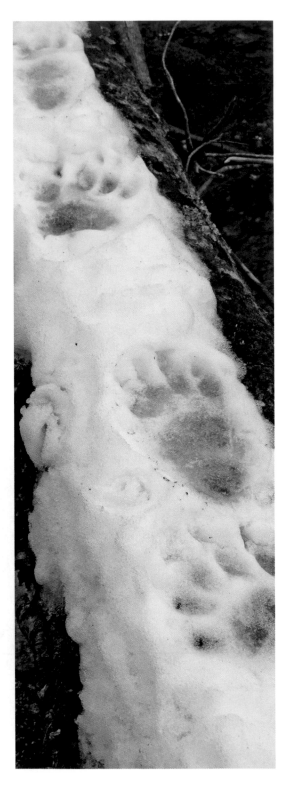

there—it's in me. On the trails, the views, the spring wildflowers, the rime ice all make my breath snag. But I don't have to be on a mountain to be awed by the natural world. Hiking helped me discover my love of cheering for others and being cheered, but sharing my joy is certainly not trail dependent. Hiking helped me discover what I have in me, but it's in me, not in hiking.

Somehow this knowing doesn't make me feel any better. Clearly, my resistance is strong and I dig in my heels. I'm acting like this is some terrible phenomenon that is happening just to Pat and me. But it's not, and I know it. It's life. Something is remarkable—a new relationship, a job, a hobby, a physical activity, a new friend, a challenging project. You are on top of the world. You find yourself marveling that life can feel this good. And then, one day something changes. The relationship no longer makes you smile, the job no longer feels rewarding, the project ends, your friend lets you down, your knees start to ache, you get older. The magic seeps out and the joy is gone. It happens all the time. Our tasks are to recognize when it happens, to let go of what no longer works, and to move on to whatever may be next. We let go in our own time. It can take years or minutes. We choose.

I choose.

It is Saturday, and Pat and I are not hiking. I am doing laundry, running errands, spending time with Don. I miss the thrill of getting to the top of a mountain with Pat. I miss the feeling that I have done something really worthwhile today. I miss having deep conversations with Pat. But I find joy in relaxing with Don. The week goes by and it is Saturday again and Pat and I are not hiking. I am doing laundry, walking the dogs, writing this report.

Sitting in my office and working on my computer, I look at our hiking pictures, framed and placed on surfaces all around me. Grief swells, filling me until I turn away. The sadness of not being on a mountain, of not looking out at views that can bring me to tears feels so gut-wrenching that I look away from the photos and banish the memories as quickly as they come. I send them somewhere deep within, to an airtight, walled-off room so inaccessible that it will take days before they work their way back up to my surface. I wonder how long it will be before I can look at a picture of Pat and me on a mountain summit without pushing the memory and its accompanying sadness away.

Pat and I continue to walk our dogs, run, and go to strength-training classes together. Sometimes it is hard to see her. There are moments when her face is so full of pain I have to look away. As we sit together, having coffee, and I see tears roll down her cheeks, indicating her desperate wish to be back on the trails, it brings that pang of loss into the pit of my stomach. If I push it back down to its cell, then I am not available to Pat or her grief. If I sit with Pat in that awful space, it feels almost unbearable. I wonder what to say. How do we talk with each other about this?

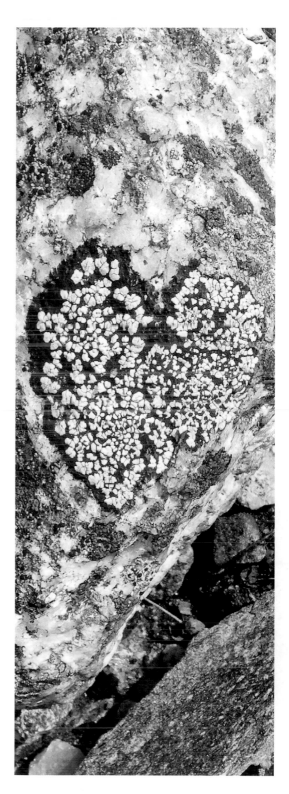

How do we call it quits to hiking when it feels like not hiking means the end of our friendship? And the end of our physical fitness, which has taken years of hard work to build? And the end of our ability to inspire others with our stories?

That's how I feel when I am in the grief space, Pat next to me, Kleenex between us.

Looking at our situation through the lens of "holding on," of desperately wanting our hiking to go on forever, leaves me with nothing to look forward to. I'm stuck doing what I don't want to do, because I don't want the joy to end, even though it already has. I am living with the fear that there is only so much joy available to any one person and I've already had my fair share. I got that from my parents who believed in "limited fun." Whenever the four of us kids were having a ball, they would yell at us to stop. Stop having fun? Why? Is there a maximum restriction to how much fun a person can have in one life? I don't believe that. Thinking there is a limit to anything—love, fun, potential, money—is the glass-half-empty instead of the glass-half-full view of life.

Eventually my positive attitude kicks back in and I find myself looking through an optimistic lens. Immediately I am in a totally different place. I know I will be friends with Pat forever. We have been through too much and know each other so deeply that we will stay connected for the rest of our lives. This I know.

And losing my physical fitness? Come on! I don't have to lose my physical fitness unless I choose to. I know what I have to do to stay in shape. It's not easy, but it has never been easy.

And then there is the fear that clogs my airways when I think about it, the fear that I will lose my ability to connect with and inspire others because I no longer have a hiking story to share. But here is what I know. It is not my stories that inspire others. It is not about what I do. It's about who I am. People connect with a spark in me that they also feel in themselves. I picture it like a light coming from within, and it shines through me in my words, my expressions, my eyes and my actions, revealing my heart. And others recognize it instantly because that same light is also shining in them. They feel it vibrate within them, and a deep connection is made. That is inspiration; it is a two-way street. Heart meets heart. It is not me or you; it is something monumentally wonderful that happens between us. And it comes from me being me, and you being you, and the presence of my heart with your heart. And that spark, and monumentally wonderful moment, is what makes life worth living.

Climbing mountains is just one manifestation of Nancy, as is running the Pumpkin Festival, raising my children, making my house into a loving home, and our It's Not About the Hike website and presentations. What might be the next manifestation? There are endless possibilities! And what is next could be even better, bigger, more fulfilling, more inspirational, have deeper

meaning, and be even more true to me. It's hard to imagine something being better than the last five years of hiking with Pat, but I know there is a whole world out there that I can't even begin to understand, with endless promise that I cannot begin to fathom. And those possibilities and promise are out there for all of us.

While I mourn hiking, the grace wave inches me ever closer to another door. In between the tears of loss, I see the glimmer of a new life and a new goal, like the sun peeking over the rim of the Grand Canyon as a new day dawns.

Circumstances are lining up for Don and me. Our daughters, Kelly and Jess, are now married and have started their own lives in their own homes, leaving us in a big house that we no longer need. Don has a temporary job that will last nine to twelve months. All of a sudden, staying put isn't so important in our lives. The world opens up for us in a brand new way.

One day it hits me. "Hey!" I say to Don. "Maybe this is when we are supposed to travel across the country, while we are still healthy and can explore. It's been on our Life List forever.

We've always wanted to do it. Maybe that is what we are supposed to do! We could sell the house." I pause, letting in how incredibly hard that would be. But it doesn't dull my enthusiasm. "Buy an RV and just go! See all the national parks, check out a few baseball stadiums, visit family and friends we haven't seen in forever. Yes! That is what we are supposed to do!"

Let go and move on takes on a whole new meaning.

So I go shopping. I buy a huge map of the United States, a whole mess of different colored map pins, and books on the national parks, state parks, and scenic byways in the United States. Don and I go to an RV Superstore and decide that smaller is better. Then we talk to a real estate agent about selling our

house. *Holy shit! What am I thinking?* a voice inside me screams. The idea of selling the spacious, light, plant-filled home where we raised our children, its walls covered with family photos and infused with love, and living in a twenty-three-foot motor home for a year fills me with exhilaration and trepidation. But this is the grace wave. And I am on it. This is what I am supposed to do. I can fight it, or I can go with it. I can go kicking and screaming, or I can go enjoying the ride. My choice.

I am driving with Pat when I get my next revelation. I don't want to stop hiking. I just want to have a life beyond hiking. For five years hiking was my life. Just about everything I did was about staying fit for hiking, choosing the next mountain and trail, packing

for a hike, hiking, recovering from a hike and then writing about the hike. Now I want hiking to be a part of my life, leaving room for other things.

When I tell Pat that I don't want to stop hiking I feel a huge wave of rightness shower me with relief. I let that sink into my being. I am so glad! Hiking is not done. It is just going to be different. Less often, less arduous, slower paced, more fun. We can still hike, still write hike reports, still give our hiking presentation. But my life won't be defined by hiking; it will be defined by me.

It's not about the hike. It never has been. These past five years, blessed by my friendship with Pat and by climbing to mountain summits almost every Saturday, have been the most incredible, difficult, exhausting, exhilarating,

meaningful, glorious years of my life. From the first hike to the last, I have grown more into the person I am. I have found more strength, understanding, compassion, resilience, courage, determination, joy and beauty—more everything in me.

It's not about the hike. It is about who I am as I live my life; hiking, cleaning out my home, throwing away cherished possessions, sticking pins in a map of the U.S., and shopping for a motor home. I am more fully me.

When Don and I climb into our RV and head across the United States, it will not be about the journey from the East Coast to the West Coast and back, it will be about the journey within. It will be about who I am, one baseball stadium and one national park at a time.